"MacEwan helped shatter the colonial state of mind of Western Canadians who had assumed that nothing worthwhile could originate in their own land, that all heroes were foreigners, that nobody worth writing about—let alone reading about—had dwelt in their midst."

~Rusty Macdonald

"MacEwan has spent an endless amount of time tracing the histories of Canadians whose lives deserve to be better known. The literature of Western Canada has been enriched both by Grant MacEwan's efforts and by his unerring ability to depict his characters as human beings."

~*Sundre Round-Up*

"Grant MacEwan is the leading popular historian of Western Canada . . . no Western Canadian writer has done more to bring to life the popular history of the region for the ordinary reader."

~*Prairie Forum*

"If any one writer can take the credit for saving Western Canadian history from the dusty shelves of academics or even total neglect, it is Grant MacEwan."

~*Red Deer Advocate*

"Western Canada's highly acclaimed and most widely read popular historian."

~*Calgary Herald*

A Century of Grant MacEwan

SELECTED WRITINGS

Introduction by Donald B. Smith
Edited by Lee Shedden

BRINDLE & GLASS PUBLISHING

National Library of Canada Cataloguing in Publication
MacEwan, Grant, 1902–2000
A century of Grant MacEwan : selected writings.

Includes bibliographical references.
ISBN 1-894739-00-0

1. Canada. 2. Canada—History—20th century. I. Title.
FC3675.1 M234 A2 2002   971.06   C2002-902669-5
F1060.92.M24 2002

Cover photos: MacEwan files

The following selections have been reprinted with the kind permission of
the publishers: "Western Canada's Foremost Storyteller," Alberta Historical
Society; "Fred Kanouse: The Trader," "Trail to Disaster," "The Pulling
Contests," and "A Cowboy's Horse," Fifth House Publishers; "Bedson's
Buffalo," Alberta Sport, Recreation, Parks and Wildlife Foundation; "The
Plains 'Noblemen'," Éditions des Plaines; "Horse Race Down the
Mountainside," Rocky Mountain Books; "Water Pleasure: A Raft on the
South Saskatchewan," NeWest Press.

Brindle & Glass Publishing
132 Hallbrook Drive Southwest
Calgary, Alberta
T2V 3H6
www.brindleandglass.com

1 2 3 4 5 06 05 04 03 02

PRINTED AND BOUND IN CANADA

This book is dedicated to the memories of Alec McEwan and Bertha Grant McEwan, and other pioneer spirits sung and unsung who helped shape the history of the West.

≁

Table of Contents

Introduction

~

Western Canada's Foremost Storyteller
Donald B. Smith

In the spring of 1966 the Historical Society of Alberta honoured Grant MacEwan for "the most outstanding contribution to Alberta history."[1] The newly appointed lieutenant-governor of Alberta, then sixty-three years old, appeared to have reached the high point of his career as a Western Canadian popular historian. But appearances can be deceiving. Thirty plus years, and thirty plus books, remained ahead of him. He had only begun to make his contribution to our understanding of ourselves and of our region. How did Grant succeed in bringing the natural and human history of the West before a wide reading audience? What brought this well-known agricultural specialist in his forties to write on the human history of Western Canada?

Grant's extraordinary energy and organizational skills help to explain his success in popular history at a time when he had numerous university, community, and later political commitments. Born in 1902, he grew up on a pioneer farm just north of Brandon, Manitoba. After several years in Brandon itself, he spent his teenaged years on the family's new farm in the Carrot River valley near Melfort, Saskatchewan. Early in his life he developed work habits of long hours, marked by efficient use of time.

Grant's knowledge of Western Canada's rural past came from his farm upbringing, as well as from his university training and teaching. In Saskatchewan he walked two miles each way to school. En route the teenager studied the flora and fauna, acquiring the deep knowledge and appreciation of nature which appears throughout his work. He knew intimately of what he wrote. On the family farm he lived through the entire early twentieth-century prairie experience, from breaking virgin sod with horse and plough to the full mechanization of agriculture. His years of study at the Ontario Agricultural College in Guelph, Ontario, and graduate work at the Iowa State College of Agriculture, as well as his teaching at both the Universities of Saskatchewan and Manitoba, deepened his understanding of Western Canadian agriculture.

The future historian of prairie Canada knew how to communicate easily with the public. While at the Ontario Agricultural College, one summer he sold nursery stock throughout southwestern Ontario. He sold as much as the average experienced salesman his first week, and every subsequent week his sales went higher. Meeting and talking with strangers came naturally to him. Later, as a professor of animal husbandry at the University of Saskatchewan, he loved giving community talks and judging at cattle shows. By the early 1930s the young professor had established a reputation as a gifted and popular speaker on agricultural topics, and on others as well. But when the University of Saskatchewan decided to emphasise scholarship and pure research rather than contact with the public, Grant's interest in the institution declined. He seized the chance in 1946 to become the Dean of Agriculture at Manitoba with the assigned task of taking the university out to Manitoba farms.

Grant had all the necessary attributes needed for recording and writing on Western Canada's past. But he only began to write on human historical topics in his forties. Like many Canadians before and since, he had a negative experience with history in school. His Ontario-born father and Nova Scotian-born mother had brought him up with tales of stamina and courage in the pioneer period of Canada's past. But in public school his teachers deadened rather than deepened his interest. Years later Grant told his son-in-law historian Max Foran that his teachers actually made him "hate history": "The only history I got in my school years was English history. There was no such thing as a recorded Canadian history. There was no textbook. The teachers didn't know anything about Canadian history." Dates of kings and far-away wars held little appeal for him.

Arthur Silver Morton, a distinguished Canadian historian at the University of Saskatchewan, re-awakened Grant's interest in Western Canada's past. A diary entry in 1938 refers to their joint search for the sites of old fur trading posts in Saskatchewan. Grant wrote: "I have this year been favoured with the opportunity of acting as the chauffeur of the grand old man of history, Prof. A.S. Morton." Years later he dedicated his book *Cornerstone Colony* to his friend, who had kindly acted years earlier as his "self-appointed private tutor in western history." History now became the young professor of animal husbandry's hobby. Western Canadian history became the subject of more and more of his after-dinner speeches. Ideas received from Professor Morton took shape leading Grant to prepare several CBC radio broadcasts.

Grant loved agricultural writing. During his honeymoon in 1935 the work-driven newlywed brought with him the manuscript of his first textbook on agriculture, a co-authored study. During idle moments he worked on it during the trip. Three more textbooks on agriculture followed, one also co-authored, the other two with Grant as sole author. At the same time as he wrote university texts he kept up his popular writing, contributing more and more to newspapers to reach a wider public. In the 1930s he wrote for, among other publications, the *Western Producer*, the *Saskatchewan Farmer*, the *Free Press Prairie Farmer*, and the *Family Herald and Weekly Star*. His wife Phyllis Cline, a former teacher, allowed him the freedom to plunge fully into his writing by supporting him in his many university and community commitments. Early in their marriage Phyllis once counted forty nights in a row that Professor MacEwan had been called away on one sort of public service or other. After the birth of their daughter Heather in 1939, Phyllis raised her largely on her own.

In his agricultural textbooks and articles, Grant spoke directly in plain words. As *Country Life*, the respected British Columbia farm journal, wrote in March 1946 of his fourth textbook, *The Feeding of Farm Animals*: "Prof. MacEwan is not addressing students in academic language; he is talking to fellow farmers in the language which they themselves use and understand, without interpreter nor dictionary." He would bring these same communication skills to his human historical writing.

Grant's first history book, *The Sodbusters*, appeared in 1948. The manuscript originated six years earlier in a four-part CBC Radio series, which the network continued in 1943 and 1944. Grant's interviews with old-timers, as well as his own library research, furnished him with the ideal topic, the "Sodbusters," the pioneer farmers and colourful individuals who opened up the Canadian prairies. To supplement the radio portraits previously prepared Grant added new biographies bringing the total number to thirty-seven.

The Sodbusters reveals Grant's marvellous gift for anecdotes, the raisins in the dough, essential to popular writing. Speaking of the days of the whiskey trade in southern Alberta in the early 1870s he wrote in his essay on Fred Kanouse: "Those on the frontier at that time didn't ask personal questions about 'the past,' and didn't tell much. Actually a man was more likely to achieve old age if his interests in history were not too highly developed." Throughout his book Grant included insights that indicated his intimate knowledge of the western range, little facts such as cowboys' love of chewing tobacco, as it "helped to counteract the dust when driving cattle." Throughout the volume the author's love of the early ranching period shines through, a time when "there was no barbed wire to restrict the cattle, and a man could ride five hundred miles in any direction without opening a gate."

Just before leaving the University of Manitoba in 1951 Grant wrote *Agriculture on Parade*, an interesting history of Western Canadian fairs and exhibitions. He accepted the assignment on 16 January 1950, and delivered the manuscript to Thomas Nelson and Sons, his Toronto publisher, on 6 August of the same year. In this same time period the Dean of Agriculture also faced an extraordinary number of unexpected interruptions occasioned by the great Winnipeg flood of 1950. Max Foran, editor of his diaries, summarizes. First came the evacuation that spring of seventy-five thousand people, including Phyllis and Heather. "Then, at night, MacEwan manned the graveyard shift on the sewer gang in an effort to keep the sewers open. During the day, his time was spent mainly in trying to feed the university livestock from a rowboat. Following the flood, he was a member of the three man Red River Valley Board which administered over thirty-five million dollars in rehabilitation funds from the two levels of government." Yet, despite all this, he finished his manuscript in record time.

Agriculture on Parade contains the statement that the story of Western Canadian exhibitions and fairs, "should be recorded as a chapter in that unnamed, unwritten but greater work which we may for convenience call the Romantic Rise of Western Canada." This became Grant's next book.

Between the Red and the Rockies, published in 1952 by the University of Toronto Press, Canada's foremost academic publisher, told the story of one and a half centuries of agriculture in Western Canada. Grant's foreword includes this statement of belief: "The agriculture of Western Canada . . . has a personality that is rich and colourful. The story of its romantic rise should reveal entertaining, academic and cultural values and is one that should be told in school and college classrooms." The *Saskatoon Star-Phoenix* noted its straightforward prose, "readable by people who never seeded a crop or knew whether the cattle in the pasture they passed were Holsteins or Herefords."[2] Other reviewers agreed on its value as a popular introduction to the topic.[3] Hilda Neatby of the Department of History at the University of Saskatchewan enjoyed reading the volume, "written with the verve and zest of one who loves the story he has to tell"; but she did voice serious concerns. The book lacked documentation, a bibliography, and analysis. The author, she added, was no historian: "He lacks the historian's faculty for combining mastery of facts and logical analysis with that exercise of imagination necessary to produce one whole clear picture of the past."[4]

One could argue that Professor Neatby, and many future reviewers of Grant MacEwan's books, misjudged his intentions. He wrote for a general audience. Grant aspired to be a good teller of stories, and not to analyze or to provide the latest interpretations. The agricultural expert came to human history with a sense of urgency. He wanted both Western and Eastern Canadians to know Western Canada's past. As he told Max Foran in 1983: "My own parents belonged to a generation which came in soon after the railroad arrived. I knew that they had a story and that there were people around me who made me laugh and inspired me with their stories, but that nothing was happening to record their memories." As Grant was the first to admit: "I wasn't an historian by training. I stumbled into it."

Grant's first three history books were published in Toronto. After completing his next manuscript in 1956, Grant sent it off to Ontario. The manuscript carried the working title, "Boozological Bob—Alberta's Prize Personality." It was a biography of the life and times of Bob Edwards of the *Calgary Eye Opener*, the most outrageous newspaper in early twentieth-century Western Canada. No one had ever written a full study of him. At the end of his enquiry letter Grant mentioned: "I think that I should add just this, that if and when a book is published on Bob, the people of the West will go for it enthusiastically."[5] But Grant's track record, and assurances of a Western Canadian market, were not good enough. Thomas Nelson and Sons turned the book down, as did the University of Toronto Press, and Macmillans, all large Toronto publishing houses.

Fortunately the Institute of Applied Art, educational publishers in Edmonton, and the only book publisher in Alberta at the time, took a chance on the manuscript. They brought it out as *Eye Opener Bob* that October. It proved a great success. As *Time* magazine reported on 23 December of that year: "Bookstores in Calgary and Edmonton have a hot new bestseller in their racks, and it is home-grown."[6] The *Calgary Albertan* published a particularly warm review, one which captured exactly what Grant had tried to do: "Old-time Calgarians will lose forty years while they are strolling through this book. For them it is a privilege. The younger generation and the newcomers have a duty to read it, for only thus will they know that Eighth Avenue is hallowed ground."[7]

Eye Opener Bob ranks as one of Grant's best books. In Bob Edwards, a noble man who fought a losing battle against alcoholism, he had the ideal character. In Grant's words, the best subject for a biography is "somebody who achieved something, wasn't all saint and wasn't all sinner. But a little of both . . ." Grant located copies of the *Eye Opener*, and read them carefully. Throughout he indicated the issues from which he took his information, and mentioned in his text the old-timers he consulted. The richness of *Eye Opener Bob* becomes all the more apparent when compared with his later book about Bob Edwards's great friend, the celebrated Calgary lawyer and orator, Paddy Nolan. *He Left Them Laughing When He Said Good-bye* was written in the mid-1980s, too long after Nolan's demise in 1913. Few stories remained to be collected. By contrast, in the mid-1950s individuals still remained in Calgary who had known Bob Edwards, who died in 1922, quite well.

Grant arrived in Calgary in 1951, shortly after he ran unsuccessfully in a Brandon federal by-election. By entering the electoral race he had to resign his academic position at the University of Manitoba. In Calgary he obtained a position as the Beef Producers Council's general manager, a perfect day job from Grant's point of view, as it left him with plenty of time for other interests, including writing. He quickly became involved in community activities, winning a seat on city council in 1953, and then election to the provincial legislature in 1955. After becoming a MLA he remained an alderman but resigned from the Beef Producers Council. To continue his writing he took an office in the Maclean Building downtown (since demolished). He bought some second-hand furniture and decorated the walls with prints of the Old West by the American cowboy artist, Charlie Russell. In his small, low-priced office, his "hole in the wall," Grant produced in the late 1950s *Eye Opener Bob*, and several other very successful books.

Calgary changed enormously in the 1950s. Grant arrived at a time when the huge influx of newcomers during the city's oil and gas boom pushed aside tales of early Calgary. He arrived just in time to record stories soon to disappear. One must appreciate the context. The Glenbow Archives and Library, that wonderful repository of Western Canadian history, only began in 1956. In late May 1957, Grant urged the Men's Canadian Club of Calgary to work for more historical research and for the preservation of old Calgary records. "The ideas and records of the past are like the passenger pigeon, once they are gone they are gone forever."[8]

As a popular historian Grant felt biography furnished the best approach to the general public. "Farm raised and resourceful," is how he described Colonel James Walker. Clearly in his eyes the former mountie was a role model for young people. He once mentioned to his son-in-law Max Foran, "I believe that biography is the best way to inspire young people. Kids need heroes."

Grant resigned as Alberta Liberal leader in 1959, returned to the city council, and became mayor of Calgary from 1963 to 1965. Appointed lieutenant-governor of Alberta in late 1965, he served until 1974. He kept writing; he simply could not stop. When a reporter asked him in 1967 if he planned to write another book, Grant replied: "That's like asking an alcoholic if he's going to get drunk again."[9]

Three months after his "retirement" as lieutenant-governor in 1974 the University of Calgary appointed him to give a credit course in the History Department, "From the Red to the Rockies" on the exploration and settlement of the Canadian Prairies.[10] He also undertook to give two lectures a week at Olds Agricultural College on the history of Western Canadian agriculture. In the following year he began giving a Western Canadian history course for seniors. At the same time he kept up his publication of books on Western Canada at white heat, producing more than twenty books over the next ten years.

Grant's extraordinary ability to manage time helps to explain the prolific publications. If not travelling he would get up early in the morning, or stay up late at night to jot down a few extra sentences. He also wrote on trips. Grant could write anywhere, on buses, trains, airplanes, but he preferred buses. He worked from files on his chosen subject. Through reading, research, and interviews he collected information which he put in a file. When the file on a subject became thick enough he began his book. He wrote out by hand the first draft, then transcribed it himself on his Royal portable typewriter. As he transcribed, he revised the text and polished the language. After a few handwritten corrections off the manuscript went to his publishers.[11]

Grant's lack of analysis, his poor documentation of sources, and his invented dialogue worried some academics. But they recognized his extraordinary ability to reach the general reader. "MacEwan has certainly told a good story in this book, although it is not necessarily good history," one academic wrote of *Sitting Bull* (1973). Another disliked the author's uncritical approach in *Charles Noble* (1983), yet added: "MacEwan writes well and tells a good story."[12]

What did Grant think of his academic critics? If their reviews upset him he never mentioned it, with just one known exception. In a 1984 newspaper article a hint of his discomfort appears. In one rare outspoken moment the eighty-two-year-old author replied to a reporter's question about *Marie Anne*, his just-published book on Louis Riel's grandmother, Marie-Anne Lagimodière, the first French Canadian woman to cross the Canadian Shield to the Red River, and then beyond into what is now Saskatchewan and Alberta. On account of the lack of documentary information Grant wrote the book in a fictionalized manner. He invented several characters, and wrote dialogue for them to create a living, moving story. When the reporter asked about the academic community's possible reaction, Grant replied: "I don't know what the scholars will think of it. Nor do I really care. I'm not writing for them, I'm writing for Canadians."[13]

W ell into his eighties the former lieutenant-governor kept up his rigorous community commitments, as well as his historical writing and research. One day in early 1986 deserves to be remembered. Invited to participate in events at Edmonton's Grant MacEwan Community College, Grant rose in the early hours and boarded a Greyhound bus for the four-hour trip north. In Edmonton he visited the several college campuses for "Grant MacEwan Day," then asked to be dropped off at the

Edmonton public library to do some research for a few hours. Just before his hosts returned to drive him to the elegant college dinner, Grant changed his clothes in the library's public washroom. As the evening's guest speaker he spoke for twenty to twenty-five minutes on public service and the life of Saskatchewan's Tommy Douglas, who had just died. Then, at his request his hosts drove him back to the Edmonton Greyhound bus station for the four hour return trip to Calgary. He returned home around midnight. He was then eighty-three.[14]

After the death of his wife Phyllis in 1990 Grant's life became quite lonely. The den in his home on Hallbrook Drive in southwest Calgary became his refuge, with magazines, papers, and books lining the walls from the floor to the ceilings. He published two more books, *Coyote Music and other Humorous Tales of the Early West* in 1993; and *Buffalo: Sacred and Sacrificed* in 1995. He still had fun giving historical talks. *Seniors' World*, an Alberta Seniors' magazine, reported in January 1995 a recent address of his at the Golden Age Club in Calgary. The ninety-two-year-old popular historian spoke on "Funny and Humorous People," a tribute to the foothills personalities, bold and creative, who made nineteenth-century Alberta so unique. He spoke of Bob Edwards, Paddy Nolan, and several early Eastern Canadian characters in Alberta. Then, he added: "When the smart and daring people left Ontario for Alberta, that left a pretty boring province back East." The crowd roared. Grant still knew how to work an audience.[15]

He lived in the mid-1990s in his own apartment in downtown Calgary, near his beloved Glenbow Library and Archives, and the Local History Room of the Calgary Public Library on Macleod Trail. In 1997 he moved to the Beverly Centre, a long-term care facility in southwest Calgary. There he completed the dictation of his final book to his son-in-law Max Foran. *Watershed: Reflections on Water* appeared several months after his death on 15 June 2000.

On 6 May 2000, Grant made what would be his last public appearance. At the Alberta Book Awards Gala in Calgary, the Writers Guild of

Alberta presented him with a Golden Pen Lifetime Achievement Award, given for significant literary contribution and/or literary achievement. To date the award has only been previously been given to one other individual, the late W.O. Mitchell in 1994. Grant, ninety-seven years old, ended his magnificent acceptance speech with these words of encouragement: "I tell the young people, who haven't had many books published, 'Don't give up, the best books are yet to be published, the best have yet to be written, the best books are yet to be read.'"[16] The spirit of this remarkable man who believed so intensely in Western Canada, and who lived throughout almost all of the twentieth century, lives on to inspire us in the twenty-first.

ACKNOWLEDGEMENTS

Grant's good friend Mary Mjolsness kindly showed me her excellent clipping files on him. She has since donated them to the Glenbow Library. In addition, Mary lent me numerous volumes from her complete collection of Grant MacEwan books. I am also grateful to Lee Shedden for his identification of important book reviews in the Grant MacEwan fonds, University of Calgary Library Special Collections/Archives, which I had missed, particularly in Acc. No. 392/86.14, 2.54. Special Collections/Archives has a very rich collection of materials on Grant. Wonderful collections of clippings about his life appear in both clipping files of the Glenbow Library, and the Local History Room of the Calgary Public Library, Macleod Trail branch, both favourite haunts of Grant. My thanks to all.

From Grant MacEwan's Journals (1986)

EDITED BY MAX FORAN

December 25, 1926 At home all day. I have persuaded Mother and Dad to take a holiday at the West Coast and I will remain home and hold the fort.

January 3, 1927 I had a phone message from J.G. Robertson, livestock commissioner, asking if I would return at once and conduct some work for the branch at Moose Jaw. My reply was "No." I will run the farm this winter.

January 5, 1927 I'm alone on the farm and have about sixty head of cattle, horses and a house full of hens. Mother left bushels of food including two large batches of brown bread (the kind of black stuff which she alone can make) and froze it in the fresh state. I've also laid in a pail of jam and a case of canned tomatoes.

January 17, 1927 Batching is going fine. Meals served at all hours. I baked a pan of biscuits and the dog liked them so well that I gave him the entire batch. D.N. Jamieson has been here twice for meals. I told him that if he took a good dose of salts prior to one of my meals and another after, the chances are that the meal would never hurt him.

About forty degrees below this morning and much of the day. One old hen laid a frozen egg. Some of the neighbours thought that a joke but the poor old hen didn't see the joke.

January 24, 1927 Forty-four below this morning. When I was through milking, I had a pail full of shreds which looked like macaroni. Each squirt of milk froze before it settled.

February 16, 1927 Beauty calved rather unexpectedly this afternoon. I put the cattle out this morning and went to the valley this afternoon, returning about 3:30. Immediately upon my return I put the cattle in the stable but old Beau was missing. My next job was to find Beauty and her calf. I was sure the latter, if born on this severely cold day, would be dead, but I was hopeful. I hitched the big team to the stoneboat and began the search. It was bitter cold and darkness was falling. After exploring the bluffs, I turned to a straw pile on the southeast quarter and, sure enough, there was Beauty and her bull calf—the calf quite white with frost. It was badly frozen but still alive. I placed it on the boat and held it there while I drove with one hand. It was cold. I froze several fingers before I got home but that was all right as long as I saved that bull calf.

February 17, 1927 Beauty's calf is living in the kitchen of the house along with me. I brought him in to get thawed out last night and each time I return him to the barn he freezes again. His tail and ears become quite stiff and even his nose freezes. It looks as if I'll have to keep him in the house all winter even though his house manners are the worst in the world. I carry him to the stable for a suck about five times during the day, and he is awfully happy to suck in the stable and sleep in the house.

February 20, 1927 Beauty's calf is still in the house and his manners are not improved. I plan to try him in the stable again tomorrow and to protect his ears I have made him a cap or head gear out of an old sweater. It has the dandiest ear pockets. I will also bandage his tail and put him right in an old woollen sweater.

March 1, 1927 Attended a public lecture in Melfort by J.G. Haney of the IHC demonstration farms. Then I stayed up all night to write the lecture up for *Melfort Moon*. (EDITOR'S NOTE: J.G. Haney was a representative of International Harvester. MacEwan's report on the lecture for the *Melfort Moon* marked his first piece of public writing.)

March 11, 1927 Poor old faithful Scotty was sick last night and I thought he was going to pass out but he is somewhat brighter looking today. I was moved to writing a poem to him last night, but my poetry is so rotten that when I wrote a poem to a dying dog, the dog didn't die.

~

June 7, 1937 My father, while loading a car of cattle for the Saskatoon spring show, broke and crushed his wrist and was taken immediately to the hospital. According to the story as told, he heard the bones collapsing and immediately called to Mother for the whiskey bottle. At the hospital, he was placed on the table, given chloroform and the bones set. While under the anaesthetic, the doctor, Dr. McKendry, pulled out the last nine teeth in the old gentleman's head.

Evidently, the doctor had been trying to persuade him to have these removed for a long time but he would never take time to have it done. Dad went home twenty-four hours after being admitted to hospital, nursing a big cast on his arm and toothless. Phyllis asks me if I'm a philosopher and quotes Socrates, "Marry by all means. If you get a good wife you will become very happy; if you get a bad one you will become a philosopher—and this is good for every man!"

June 17, 1937 Up at 5:30, Coles and I drive to Henry Chapman's at Belle Plaines, saw an excellent two-year-old (Gallinger bull) and a few good cows. From there back to Regina and to the Jail Farm where we inspected a recent shipment of fifteen young boars from Ontario. The Percheron Stallion Rumulus looks splendid.

At the Jail Farm this morning, I acquired a pair of young orphan skunks, just walking. The mother was killed yesterday. The skunks arrived home with me this evening and although slow to take milk, after they had taken it, took a new and better lease on life. The sudden change from a creature of the wild to a devotee of man has occurred in eight hours.

June 18, 1937 Skunks doing well and already part of the household.

June 29, 1937 Saskatchewan crops pronounced the worst in history.

Saskatchewan wheat estimated today at 90 million or six bushels per acre average, which is two bushels per acre under the former low (1936). The situation over the entire province, with exception of a few small areas, is critical.

June 30, 1937 101 °F in shade (official) with strong hot south wind; a devastative day.

July 8, 1937 After judging this evening, I visited John Burns and discussed biographical sketches of his late uncle, Pat Burns. (EDITOR's NOTE: This marked the beginnings of MacEwan's ongoing interest in Pat Burns which culminated in a biography over forty years later. While John Burns was very cooperative, MacEwan realized even then the paucity of written records pertaining to Burns's personal life.)

July 9, 1937 Calgary to Saskatoon. The country for three hundred of the four hundred miles travelled looks desolate.

July 19, 1937 The skunks acquired on 17 June and descented on 12 July, disappeared this morning. Their departure was a tragedy in the MacEwan home.

July 21, 1937 The skunks were found this morning in a deep toilet hole under the dressing room at the University Stadium. I managed to snare them with a piece of wire and draw them up. They spent most of today devouring food. After their arrival home, we disinfected them and reinstated the prodigals.

July 22, 1937 Judged Ayrshires at Saskatoon Exhibition. We began cutting Apex wheat on the University Farm. The crop is early and poor but miraculous, nevertheless, when one considers the absolute deficiency of moisture.

August 26, 1937 My share of royalty on six months sales of "Science and Practice of Canadian Animal Husbandry" received today—$36.75. Total sales from September 1936 to 30 June 1937 were 420 copies.

August 28, 1937 The skunks have constipation. They have each had a dose of olive oil. We have between sixty-five and seventy loads of Russian thistles in the silo and ceased to ensile today. Can molasses was added to a part as a trial, the hope being to check putrefaction of the proteins by furnishing more available carbohydrates for bacterial attack. I expect to know a lot more about Russian thistles after this year. Phyllis and I tried Russian thistles for greens at dinner on 22 August and found the immature plants very much like spinach. (EDITOR'S NOTE: MacEwan recalls that the only yield from the University's one thousand crop acres was two hundred loads of Russian thistles. The resulting experimentation with them as fodder was not overly successful. They were low on palatability and were intensely laxative. At their best they could be utilized as an emergency measure. Phyllis MacEwan remembers being somewhat appalled at being asked to experiment with them as salad as at that time they had not been tested on cattle. Certainly she was even less impressed at her husband's comment that one would never know if they were good for cattle without personal experimentation. Both admit that the thistles "were not very good to eat.")

≈

EDITOR'S NOTE: MacEwan speaks fondly of his trips with Arthur Silver Morton whom he refers to as "the Dean of Western Canadian historians." Morton was the expert and MacEwan the labouring apprentice. Morton, a noted authority on the fur trade, possessed an uncanny ability to ferret out the precise location of long-disappeared fur trading posts. He was, however, hopelessly impractical in the bush where, clad in a suit and hat, he would wander about oblivious to everything but his quest. MacEwan recalls that he "had the dickens of a time keeping track of the old man." Certainly it was Morton who provided the greatest single influence in the shaping of MacEwan the historian.

September 15, 1938 Professor Arthur Morton and I left early this morning to search for sites of old forts and trading posts in NE Saskatchewan.

We began our search on the Upper Assiniboine, north of Canora, and made our night camp on the riverbank.

September 17, 1938 Efforts rewarded by the discovery of the sites of Carlton House (Hudson's Bay Co.) and Alexandria (North-West Co.) on the south side of the Assiniboine on SW33-32-3 W2. Only the small holes marking the old cellars, some below the bastions, remain. Carlton House was built in 1790 and abandoned about 1820.

This evening we journeyed NE to a small lake on the shore of which we searched for Peter Grant's trading house, but the exact location could not be discovered.

September 18, 1938 This morning we drove north from Pelly to the site of old Fort Livingstone, first capital of the Northwest Territories 1876–1877. "Here Lieutenant Governor Laird and His Council were sworn into office on 27 November 1876, and here on 8 March 1877, was held the first session of the North-West Council."

Our next jaunt was to look for Belleau's House on the east side of Snake Creek, about four miles west of Pelly. Unsuccessful.

To Old Fort Pelly, the Elbow of the Assiniboine and the Indian Reserve farther west. At the Reserve we were joined by Mr. Gilchrist (a Puchlinch man whose wife was a Galt Scot), and we searched the riverbank for a fort we did not find. Likewise, our search at the Elbow was fruitless, but we explored the site of Fort Pelly and also that of Old Fort Pelly from which location the post was moved on account of floods. Carlton House was superseded by Fort Hibernia and the latter by Fort Pelly. Fort Pelly was built about 1827.

September 19, 1938 We sketched the site of the old fort and drove on to look for Cuthbert Grant's house on the Assiniboine near Runnymede. We located the site on SW 14-28-31 W1. I picked up a button probably worn by my namesake. Cuthbert Grant was father of the half-breed Cuthbert Grant who led the rebels in the massacre of Seven Oaks.

The Old West 1754–1881

Anthony Henday: An Old Smuggler
Who Made History

If Anthony Henday, raised on the Isle of Wight just off England's south shore, had a profession, it was that of smuggling. When he was caught at it, his punishment was banishment from the island. He went to London, and being a bold and enterprising fellow, he was soon employed again, this time with the Hudson's Bay Company for work at distant York Factory.

There at the fort beside the mouth of the Hayes River, Governor James Isham was worried by reports of French traders from Montreal building on the Saskatchewan River and getting furs from Indians on their way to the Bay. Isham needed the trade and, recalling Henry Kelsey's journey to the interior in 1690, decided to send somebody into the region to persuade the natives to bring their furs all the way to the Bay to trade.

He called for volunteers, and Henday, who had been working as a handyman/labourer, said that he would go. By good fortune, a small group of Indians from deep in Blackfoot country was present at the Bay, and its leader, Conawapa, invited Henday to share his canoe. The two men became close friends. The group departed on 26 June 1754. They travelled up the Hayes River and reached the French post, Fort Paskoyac, on the Saskatchewan River twenty-six days later.

Calling at the French post, Henday had an opportunity to test his unpolished diplomacy. He and the French trader viewed each other with mutual distrust. Fortunately, Henday had been instructed to keep a journal:

"On my arrival, two French men came out, when followed a great deal of Bowing and Scraping between us

and then we entered their fort—or more properly a Hogstye for it was no better. They asked me where the Letter was [presumably a letter of authority]. I told them I had no letter, nor did not see any reason for one, but that the country belonged to us as much as to them. He made answer it did not and he would detain me there and send me to France. I said I knew France as well as he did and was not afraid to go. . . ."[1]

Henday's party returned to canoeing, but not for long because the Indians heard that their families were camping in the Carrot River Valley, and, abandoning their boats, the party set off on foot. The park country through which they travelled was rich in wild game, and the trip was made pleasant, according to Henday, by "feasting, smoking, drinking, dancing and conjuring." And if other luxuries were needed, his journal indicates that he had those too: "As I am looked on as a leader, I have ladies of different ranks to attend me."[2]

They moved out onto the prairies and passed, by Morton's estimate, northwest of today's Humboldt, crossed the South Saskatchewan River near Clarkboro, and continued to a point low on the Red Deer River. Then, following that river upstream, Henday and his friends met a band of Blood or Blackfoot Indians east and north of today's city of Red Deer. Henday was the first white man these people had seen. For Henday, it was the best encounter with the native people he was to have. They had two hundred tipis standing in two straight rows and were the first Indians seen riding horses.

The chief was a man of fine bearing and friendly, but he was unenthusiastic about going as far as the Bay to trade. Why? His reasons were clear and almost convincing: they were getting all the guns and beads they needed from the French without going so far. More than that, the chief's people were prairie Indians and were not accustomed to canoe travel; the food upon which they lived was buffalo meat and pemmican, without which they might starve on a long trip. Henday and his friends didn't argue. They moved on toward today's Rocky Mountain House to winter. There the mountains stood gloriously clear, and they were able to gather many furs.

In the spring, they moved toward the North Saskatchewan River and home base. Paddling downstream was faster and easier than paddling up. They made the mistake, however, of stopping at Fort La Corne, where the French brandy proved irresistible, with the result that Henday's stock of furs intended for York Factory was recklessly bartered away to his French hosts. He tried to replenish his supply of furs as he travelled, but at Fort Paskoyac the same mistake was made and the furs were all but lost. On 20 June—almost exactly a year after leaving—Henday was back at York Factory. He was forced to explain why he didn't have a full load of furs but was able to report that he had seen mountains with snow on them and Indians riding horses. He hadn't met many Indians who were ready to bring their trade to the Bay, though, so the trip was not instantly rewarding, but the message about taking the trade to the Indians should have been fairly clear.

From *Grant MacEwan's West: Sketches from the Past* (1990)

With Face to the West

When it became apparent that the new house being made from pine logs would not be ready for the newlyweds on their wedding day, 21 April 1806, Jean Baptiste Lagimodière arranged for the use of a cabin on an adjoining farm. The rented structure was not handsome, but it would break the wind and turn most of the rain for a few weeks. The setting was lovely—hills with the hue of a bluebird's feathers to the north, heavy maple trees to the east, and the Maskinonge River within a stone's throw to the west. Marie Anne's cup of happiness was running over and Jean Baptiste should have been busy enough with tasks on the new farm to ensure contentment. In addition to the completion of the house, there were logs to cut and split for rail fences, stumps to be demolished, ploughing with a pair of black Normandy oxen borrowed from the seignior, and the preparation of a garden plot shaped to fit Marie Anne's precise specifications.

Jean Baptiste could be a good worker as long as he was interested, but he had a record of restlessness, and whether his wife recognized it or not, his love of adventure was quite capable of overruling his dedication to menial tasks. That characteristic could, and did, spell trouble for a new wife.

For anyone with wanderlust in his bones, the spring season presented the biggest temptations. Before the new house was completed, Marie Anne detected a change in her husband's manner, almost as clear as a rabbit's changing coat at the same season. He was talking more about the Northwest where he had lived for four years. He was thinking with visible nostalgia about buffalo hunts, gay times at Pembina, and friends among prairie Indians. Marie Anne liked to hear him relate his adventures in the fur country, but why this sudden preoccupation?

She didn't allow herself to think it was serious, but one evening after a heavy day with logs, her husband unburdened himself in his own blunt way. Blaming the spring months, he admitted he had been caught up by the unyielding spell of the Northwest. "You won't like this," he warned his worried wife, "but try to understand. My feeling for you, it's the same as ever, but I can't do anything to kill that urge to go back with the canoes. I've decided I can't live here—not for now anyway. I've got to go, but it means leaving you for awhile, maybe a year. Then I'll come back and we'll live on our farm and have a family, a big family. You'll be all right, I promise. You'll always be my wife. You can live with your mother or stay with my family on my father's farm."

It was the longest speech Jean Baptiste had ever made and almost as exhausting as lifting pine logs. And it was enough to strike the bride of a few short weeks with shock and pain. She buried her face in his buckskin jacket, still pungent with smoke from the tanning, and said nothing. But if he interpreted her silence as submission, he was totally wrong. Unwilling, yet, to trust herself with a reply to this cruel proposal, she kept her silence and went to bed, not to sleep but to weep and think.

By the time he retired to bed, her eyes were dry and she was ready to make her speech, a brief one, but carefully rehearsed. "Ba'tiste," she said with iron in her voice, "I didn't marry you to live alone. I married you to be with you. Now, you won't like this any better than I liked what you said to me, but I have to say it. If you go west, I go too."

Had he heard her correctly? The words stunned him as he hadn't been stunned since a drunken hunter held a knife over him at Pembina. Angry as much as shocked, the words came more easily now. "What damn nonsense, girl! Don't you know that no white woman has ever gone beyond Grand Portage or Fort William? You don't know what you'd be getting yourself into if you went out there. No girl raised here could stand the life there." With mounting impatience he repeated, "You don't know what you're talking about. Would you be able to live without a house, without a priest, and without friends?"

She nodded in the affirmative and smiled faintly to indicate that she was listening. And Jean Baptiste talked on. "You think you'd be ready to sleep on spruce branches beside the river and travel all day in wet clothes? And live on pemmican? Damn it, woman, you'd have to be crazy to think about it."

He stopped talking long enough for her to start again. She had no intention of inviting a long debate, but felt she should answer him and hoped to have the last word.

"If you really believe you must go," she said firmly, "I give you a wife's consent to do so, but in case you didn't hear me correctly before, I repeat: if you go, I go too."

His opinion was unchanged. To take an attractive young wife to that uncivilized country would be sheer madness, but he knew now that his wife was not fooling. His choices were clear and limited; he could decide to settle down at Maskinonge where his life would be dull, or he could stoop to her foolishness and allow her to accompany him to the West. The former he could not do; the latter he did not want to do.

He thought of a way to resolve this problem in his own favour. He would sign on as a North-West Company voyageur, then place the request to take Marie Anne along before William McGillivray, the head of the company. He would refuse to accept a woman passenger and Jean Baptiste's wife would be forced to remain behind.

Great idea, he thought. Of course McGillivray would not allow an idle woman to take up valuable space in a freight canoe. Jean Baptiste would go next day to Trois Rivières and put it to the company men there. Marie Anne prepared a package of food for his trip and Jean Baptiste set out on foot, just as he had embarked upon many long distance journeys before.

He met the North-West Company men but was astonished and disappointed when they did not refuse the unusual request. Calmly, they told him: "Your wife can go but you will have to pay for the extra 150 pounds of freight. And you can't expect the voyageurs to change their ways because a woman wants to travel. You know how the canoemen eat and drink and swear. It would be a mistake for you to take her, but if you are that foolish, we'll let her travel."

The decision was made and there was no time to lose. Plans for the brigade were already well advanced and crews were being recruited and signed to contracts. Jean Baptiste signed as an experienced voyageur, and it was understood that the cost of his wife's passage would be charged against his wage account.

The news travelled like a grass fire at Maskinonge. "She's going too," people were saying in astonishment. "Even Jean Baptiste admits it's an awful mistake, but you know the willpower of that girl."

The days that followed were frantically busy and by the middle of May, the Lagimodières were ready to leave with the brigade from Lachine. They took Marie Anne's forty pounds of personal luggage and Jean Baptiste's hand-carved fiddle that he had carried on the previous trip to Pembina. After tearful farewells and many well-meaning warnings, the newlyweds were starting on what Marie Anne facetiously called their honeymoon. They went first to Montreal and then another nine miles to Lachine where the company canoes were being assembled.

Lachine buzzed with activity. Cargo was piled at the river's edge and voyageurs—each with a newly decorated paddle—were milling about, impatient to be going. And the gossip on every tongue was about the young woman who was going. "Imagine, she's going all the way to Red River—if she lasts that long."

"There she is," a man was saying, pointing his paddle in her direction. "Holy Joseph, she's pretty but she must be insane. What in hell are things coming to?"

"Why would the company allow her to go?" came the response. "It's not safe for her, and it's hardly respectable for a young woman to be travelling in that company. She'll know what I mean before she goes far."

Marie Anne tried to close her ears to the gossip because she knew very well she was going anyway, regardless of what anyone said. She might die en route but nothing would induce her to turn back. Glancing up at her husband, she wondered if he had heard the current whispers, but his whiskered face gave no clue to his thoughts. If he had heard them, he'd have probably said, "Let 'em talk. Nothing short of hellfire would stop her now."

"What big canoes!" she exclaimed in his presence and received no reply. "Ba'tiste, I said, what big canoes!"

"I told you they were big," he said without smiling, then hurriedly joined the men who were loading to get the maximum of freight into the limited space. He had told her about the size, but she had to see for herself to be impressed. Each of the so-called Montreal canoes was twelve paces long and each would require eight or ten paddlers. She had not thought of canoes being big enough to carry four tons of freight and another three-quarters of a ton of voyageurs. Nothing was the way she had imagined it, and the mounting confusion made her feel ill. For a moment she was afraid she could be persuaded to abandon the adventure and return alone to Maskinonge. She walked away from the scene and quickly recovered the confidence she needed.

She watched Jean Baptiste and his fellow workers toiling in the sun, fitting what seemed like big packages into small cavities, bundles of trade goods, food supplies, personal effects, kegs of rum, guns, hatchets, kettles, and a few tents, one of which was for her and Jean Baptiste if they wanted it. Indeed she did and would be grateful for the privacy it would provide.

Men talked in loud voices and as the time for departure drew near, excitement ran high. The men were jubilant as they sought to get acquainted with those with whom they would be sharing a canoe. The Lagimodières would be travelling in a brigade of four canoes. With ten men in each canoe and a woman in one, there would be forty-one people together at the camping hour. The men would have to co-operate; time alone would tell if the presence of a young woman would have an influence upon the rough and ready voyageurs. Ahead were two thousand miles and several months of travel, day after day of exposure to hot sun and driving rain, and an unchanging diet of corn meal and fat pork.

Ultimately, there would be the triumphant arrival at Fort William, Red River, or whatever the chosen destination.

Taking her place in the centre of the canoe, Marie Anne recognized another testing hardship—that of sitting in a cramped position day after day amid the bales of freight. She might have wished she could periodically get out and run behind as she had done many times when travelling by sleigh in winter seasons. There'd be no such freedom here.

She had no fear of being hungry, but suspected that the quality of the food and the manner of dispensing it would become monotonous, even nauseating. Her daily ration of one quart of cornmeal and an allowance of fat pork—same as that for the men—sounded unappetizing and dreary. But the loaded canoe, riding low in the water, gave proof that luxuries were out of the question, and she said again to herself: *If Jean Baptiste can do it without complaining, I can too.*

There was much waving and weeping at the moment of departure. Then, as if to ease the sorrow of separation, the voyageurs, responding to the bowsman's signal, broke into a favourite paddling song, matching its rhythm to the motions of their paddles:

Derrière chez nous il y a un étang,
En roulant ma boule,
Trois beaux canards s'en vont baignant,
Rouli roulant, ma boule roulant,
En roulant, ma boule roulant,
En roulant ma boule.

Le fils du roi s'en va chassant,
En roulant ma boule,
Avec son grand fusil d'argent,
Rouli roulant, ma boule roulant,
En roulant, ma boule roulant,
En roulant ma boule.

Marie Anne was calm but in no mood for singing. Regardless of her spirit, the uncertainty of the days ahead was awesome. Still, turning back was not in her thoughts. She would try to keep herself occupied, doing what she could to help or cheer the men in her canoe. Speaking for all to hear, she assured her own man that she would carry her own belongings over the portages. Amused smiles on ten male faces indicated doubt that she could do it. She, too, was slightly amused at their reaction, and repeated silently that she would show them that being a woman did not make her helpless. For the first night, the brigade camped on the westerly end of Montreal Island where travellers paid their respects at the Shrine of St. Anne, the patron saint of Brittany. Marie Anne placed her offering in the gift box, the last she would see for months, maybe years. Then, facing the shrine and making the sign of the cross, she said a simple prayer for protection and peace; "Oh Mother of Jesus, keep us from the dangers of rivers and lakes and violent men. And watch over all at Maskinonge until Jean Baptiste and I return to that place. Amen."

Everybody slept on spruce boughs, the hardened voyageurs under overturned canoes, and the Lagimodières in their small tent. Marie Anne could not sleep, not even with the reassuring arm of Jean Baptiste around her. Spruce needles pierced her tender flesh, and she could not tear herself away from a review of the first day's events and the prospects for the shapeless days ahead. She heard the bowsman's call to rise and was glad the night of mounting physical discomfort was over. By the time the teapot hung over a campfire was hot, the canoes were reloaded, and minutes after sunrise, they were ready to move out against the strong current of the Utawa River.

The old hands warned the novice voyageurs that because of portages and rough water, travel on this stream would be slow and heavy. But after an hour on the water, the bowsman would select an inviting riverside location and order a brief stop for part two of breakfast. Crewmen had their cup of tea before sunrise; now they would devour their cornmeal mush and fat pork, practically the same fare as at other meals. The only variation would consist of an occasional addition of fresh fish taken from the river.

With every halt for meals or portages, the bowsman was the first man to jump into the shallow water at the shoreline to steady the canoe as others disembarked. He was followed into the water by the steersman and then the paddlers. Marie Anne, the last to leave the boat, would be spared from a wetting by being carried on her husband's strong shoulders. Paddling on a river with many portages, the men's clothing was never dry before it was time to jump again into the water near the shore.

Voyageurs knew their days would be long and, with or without portages, they would be tiring. On a river, they complained about the portages, but on a lake where a day's paddling might be unbroken except for brief intermissions for a smoke, they might wish for the change of pace offered by a portage. No wonder their moods varied like March weather; they sang, complained, laughed, and cursed their occupation but remained intensely loyal to it. Marie Anne had tried to prepare herself for work and danger, but the monotony of sitting at the exact centre of the canoe, hour after hour, was something for which no preparation could be effective; and the cramped position caused her legs to ache cruelly. The tasks for which she could assume responsibility were limited. She won the gratitude of the men in her canoe by doing all the mending and the preparation and cooking of fresh fish when the men were engaged at a portage. These were useful chores but hardly satisfying for one accustomed to a much wider variety of activities. More than once Jean Baptiste saw her eyes fill with tears and knew that she was thinking of dear old Maskinonge, or suffering from leg cramps. For good reason, he worried about her, and although he ceased to talk about it, he still believed that she should not have come.

Even as he thought about it, bullets whistled over the bow of the boat and the voyageurs crouched low and reached for their guns. "Indians!" they said with one voice. "Keep low, they'll likely shoot again." No native figure was in sight, but one of the men replied with a shot to remind anybody within range that canoemen can shoot too.

The men had neither the time nor the will to engage in a war with the tribesmen, but here was a convincing reminder of another hidden danger for which they should be prepared, and paddling resumed at a faster pace.

Lake Nipissing's blue water and green border offered the brigade their first lengthy spell of canoeing without the necessity of periodic portages, and the miles passed pleasantly. Lake water, of course, could be rough enough to toss loaded canoes like corks in a washtub and, wisely, the men chose to travel close to the shore to permit a fast retreat to some nearby cove in the event of a sudden squall. But Nipissing remained calm and the only squalls came from the cormorants.

On Rivière de Française, the current favoured the canoes all the way, but presented five portages, all short ones. Then the party seemed to coast right into Lake Huron, the sight of which brought shouts of welcome from the men. The days on Huron passed without incident except for drenching rains from which there was no protection, forcing everybody to sleep in wet clothing.

Then there was Lake Superior, big and treacherous, with all the characteristics of an inland sea. The sun was setting when the brigade moved through the narrows and halted for a night camp on a stretch of white sand. The lake was peaceful and might have passed for the Sea of Galilee on a calm evening. As usual, Marie Anne gathered wood and started a campfire while the others joined in the routine of unloading, beaching the canoes, and making ready for the extra ration of rum that would honour Lake Superior.

Superior would be the last long leg of the journey to Fort William, at the end of which there would be relaxation and celebration. It was a pleasant prospect. And despite tired muscles, the rum induced the men to sit longer at the fire to sing some French songs and exchange stories. Steersman Dorian, as always, had stories from earlier adventures on this route. He told about the swimming moose that upset his canoe on Lake Superior, and then about a big wind storm on the same lake—a typical Dorian exaggeration—so strong that it picked up his loaded canoe, carried it the full distance of a paddling day, and set it down without loss of either cargo or men.

Marie Anne joined in the laughter and Jean Baptiste said he was glad that she hadn't forgotten how to laugh. But there was one voice more sober than the others, that of the bowsman. He agreed that progress to date had been good, and there would now be the advantage of straight travel, without the time-consuming portages, all the way to Fort William. "But by Gar," he said as he eased himself off the sand to make his bed under an overturned canoe, "you know you can't trust this old lake. I've seen the damnedest storms on this water. Sometimes they came up so fast that nobody had time to pull a waterproof over his shoulders or get a boat to shore. I tell you, a storm can come up just like my old woman's temper."

Jean Baptiste had no stories to tell but when he and Marie Anne finally retired to bed, the rum was still having its effect and he was in a mood to talk.

"Good men in this crew," he said. "Best I've travelled with."

"They seem like good people," she replied. "I guess we've been lucky in getting along so well. Maybe a woman in the crowd can bring good luck. Think so, Ba'tiste?"

He snickered and said nothing. She tried him with a more important question: "Ba'tiste, are you glad I came, or do you still wish I had stayed home?"

He wasn't ready for that question, and stammering slightly, replied: "Sometimes . . ." then held her more closely, making additional words unnecessary.

Lake Superior in the morning light looked beautiful, calm, and innocent. The voyageurs' hearts were light and Marie Anne's voice mingled with the others as paddling songs—unusual at early morning hours—echoed across the water.

Suddenly, the big lake seemed to erupt in anger. With hurricane force, the wind assumed command, and men turned their canoes toward the shore and paddled furiously. Here, without warning, the travellers were caught in the dangerous test of which they had been warned. Boats rose and fell as waves broke over them. Marie Anne was frightened. Having no paddle with which to take action, she closed her eyes and prayed for deliverance for all those battling desperately against the driving wind and waves.

There were signs of panic among the men. That would only weaken their chance of survival, and Marie Anne found the strength to make a show of composure. Crouching low and clinging to Jean Baptiste's ankle, she shouted to the men that they were doing well and must keep it up. Her words may have been lost in the howl of the storm, but it helped to bolster her own spirits. A huge wave broke overhead and she struggled to bail water from the boat, praying silently for divine rescue.

Turning to see how her own canoemen were getting along, she caught a glimpse of one of the other canoes in trouble, and cried out; "Oh God, they need help over there." The other boat was almost swamped and the crew were throwing freight overboard, bailing water, and fighting with all their strength against the waves.

"Pray, Marie Anne, pray," she was saying to herself, but even as she said it, the other canoe tipped and disappeared under an enormous wave. Momentarily, all traces of the boat were erased and then it reappeared, bottom side up. The men from the overturned canoe went under, then came to the surface, struggling. Marie Anne could count eight of them in the water but knew they had no chance of swimming to the shore, and only a slight chance of being picked up by one of the three remaining canoes.

"Come this way," paddlers in Marie Anne's canoe bellowed, but the wind hurled the words back at them. Rescue seemed hopeless. It was all that men in the upright canoes could do to stay afloat, but the young lady could sit still no longer. Defying instructions to remain low and hold both sides of the canoe, she stood erect and shouted frantic words of encouragement to the strugglers in the water. It did no good, and a mountainous wave cut off her view. Only a tug from her husband's right arm pulled her down and prevented her from toppling overboard.

When visibility improved somewhat, she thought she could still see eight men in the water making perceptible progress. One of the men reached her canoe and was pulled over the side. A second man made it to one of the other canoes; then a third and a fourth were pulled from the water. Sad to say, two of the young men went under and did not reappear.

Marie Anne felt sick but knew this was no time to surrender her strength. The storm raged on and their lives remained in imminent danger; nobody was sure of surviving. She sank back into the squatting position and took a firmer grip on Jean Baptiste's ankle. The assurance that he was still there gave her fresh courage, and from the depths of her memory came the words of the old medicine man who spoke years earlier beside the little Maskinonge River: *She will live long. Many times will her life be in danger but she will live long.*

There was another reason why she must live. She thought of the child she believed she was carrying and of which she had not yet said anything; the thought seemed to rout her fears. Jean Baptiste must be told now, she decided. It would help him too.

"Ba'tiste," she called loudly as a splash of lake water struck her face. "Are you listening? We must live. Do you hear me? We must live for the child, your child, our child under my heart. We must live."

What a moment to reveal such information! But his eyes acknowledged that he heard. At the same instant, he heard the bowsman say, "The wind is dropping, boys. We're going to make it." Even the hardened old voyageur was moved to add: "Thank God."

All except the two men who were lost succeeded in reaching the lake's north shore. Exhausted and sad, they ate their corn meal and pork and wasted no time in preparing their beds. Even wet clothes and bedding would not prevent them from resting and catching snatches of sleep.

In the seclusion of their tent, the Lagimodières talked about the baby Marie Anne believed she was carrying. Jean Baptiste tried to say something of the joy his wife's words brought to him, but sharing what was in his heart was not something he did easily, and he did little more than mutter some indistinct phrases. But his wife understood and wondered if their child would be the first of its race to be born in the new country.

He thought it likely that it would be; then, speaking like her guardian, he said: "You must take care of yourself. I will try to help you. You have to stop taking risks. Our baby comes first." He tried to find adequate words to tell her how much the men had admired her readiness to wade ashore after the storm in order to spare them as fully as possible, and that they were grateful for the encouragement and strength her words brought to exhausted men still battling with their paddles.

Many times during the night, men quit their beds to throw more wood on the fire and hover close to the flames until some warmth penetrated their wet clothes. Morning dawned bright and clear as though nature was trying to atone for the cruel treatment of the previous day. Nothing, however, would blot out the memories of that struggle, and nothing would remove the sadness occasioned by the loss of two colleagues. The men could carry their sorrows with them but as they knew very well, they would be expected to reload and be on their way to Fort William.

With a delay of an hour or two, the brigade was again in motion, this time with three canoes, three-quarters of the freight, and thirty-eight men instead of the original forty. They paddled closer to the shore line, thereby taking less chance of being caught in another storm. But in the remaining days of the journey to Fort William, paddling conditions were ideal and morale returned slowly but surely.

A young Easterner making his first trip to the West found the lake to be distressingly big and asked why people didn't call it Superior Ocean. He was a happy fellow when he heard Dorian call out, "Cheer up! Tomorrow we'll see Fort William."

From *Marie Anne: The Frontier Adventures of Marie-Anne Lagimodière* (1984)

Laidlaw's Pigs

Lord Selkirk selected the site for the Hayfield Experimental Farm, west of Fort Douglas, when he was at the Colony in 1817; but the decision to embark upon the program was made earlier and the Earl's choice of a man to be manager of the farm was already on his way to York Factory. The appointee, William Laidlaw, was a young man of enterprise who had farmed successfully in Scotland. Selkirk's instructions to him were to develop this Red River property as a dairy farm and make it useful as a public demonstration. The money needed would be forthcoming.

Laidlaw arrived at the Settlement after freeze-up in the autumn, burdened sufficiently to try any ordinary human patience with the most uncongenial and uncooperative travelling companions in the form of seven pigs for the Settlement, the first of their race to reach that place. Had he done nothing more than deliver the pigs under the most difficult conditions early winter could impose he would have earned a place in history.

Of course the settlers should have pigs as well as cattle, sheep and horses, even though members of the swine family seemed particularly foreign to this western land. Transporting the selected specimens across the Atlantic presented no great problem because the masters of sailing ships often carried pigs to consume waste and furnish fresh meat on long journeys. But conveying these, the most obstinate of farm animals, from York Factory to Red River was an undertaking presenting the most extreme difficulties, especially when the season was far advanced and frozen lakes and rivers could put a sudden end to travel by canoe.

But Laidlaw saw this as the first test of his stewardship and was determined to finish what he had undertaken. Proceeding from York

Factory, the pigs—by this time weighing about one hundred pounds each—were cooped up in a section of the canoe, which worked well enough. Daily, however, he became more aware of the danger of his boat being arrested by ice. Before reaching Jack River, winter weather brought all travel by water to an abrupt end and Laidlaw knew he must abandon the precious porkers or transport them by sled. Obtaining the necessary sleighs and toboggans and dogs to provide motive power, he wrapped the pigs in buffalo robes to prevent them from freezing, then tied each one down to the sled. The pigs protested with squeals to be heard for miles in the frosty atmosphere, and the hungry sleigh dogs, lusting for a taste of pork, had to be muzzled to prevent them from attacking.

Supplies of pig feed carried all the way from Scotland were running low and Laidlaw sensed the danger of losing his pigs through starvation—until he reached Jack River where he found an abundance of fish available for pig feed. He gave instructions about cooking the fish before feeding but apparently the helper did not obey orders and fed frozen fish which, in Laidlaw's opinion, accounted for the deaths of three animals. The remaining four, however, still carefully clothed in buffalo coats, reached Fort Douglas to command as much attention as if they were Bengal tigers. There they stood, the only members of their race in half a continent and, in terms of effort, surely the most expensive pigs ever bought for breeding purposes.[1]

From *Cornerstone Colony: Selkirk's Contribution to the Canadian West* (1977).

Rowand of Fort Edmonton

Fort Edmonton was the scene of stirring activities. It was always in a position of danger because of its location in relation to the Blackfoot and the Cree, both of whom came that far north. When the two enemy groups met, battle could be expected, but company men wanted to trade with both tribes, and the risks were accepted.

Trade in furs was the reason for the fort's existence, but boat-building and pemmican-making were sidelines for which the place gained fame. In 1850, there was also a small farm of about fifty or seventy-five acres under cultivation, on which wheat, barley, and vegetables were grown.

It was Chief Factor Rowand, however, who gave Fort Edmonton its distinctiveness. Rowand was an Irish-Canadian, born near Montreal in 1787, who started working for the North-West Company while still in his teens. He became chief factor at Fort Edmonton in 1823, remaining in the position until his death in 1854. His way with Indians was unusual, for although he tended to bully them, he still won their respect. Rowand had a well-filled medicine chest, which he used freely, thus gaining his reputation as a medicine man. Even the romance leading to his marriage to an Indian girl resembled something from a storybook. One day when he had been hunting, his saddlehorse returned without him. An Indian girl who may have been dreaming about living in his big house suspected trouble and rode out to search for him. She found him with a broken leg. After she managed to get him on her horse and bring him back to the fort, she set the fractured limb and cared for him. As a result of her kindness, he married her.

In becoming Mrs. Rowand, the girl soon moved to occupy the biggest house west of Toronto. It was strictly John Rowand's idea and became known as Rowand's Folly. Made from squared logs, it was seventy feet by sixty feet and three storeys high. The long balconies were just right for Colin Fraser of the Hudson's Bay Company who liked to pace slowly back and forth as he played his famous bagpipes, filling the river valley with Highland strains.

There were other Rowand innovations, making early Edmonton a place of distinction. The Chief Factor liked racehorses, and when Alexander Ross visited in 1825, Rowand had a two-mile racetrack near the fort. There was also Rowand's famous icehouse, made for storing buffalo meat. It was a big pit in the riverbank and, as soon as the ice was sufficiently thick on the river, men were directed to cut pieces and pile them around the walls. Then, having prepared the ice chamber, Rowand's men went hunting to try to fill the pit with buffalo carcasses. Sometimes buffalo herds were within gunshot of the fort walls; sometimes they were far away. Rowand wanted his meatpit to be full in case of a scarcity in the herds later in the winter, and as many as five or six hundred unskinned carcasses were piled in the icy cave and frozen. The big appetites of 150 or 200 people and many dogs living inside the stockade demanded red meat and lots of it. Governor George Simpson regarded Rowand as the best of the traders in his far-flung fur empire. Everybody knew him as a bustling and vigorous fellow with a fiery temper. It was during a fit of anger while visiting Fort Pitt that he dropped dead. Friends buried him there, but somebody recalled one of Rowand's last requests: namely, that his bones ultimately might rest close to Montreal. George Simpson, who was by this time knighted, authorized that the body be removed and taken to the East, but such an order presented problems at a time when transportation was still at the cart and canoe stage. The story is told that the remains were placed in a barrel containing rum and taken by Sir George Simpson's canoe to Fort Garry. Voyageurs were superstitious people, however, and the idea of carrying a dead body or the bones of a dead man produced growing unrest, and to avoid a rebellious refusal to carry the barrel any further, Simpson sent it with a fresh and unsuspecting crew to Hudson Bay, to be taken by sailing ship to London and then rerouted back to Montreal. Finally, after being shipped many thousands of miles by water, John Rowand's bones were laid to rest exactly where the great fur trader had requested.

From *West to the Sea (A Short History of Western Canada)* (1968)

Maski-pitoon: "He Stands Alone"

Friends and foes alike feared the Cree Chief, Maski-pitoon. Nobody wanted to argue with him. A man of terrible temper, he scalped one of his wives in a moment of rage. Although the unfortunate woman survived, she carried the ugly mark of matrimonial violence for the rest of her life.

Like Saul of Tarsus, this tough and cruel fellow breathed "threatenings and slaughter," and like the same Saul, caught a vision of a better way of life, changed completely and became a gentle person, on the best of terms with many of the early missionaries. Although the churchmen tried to take full credit for the amazing transformation, the clearest evidence shows that this Indian had caught the idea and obtained the guidance directly from the Great Spirit, in just the way Indians expected to obtain inspiration and truth.

In his appearance Maski-pitoon was typically Cree—medium in height, straight in posture, bowed in the legs and heavily muscled. His hair was long and black and his facial features were sharp as though shaped by an artist's chisel. The marks of a fine intellect showed through the angry scowl which seemed to be an essential part of the office of Chief. "A kingly-looking man," said John McDougall when he met him in 1862. An old injury left one arm with an abnormal twist, accounting for his name which in Cree meant "One Whose Arm Has Been Broken." But a mere arm defect was not enough to handicap the man's activities on hunts and war fronts.

Not much is known of Maski-pitoon's early years although Rev. R.T. Rundle encountered him in 1841 and was impressed by an obvious depth of character behind a rough exterior. Already he had a fine array of long-haired scalp trophies, mainly Blackfoot and Sioux.

Anything Maski-pitoon undertook to do he did thoroughly and his followers watched with a mixture of fear and pride. He won the right to become Chief by undisputed performance, passing the harshest tests. A savage fighter, he never flinched from danger, and was cruel and uncompromising in revenge.

But in addition to all else, he was a man with an enquiring mind and many of the immigrant whites were impressed. Missionaries of various denominations were anxious to win him to their beliefs and one after another tried to persuade him to abandon what they called his pagan ways and embrace the white man's religion. But Maski-pitoon was not convinced that the newcomers' faiths were in any way better than his own.

Artist Paul Kane, making a sketching trip across the continent, saw Maski-pitoon near Fort Pitt in 1848. That would have been seven years after the Chief met Rev. Rundle. At this time, as always, Maski-pitoon was on good terms with the churchmen while resisting their proselytizing overtures. As told by Kane, the Indian's words at that time made him seem like one of the pioneers in the ecumenical movement. Arriving at the Cree camp, Kane and his friends went to the lodge of "the Chief named Broken Arm" and were invited to sit on buffalo robes "in the best part of the tent." Food was provided and then the Chief, having cut tobacco and filled a handsome stone pipe, took a few whiffs and passed it around.

"We sat up very late talking to the Chief who seemed to enjoy our society very much," Kane wrote. "Among the topics of discourse, he began talking about the effects of the missionaries amongst his people and seemed to think that they would not be very successful; for though he did not interfere with the religious beliefs of any of his tribe, yet many thought as he did . . . As Mr. Rundle (Wesleyan) told him that what he preached was the only true road to heaven, and Mr. Hunter (Anglican) told him the same thing, and so did Mr. Thebo (Roman Catholic) and that they all three said that the other two were wrong, and as he did not know which was right, he thought they ought to call a Council amongst themselves . . . but until they agreed, he would wait."

Broken Arm then related a Cree legend concerning a member of his tribe who had accepted Christianity and lived as he was instructed by the church missionaries. When he died, he was taken up to the white man's heaven but he was not happy there. All things the white man loved were present but they were not what the Indian could enjoy. The spirits of his ancestors were not there to welcome him. There was no hunting and no fishing. There was none of the fun of horse stealing. Sensing the Indian's sadness, the Great Manitou called and enquired why he was not happy in such a beautiful place. The Indian admitted the surroundings were attractive but told how he missed the spirits of his own people. He was lonely. The Great Manitou was sorry that he could not move this man directly to the Indian heaven but because "he had been a very good man, he would send him back to earth again and gave him another chance." Maski-pitoon did not want to be caught in the wrong heaven.

Here was an Indian given to independent thought and, with passing years, his analysis of Native customs led to a complete change in his outlook and way of life. Indeed, the most exciting part of his career was after he became a man of peace.

Nobody can be sure how or when the radical idea of a peaceful Indian community came to him but come it did, leaving him disturbed until the questions arising in his mind were settled. His first conclusion was that tribal customs, no matter how firmly they were established, should stand up to the test of reason.

Maski-pitoon may have discussed the questions about behaviour with John McDougall from whom he would have received encouragement, but there would be extremely little sympathy from his own tribesmen. He talked with the Medicine Man but it was a waste of time. That wise man of the tribe scorned such an unorthodox thought; why, living without war would be as unthinkable as an eagle living without claws or a buffalo without horns.

Next, Maski-pitoon consulted an uncle, old and blind, and received some help. "It's your decision," said the old man "but don't give up yet.

Take three black feathers to represent hatred, cruelty and war and take three white feathers to represent sympathy, honesty and peace and go into the hills with them. Decide which ones you will keep and live with."

The Chief knew he had to seek solitude and commune with the Great Spirit. If it was right to consider a peaceful existence, the Great Spirit would tell him. It would be the direct approach in a search for truth, and most logical. Maski-pitoon did not have to explain his exact purpose in going away to the forests and hills for a few days in this manner because Indians did it often and generally found help.

Taking no food and no sleeping comforts, the Chief went on his way toward the mountains, alone. He knew the country and had no fear of becoming lost but he was travelling without bow-and-arrow or gun, and when he became hungry he would be obliged to eat berries, bark or roots. At night he would relax on Mother Earth and pull some pine boughs over himself. And when it rained he would seek the shelter of a big spruce. He would not hurry but would become wholly a citizen of Nature's community, meditate, and pray. It might take a day; it might take a week. Time did not matter; it mattered only that he be in the mood to hear the message when the Great Spirit would communicate to him.

It came in a dream, clear and positive. The voice told him to carry the white feathers in his hair and burn the black feathers. Maski-pitoon listened for more. All people and all animals were part of the Great Spirit's family. He had equal concern for all. Needless killing was wrong. Anyone with an understanding and conscience should work for peace in that community of living things. All this made sense to Maski-pitoon and he turned toward home, wearing the white feathers in his hair.

He was now convinced, but what could be done about it? As he knew very well, it would be difficult to persuade his own Crees that any new way of living would be better than the one with which they were familiar. And to win over the enemy Blackfoot, with whom the Crees had fought about as often as the tribesmen met, would be still more difficult. For any lesser personality there would have been no hope of gaining even a hearing on the subject of inter-tribal peace, but Maski-pitoon commanded respect tinged with fear. He called his Cree followers together and asked them to consider seriously the merits of his proposal. The Crees were amazed—even shocked—at the idea being presented by one whose reputation was for killing. They would have to think it over. They talked about it and some thought the idea was ridiculous, but most of them agreed it was worth a trial. Maski-pitoon knew that it was now up to him to take the proposal to the enemy Blackfoot. But how was that to be done when Crees and Blackfoot, without means of communication, simply shot each other on sight? In the circumstances he would have to wait for an opportunity, and it came.

The Crees were hunting in the area of Wetaskiwin when they came upon a small band of the Blackfoot travelling to Fort Edmonton to trade. Cree guns far outnumbered those of the enemy this time but instead of annihilating the Blackfoot braves on the spot, the Crees brought them to camp as prisoners and placed them on display before the Chief. In looking them over, Maski-pitoon identified one as the murderer of his father. The Chief gazed intently and the Blackfoot, knowing the reason for the special interest, cringed with fear, convinced that he would be slain immediately. Even the Crees standing nearby supposed the urge for revenge would override the recently adopted ideals.

Speaking quietly, Maski-pitoon called for his best leather coat and when it was brought, he addressed the Blackfoot:

> You are a murderer. You killed my father. There was a time when I would not miss the chance to kill you quickly to settle that old account. But I have found a better way and I am not going to take your life. I am going to let you go, hoping that you will support my plan for peace between Crees and Blackfoot. Because you killed my father, you must now be a father to me. Take the message to your Chief and your friends that Maski-pitoon is serious in his

hope that these two tribes will cease their killing, and live side by side in peace. And now, I ask you to return to your people wearing my best coat which I am presenting to you. I shall expect you to pass my views to your Chief and assure him that I am ready to meet with him and talk at any time and any place. Now, be going.

Astonished, the Blackfoot replied: "Never have I heard anything like this. These are the words of a wise and good man. My people will be glad and say: 'Maski-pitoon is the bravest of them all.' You must come to our camp and I will be your guide and your guard to ensure safety."

Some time later Maski-pitoon and six or seven Crees were on their way into Blackfoot territory for the crucial discussions. But while they were still far from the Blackfoot camp an enemy war party swooped down with murderous yells, no doubt contemplating some easy scalps for their belts. The shock of sudden attack sent the Crees to flight, leaving only Maski-pitoon, standing erect and alone, with neither gun nor show of fear. As they rode in for the kill, the Blackfoot men were astonished at seeing a defenceless Cree showing no inclination to escape, and they dropped their guns to stare.

At this point, a Blackfoot recognized the Cree Chief and shouted: "It is the brave Maski-pitoon, of whom our Blackfoot brother told us. He stands alone. We want him to tell us what he told our brother."

Gladly, Maski-pitoon explained his hope of discussing peace with the Blackfoot Chief and immediately the warriors from the south offered to escort the Crees in safety to the Blackfoot Chief's tipi. The Indians of the two tribes went on their way to the Blackfoot encampment and there the two leaders smoked a pipe of peace and entered into a pact to end the constant fighting, the first of its kind in prairie country. From it came the name, Wetaskiwin, meaning Hills of Peace.

The change in Maski-pitoon surprised everybody. In 1865, he told John McDougall of his sorrow in learning that his own son had been on an expedition to steal horses from the Stonies at Pigeon Lake. It was a strange reversal of sentiment. "All men are now my friends," he said, "and especially all missionaries." He did not say that he was accepting the teachings of the missionaries in their entirety but he did say that if he ever fought again, it would be on the side of the missionaries. Then, looking directly at John McDougall, he added: "I will pray the Great Spirit to help you to gain power over young men."

The McDougalls, quite wisely and properly, did all in their power to cultivate the friendship of the Chief. After establishing their mission at Victoria, northeast of Fort Edmonton, they saw much of him. A room in the McDougall home was made available to him at all times and there is reason to believe the Chief used it quite freely, and the increasing number of contacts between Indian and missionary was mutually helpful. John McDougall's writings carried many references to Maski-pitoon, giving one of the best insights to his character.

There were two or three peaceful years but pacts had to be renewed. On one of the trips into Blackfoot country, Rev. George McDougall and John McDougall accompanied him and the discussions were successful; but on another occasion, presumably in 1869, Maski-pitoon and a few of his followers rode again into the Blackfoot country and into the Blackfoot camp to renew the understanding with the neighbouring Chief, and this time there was tragedy. Dr. Edward Ahenakew, with a fellow-Cree's interest in what happened, related the circumstances as he heard them from Chief Thunderchild.

It was late summer and the little group of Crees going on the peace mission included one of Thunderchild's cousins. When nearing the Blackfoot camp, Maski-pitoon raised a Hudson's Bay Company flag and a party of Blackfoot responded by raising a similar flag and coming to meet the visitors. "But suddenly, a foolish young Blackfoot arrives unnoticed and unsuspected," Dr. Ahenakew wrote. "He rides around fast and shot Broken Arm dead." The Blackfoot Chief, who had grown to admire and like Maski-pitoon, was stunned and saddened. The Crees were angry at the murder of their Chief and were ready to go to war.

It is the story of a man with a record of brutality becoming a man of goodwill, and justifying the remark from the editor of the *Regina Leader* that he was "a courteous, hospitable gentleman of Nature."[1] Maski-pitoon, as an apostle of non-violence, in his pursuit of peace and in his death at the hand of an assassin, seems to qualify as the Mohandas Gandhi of the Canadian plains.

From *Portraits from the Plains* (1971)

Political Comedy at the Portage

While Confederation was still a new word in the East, the West witnessed two attempts to fill the constitutional vacuum, one in the Provisional Government called New Nation, under Louis Riel, and the other, the Republic of Caledonia, an infamous invention of Thomas Spence. Motives were totally different. In the so-called Republic, spectators saw a plan intended to do more for Spence than for the country.

As the Capital of the Republic, Portage la Prairie became the setting for the most unusual bit of political comedy enacted in the entire West and it would be a misfortune if that local drama in Confederation year and the year following were allowed to be forgotten.

The founder of the homespun Republic arrived at Fort Garry in 1866. His real purpose was cloaked in mystery and his conduct did nothing to remove suspicion. But for ambition and imagination, Thomas Spence deserved the highest praise. While still a stranger in those parts, he attracted attention by writing a letter to the Prince of Wales in London, inviting His Highness to a prairie bear and buffalo hunt with the Indians, and signing as one of the tribesmen. The letter was written on birchbark and had all the appearance of a genuine Indian effort. In due course, a very formal reply came from the British Colonial Secretary, conveying the Prince's profound regret in being unable to accept Indian hospitality on a bear and buffalo hunt.

Before long, the irrepressible Spence was off on another tangent, this time calling a public meeting at Fort Garry for the purpose of discussing a Union of all the British Territory between Atlantic and Pacific Oceans, a plan which might have won support if offered by a person enjoying better standing in public esteem. As it was, the plan invited only suspicion and nothing came of it.

Seeking new worlds to conquer, Spence moved to Portage la Prairie, doing so just when the four Eastern provinces were being joined in Confederation. The Portage of that day was a primitive community built around the mission established by Archdeacon Cochrane a few years earlier. About sixty trail miles from Fort Garry, it was a place where a man could indulge in almost any pastime except murder without fear of organized restraint.

Of course, there was need for something in the nature of government and Spence resolved to furnish it. "A Republic," said he, "is exactly what this country needs." With pronounced "do-it-yourself" tendencies, he proclaimed his plan. Who could complain? If there was objection at Fort Garry or London, the protests would be too far away to be heard and most local residents didn't care.

Having decided upon the formation of a Republic, a President was an immediate need. Such a post should be filled by the best possible man and there was no doubt in Spence's mind about who should be installed. With all the authority needed under such circumstances, he appointed himself.

So far, so good, but there were many matters to take the attention of a new president in a new Republic. A name was required and the President's choice was Caledonia; the Republic of Caledonia it would be, and every Scot for miles around agreed that no bonnier selection could have been made. Portage la Prairie would be the capital and there was the matter of defining the Republic's boundaries. Nobody within arguing distance seemed to care where Spence's territory started and stopped, and so the President ordered that the International border would be the south boundary, the Rocky Mountains the west boundary, the Arctic Circle the north boundary, and some uncertain line—about as close to Fort Garry as it was safe for Spence to go—would be the eastern boundary.

Yes, he would need a Cabinet, but Portage la Prairie had men who were ready to serve. There was no need for any democratic niceties like elections because Spence was running the show and he had friends who wanted to help. Findlay Ray was appointed Secretary of State, or something like that, and other friends were named to fill dual roles like part-time Minister of Justice and part-time police constable. Then, having policemen, the Republic needed a jail and just such an institution with bars on windows and strong locks on doors became the first public building. After all, what could be more important to the future of a Republic than law enforcement?

Nor could a Republic be expected to operate without funds. Spence decided upon tariff duties to be paid on all goods entering his domain. Strange as it seems, he was successful in making collections; even the Hudson's Bay Company is said to have contributed. Moreover, Spence balanced his budgets precisely. But by Spence methods, that was not difficult; it was merely a matter of spending available money—no more, no less—on booze for members of the Government and, thus, there was never either a cash surplus or deficit.

The Spence plan was launched without visible public objection until the administration made a major tactical error in offending two Scottish clansmen, a MacPherson and a MacLean, thereby incurring their combined wrath. The former was a shoemaker at High Bluff and, like any true son of Scotland, he objected to the payment of unjust taxes, especially when the money was being used for the purchase of whiskey to which he had no access. What MacPherson said came to the ears of Spence who lost no time in warning the man to hold his tongue.

When MacPherson showed no intention of being silent, Spence sent two of his constables to arrest the transgressor. "Bring him in dead or alive," was the order. It was midwinter and snow lay deep on the Portage Plains. The officers travelled by team and sleigh and, knowing the showmaker would be hard to handle, they thoughtfully fortified themselves with a few snorts of Republican liquor.

Upon arrival, the men found MacPherson cleaning his gun, whatever that gesture might be intended to convey. They read the charge and invited the Scot to be arrested but the accused was uncooperative. When the constables resorted to force, there was a scuffle. MacPherson sought to escape but was overtaken in deep snow. This time, with the promise of a fair trial, he agreed to accompany the constables to the Portage.

On the way, the Portage-bound party overtook a sleigh driven by John MacLean, first farmer on the Portage Plains. Recognizing his Highlander neighbour, MacPherson called for assistance. MacLean brought his sleigh to a stop and, seizing the only tool within reach, a hand auger, he advanced with some angry questions.

"What are they dain' tae ye, MacPherson?" he asked. Then, as a constable stepped ahead to block MacLean's advance, the farmer shouted: "Stand aside, ye fool, or I'll rin ye through wi' this auger."

The constable accepted the hint and stood aside. Who would be so foolish as to stand in the path of an angry MacLean? Anyway, MacPherson told his story and MacLean advised his friend to go along peacefully, at the same time promising to be at the Portage to see that there was justice in the course of the trial. MacLean hurried home to do the evening chores and, then, as good as his word, he was on the way to the capital. Somewhere along the trail he picked up three friends, hard-muscled miners who welcomed the prospect of an evening adventure, and the four men arrived at the scene of the trial just after the charge had been read. Flanked by his friends, MacLean paused, glaring angrily at the men assembled around the long table illuminated feebly with a kerosene lamp. Recognizing Spence at the head of the table, MacLean's face became flushed and his body tensed for battle.

"You," said the farmer, pointing at Spence, "sitting there like a laird. What dae ye mean? What right hae ye tae sit in judgemen' on m' friend?"

"He's charged with treason against the laws of the Republic," came the reply.

"What ye talking aboot?" MacLean snarled back. "We hae na laws. And, onyway, wha's prosecuting?"

"I'm prosecuting," Spence admitted and, in the same breath, added: "Now be quiet, MacLean, or you'll be arrested too."

"I'll no be quiet," MacLean countered, moving closer to the table. "Now, come oot o' that, ye whited sepulchre; ye know ye canna be baith accuser and judge. Quit yer nonsense and let MacPherson gae hame tae his shoemaking."

At this point, one of MacLean's friends caught MacPherson's coat-tails and proceeded to drag him away. But in an ordered Republic, such rebel action cannot be tolerated and Spence shouted an order to arrest all the intruders.

A constable moved to carry out the order but was caught in the heavy grip of a miner and hurled bodily across the table. At the same moment, the lamp was upset, leaving the room in darkness. There were sounds of heavy blows and the gasps of struggling men. MacLean's friends, it seemed, were able to fight in the dark about as well as in the light, and didn't stop until all resistance had ended. One of the miners drew a revolver and fired a shot into the ceiling and, then, all was quiet. Somebody recovered the lamp and managed to get it lit. A couple of honourable servants of the Republic lay in helplessness on the floor and the President was not in sight. When found hiding behind some pieces of furniture, Spence pleaded for mercy, explaining his importance to a wife and family. He promised to withdraw the charge against MacPherson and, for good measure, buy a new suit of clothes to replace the garments torn by arresting constables earlier in the day.

MacPherson and MacLean and the three miners set out for their homes, not realizing that they had actually delivered a death-blow to the Republic of Caledonia, also called Republic of Manitoba. About the same time, Spence received a letter from the Secretary of State in London, reminding him that his actions in setting up a Republic in British North America were illegal and he would do well to terminate the whole thing.

But the letter was quite unnecessary. The Republic was already as dead as the dinosaur race, an added triumph for Clans MacPherson and MacLean. Spence departed soon after, leaving the great expanse of country extending to the Rockies and beyond to await government of a more legitimate and democratic kind.

From *Poking into Politics* (1966)

Fred Kanouse: The Trader

I can offer two good reasons for giving Fred Kanouse a membership in the noble Fraternity of Sodbusters: he was a frontiersman of the most devastating kind, and he was one of the brave souls who performed the first ranching experiments on the plains. Yet very few people of the present generation have heard the name of Fred Kanouse, and still fewer have encountered anything about him in the records. Were it not for the tales perpetuated by a few pioneers in the southwest, there would be no story about Fred Kanouse on this occasion.

He came to the Canadian foothills in 1871. Although I have enquired diligently for information about Kanouse's career prior to that date, I can find nothing. Perhaps it is better. Those on the frontier at that time didn't ask personal questions about "the past," and didn't tell much. Actually a man was more likely to achieve old age if his interests in history were not too highly developed. This we do know, however: Kanouse came in from Fort Benton on the Missouri and travelled by way of the notorious Fort Whoop-Up, and then to a point on the Elbow River, a little west of where Calgary was located later. There he built a fort. He came as a free-trader, and I'm sure he was well supplied with guns and trading stock in barrels. He didn't come alone. Evidently four white men and one Indian woman made up the party. Only bold men ventured into Blackfoot Indian country in those years. The Mounted Police hadn't arrived. Men made their own laws from day to day—made them to fit their convenience. The Manitoba metropolis of Fort Garry, which later adopted the name Winnipeg, had a population of 271. And westward to the mountains, the plains were occupied by buffalo and Indians; white men were about as common as grizzly bears.

But just as long as a trader retained his scalp, there was profit in the Indian business, and Kanouse knew the precautions one must take. He never turned his back upon a customer, and his gun belt was as vital a part of his clothing as his pants and boots. Traders were just beginning to visualize a big business in buffalo hides. And a keg of rum could secure a lot of those robes. The wholesale slaughter that resulted in practical extinction of the prairie buffalo was about to begin.

Anyone dealing in firewater in Blackfoot territory was indeed playing with fire, and Kanouse had his full share of thrills. Shortly after the fort was established on the Elbow, one of his colleagues figured in an Indian quarrel, and the Indians, it seems, plotted to annihilate the little nest of whites. As the Indians were advancing upon the fort, Kanouse and two of his friends went out to meet them in the hope of appeasement. But Kanouse miscalculated that time. His visitors were decorated with more shades of cosmetics than he had seen before. They had not come to talk: they came for a fight, and an Indian bullet dropped one of Kanouse's pals. In the next instant a ball from Kanouse's gun eliminated the chief who was leading the braves. Kanouse was then the target for the next volley, and, though his arm was injured, he managed to get back to his fort. The little group consisting now of three men and the Indian woman, organized to withstand attack. The woman loaded the guns, and the males fired them. For three days, the Indians were unable to crack the Kanouse defences. Then the Indians retired, presumably to get reinforcements. But they must have found some less hazardous adventure because they didn't come again.

It is not easy to secure exact data about some of those pioneer episodes. But I have satisfied myself that "Kootenai" Brown, another famous frontiersman, was associated with Kanouse in that little party that took up trading on the Elbow, and that they stood together that day when Kanouse's arm got in the path of an Indian bullet, prior to the siege. This John George Brown, or "Kootenai" Brown, had quite a bit in common with Kanouse. Both were the fearless, outdoor, two-gun men when necessary. And while Kanouse was one of the first to turn cattle on the range,

Brown had the distinction of being the first or one of the first to actually settle to do some farming in what is now Alberta. A man on the frontier found himself with strange bunkmates at times, and this partner of Kanouse's was said to be a graduate of Eton and Oxford. But I take it that "old school ties" didn't mean much to "Kootenai" Brown. He had belonged to the Queen's Lifeguards. Story has it that he became too friendly with Queen Victoria or some other ladies of the court and was sent to India. But he had troubles there too; somebody got shot and Brown took passage to South America. Still he wasn't satisfied. He turned north; crossed Panama; didn't stop until he reached the Cariboo Gold Diggings in 1863. Two years there and he crossed the prairies to spend a winter trading with the Métis at Duck Lake. He arrived at Waterton Lakes in 1868, and there he and his Cree wife squatted and built a home.

But the question for which I cannot find an answer is this, "Was 'Kootenai' Brown's Cree wife the woman who accompanied Kanouse and his party to the Elbow and who loaded the guns when the Indians attacked?" I suppose it doesn't matter, but I have an idea that Brown's wife went where he went. Anyway, we shouldn't forget that this "Kootenai" Brown retired from trading to be the first tiller of the soil in what is now southern Alberta; then he was a rancher, and between 1910 and 1914 he was superintendent of Waterton National Park. He and Fred Kanouse were two of a kind, even if one was an Oxford graduate and the other didn't know for sure if Oxford was the name of a university or a Shorthorn bull. That was the way they came to Alberta, educated and uneducated, cultured and uncultured, saints and sinners. If I have judged correctly, however, the sinners were not at that time in danger of being outvoted by the saints.

The North West Mounted Police trekked westward across the prairies in 1874 and built Fort Macleod. They changed many things: no morality squad ever changed the social life of a community more than did the Mounted Police. The whiskey traders developed something related to a persecution complex and quit. The Fort Whoop-Up racketeers became jittery and went out of business. And Kanouse decided to adopt a more healthful and more dignified livelihood. He tried buffalo hunting. He was on hand with buffalo meat for the celebration when the Blackfoot Treaty was signed at Blackfoot Crossing. The meat business suggested cattle; if nobody else would put cattle to the test on the Alberta range, he would.

He went to Montana and returned driving twenty-one cows and a bull ahead of his pony. At Fort Macleod he promptly gave his cattle their freedom. Would they survive? There were two or three good reasons why they wouldn't. In the first place the Indians refused to differentiate between cattle and buffalo and would shoot cows with no more hesitation than they would buffalo. In the second place, cattle were likely to become assimilated and swept away by the gigantic herds of migrating buffalo. Then there was the northwest winter to be considered. The people in Macleod were interested spectators. Some said Kanouse must be crazy: "He'll never find hide or tail of those cattle." Came spring of '78, and Kanouse astride a saddle went out to reconnoitre. Wonders will never cease. He found his cattle, all of them, and they were in good condition. The onlookers were surprised, but Kanouse wasn't surprised. He believed that part was just as good for cattle as Montana. The next spring found more cattle on the range, and what is now southern Alberta had its first organized roundup. One wagon and sixteen men, including Kanouse, took part. It was a small round-up outfit compared with those of later years, but the cowboys worked over a lot of country. There was no barbed wire to restrict the cattle, and a man could ride five hundred miles in any direction without opening a gate. Kanouse cut his cattle out and drove them to Waterton Lakes where his old friend "Kootenai" Brown had more or less settled down. Brown by that time had a few head of his own. Kanouse and Brown agreed that they were in a good cattle country: "Anywhere that buffalo lived, cattle will do well." That was what "Kootenai" Brown told Senator Cochrane when they chanced to meet on the prairies, a while before Mr. Cochrane drove the first big herd of three thousand head to graze on Canadian soil.

It was just about that time that Kanouse started the big prairie fire. He just had to be trading, and Indians and horses offered an outlet. He got an Indian pony in a deal and discovered that the poor brute was supporting a large population of horse lice. He decided upon a kerosene treatment. Then, too, there was precedent for a white man getting a horse from an Indian by sale or trade, only to have the Indian come and steal the horse away. Kanouse knew all the tricks and was taking no chances. He would place his brand on the horse. But he made the mistake of applying the hot branding iron before the kerosene on the hair was dry, and the horse's hair took fire. The frantic animal made a dash for freedom, spreading fire as it went, and story has it that the prairie fire that resulted didn't stop until it reached the Missouri River.

Some Blood Indians who didn't know Kanouse too well did steal a horse from him on one occasion, but they didn't have it long. Learning where the horse was, Kanouse went to the Indian encampment single-handed and came away with his horse; and it is told that to assert himself he took an Indian bridle along with his horse, while the surprised Indians looked and wondered at what manner of man this was anyway.

But Kanouse was in trouble with Indians from time to time. Evidently he became involved in a dispute with some Kootenay Indians and one of their braves vowed to kill him. Kanouse wasn't one to run away from danger, and he wasn't much worried. The Mounted Police thought sufficiently of it all to warn Kanouse to stay away from the inter-mountain region where the Indians lived. That was all very well, but Kanouse had business to attend to in that area and would go. He got permission to carry his trusted six-shooter and went in. Did he remain undercover? Not Kanouse; he wasn't that kind of a frontiersman. They tell of him giving an Indian a tip to tell the avowed killer that Fred Kanouse was about. But the boasting Indian either decided to take a philosophical view of it all, or else he just lost his enthusiasm.

I know of at least one occasion when the name of Fred Kanouse appeared publicly in print. The journals show that in the year following the first meeting of the Council of the Northwest Territories, Kanouse was charged by the Mounted Police with gambling and that the accused contributed a fine of one dollar to the public treasury. The cost of government wasn't so high in those days, and police fines weren't such a luxury as they are today. But Kanouse was a gambler in the broader sense. Anybody who would bet whiskey against buffalo skins with Blackfoot in those early years was an inherent gambler, and anyone who would turn cattle on the open range while the buffalo were still in possession wasn't to be frightened by "long shots." That was Fred Kanouse, and anyone who visits Pincher Creek or Macleod—provided he makes contact with the right old-timers—may hear a lot more about Fred Kanouse and "Kootenai" Brown, and another of similar kind named "Kamoose" Taylor. Sure they were rough, but they were the "he-men" who broke trail in the southwest. They were the links between the old and the "not so old" links between trader days and pastoral agriculture in southern Alberta. 'Twould be misfortune to forget Fred Kanouse and his ilk.

From *The Sodbusters* (1948)

At the Sign of the Buffalo

As a young boy, Walking Buffalo heard the rich legends of his people. Like Traveller and Twist-in-the-Neck, he too participated in strange and mysterious events which were later woven into the fabric of Stoney history. It was from an early childhood experience that one of the most popular stories about him evolved. This tale became known as the "Grand Legend," and, as can be expected, it centred around a buffalo motif.

According to the most common version of the story, Walking Buffalo was just learning to walk when he wandered away from the Stoney camp and became lost. In itself, this incident was not unusual; since the beginning of time, children have been running away and getting lost. In most instances, there is a brief period of parental panic after which the tot is located in good health, totally unconscious of any danger. With Walking Buffalo, however, the traditional search was unsuccessful. The youngster had simply vanished like a frog in a muddy pool.

Certainly there was an air of mystery about his disappearance. Wearing moccasins, buckskin shirt, and a dirty face, he had been playing with mongrel dogs beside his grandmother's tipi one minute yet had suddenly vanished the next. His grandmother called and then conducted a fruitless search. Friends joined to comb the tree-covered ground close to the Bow River more thoroughly, but the anxious searchers still found no clue as to the whereabouts of the missing boy. As darkness descended upon the mountains and valleys, the possibility of tragedy crossed the mind of each Stoney. Could it be that a hungry wolf or she-bear had emerged from its forest home to carry the child away? Could it be that the little one had fallen into the churning river, there to be swept to a cruel death by drowning? Or did the possibility remain that little

Walking Buffalo had simply used his unsteady legs to wander into a hiding place not far away where he would be discovered shortly?

Everyone, including the medicine man, tried to help. The next morning as daylight came again, the search was resumed and extended farther from the camp. The results were the same: no trace of the child. And so, after being forced to acknowledge his own failure, the medicine man counselled united appeal to the Great Spirit.

This was a solemn occasion, something like a great tribal prayer meeting or modified Sun Dance. A fire was built on a clearing of ground, and the Indians gathered around it in a circle. Scalps and eagle heads dangled from the medicine man's belt. As he advanced toward the fire, his painted face was partially masked by a headpiece made from crows' wings. His first act was to throw incense into the flames. Next, with the air of a man enjoying his authority, he demanded silence, then ordered singing and the smoking of pipes. Finally, at exactly the correct moment, the wise one called upon the Great Spirit to tell them whether or not Walking Buffalo still lived and, if so, where he could be found.

There followed a period of dramatic silence. Then as the evening wind moaned through the nearby trees, its sound was transformed into a human voice which said, "The boy is alive and will be found with the buffalo herd."

But many buffalo herds roamed the area. Where would the right one be found? Only occasionally did big herds penetrate the higher reaches of the Bow River. Generally when Stonies hunted buffaloes, they journeyed eastward to find herds on the plains. Hence, the medicine man next prayed for a clue as to the location of this particular herd. He did not have to wait long for an answer. Scanning the night sky, the wise one discovered a blue star in the east. This was his clue. Early the next morning, Stonies, both on horseback and on foot, followed the medicine man toward the plains.

Before going far, the Indians saw buffaloes, but these were either too far north or too far south to interest the leader. He was adhering strictly to an eastward course. As the days passed, their travels brought the Stonies deeper into Blackfoot territory where attack was always imminent. Finally, a big herd was spotted directly ahead. The medicine man advised a cautious approach to allow for observation of the animals without causing them to stampede. Closing in on the herd, sure enough the Stonies spotted a small boy playing with buffalo calves. It was indeed the lost lad, uninjured and apparently quite happy.

The Indians, of course, were overjoyed, and Walking Buffalo's father impulsively called his child to him. The sound startled the animals, and with their tails held high in the air, they all fled, except for one old cow who stood close to where the small boy had been playing. Fearlessly, the cow faced the Indians, quite obviously trying to deal with this human invasion. But her thoughts were not focused entirely on the strangers; she repeatedly turned her head to observe the movements of the boy. The position of the child was clearly causing her anxiety.

After most of the buffalo herd had thundered away, the infant, instead of coming to his own people, tried to follow the animals. His small legs couldn't carry him very fast, but he was doing his best to catch up when the cow, having completed her assessment of the Indians, bounded after him and effectively blocked his escape until the Stonies could come closer.

Speaking to the Indians (as wild animals quite often did), she related the following events. She had found the waif alone in the foothills and had guessed that he required protection and food. Responding to his need, she allowed him to nurse along with her bull calf, and when the herd moved more deeply into plains country, the child followed. Now the cow was returning the little fellow to human care. Once she saw him back in the arms of his father, she turned and ran to rejoin the fleeing herd.

The child protested at not being permitted to go too. In his days with the wild stock—drinking rich buffalo milk, playing with the calves, sleeping with his body resting securely against the cow's warm flank—he had become a part of the animal community. Now the separation was unpleasant, even though the tribesmen were kind and were obviously concerned only with his welfare.

The medicine man was still in command. Because his intercessions had succeeded, he expected more respect than ever. He called for a ceremonial halt in order to remove any clinging buffalo traits from the boy's character and to restore, at the same time, his desire to be human. A fire was built, after which the medicine man uttered the necessary incantations. Tobacco smoke was blown in the boy's face, and for good measure a wisp of his hair was solemnly committed to the flames. Miraculously, the child relaxed, his ability to make human sounds and words returning. He was now glad to be back with his own people.

The legend about Walking Buffalo had a second version. According to it, the child was not found for some *months* after his mysterious disappearance. Stonies had finally been obliged to abandon the hunt. "He is dead," they mourned resignedly.

Late in the autumn, however, as evening darkness was filling the mountain valleys, members of a Stoney family squatting in their tent heard the trample of heavy feet above the noise of the wind in the pines. They placed their ears on the ground and soon identified the sound as the footsteps of a buffalo. Surprised that the animal would venture into the circle of tipis, especially during this late season; the woman listened again to confirm her suspicions. "I hear more," she remarked; "I hear a child whimpering. We must see what this is all about."

Going out in the chilly night, the woman was startled by the sight of the indistinct figure of a small boy nursing at a buffalo cow. Strangely enough, however, the cow didn't bolt as do most wild animals. Rather, she spoke to the woman and told her of finding this small and helpless infant searching for something to eat in the hills. Out of pity for the pathetic child, she had allowed him to nurse, thus saving his life.

"Now," concluded the cow, "I return the care of this boy to you." With these words, she turned and wandered into the darkness of the forest, while the boy, after being identified as the child lost long months before, was returned to his overjoyed kin.

Walking Buffalo never forgot his debt to the generous buffalo. An affection for these animals never left him. In fact, he later adopted the painted figure of a buffalo as the insignia for his family tipi.

Romulus and Remus, legendary founders of Rome, were supposed to have been mothered by a she-wolf. To have been raised by a buffalo cow on the Canadian prairies is no less plausible and no less romantic.

From *Tatanga Mani* (1969)

Birds By The Barrel

They were creatures of rare beauty, those passenger pigeons with the lustrous slate-like plumage and graceful lines. Many writers proclaimed them as the loveliest members of the big pigeon family. But their most distinguishing characteristic was their fabulous numbers. At the time of Canadian Confederation, passenger pigeons were thought to outnumber the birds of any other North American race; forty-seven years later, they were gone—extinct.

Today, the only passenger pigeons are stuffed ones with faded feathers and glassy eyes occupying museum cases. Never again will humans thrill to the sight of their kind in flight or gliding to rest on the branches of trees.

The incredible story of the passenger pigeons and their appalling fate should be required reading in North American schools. It's not a cheerful story; it is sad to think that lovely birds once filling the Canadian and United States skies now live only in books. But they teach some solemn lessons.

A few elderly Canadians remember the passenger pigeons and can tell of the huge flocks bringing shades of evening to the frontier landscape. The favourite habitat was wooded country. They frequented the eastern part of the continent more than the West but in the course of migrations, the flocks were seen in most parts—as far west as the Rockies and as far north as the Mackenzie River Valley.

So large were the flocks, according to early reports, that birds in migration sometimes cut off the light of the sun for hours at a time. Estimates of bird number stagger the imagination. Alexander Wilson, father of American ornithology, wrote about seeing a flock in Kentucky which he estimated would contain over two billion birds. Travelling in compact formation, flocks in flight presented an appearance of black stormclouds and men with guns were known to bring down as many as a hundred birds with a single shot.

The "passengers" liked the constant company of their own kind and even in the nesting season the fraternal instinct was so strong that they remained together. An area chosen for nesting might cover many square miles, with every big tree containing from one to a hundred or more of the rather roughly constructed nests. Stories are told of large branches breaking under the weight of the growing nestling squabs. And settlers in Eastern communities, loath to see anything wasted, drove pigs to nesting areas to allow the swine to fatten on eggs and young birds falling to the ground.

Norman Luxton of Banff, recalling boyhood days beside the Red and Assiniboine Rivers in Manitoba—whence one of the passenger pigeon skins in the Luxton Museum originated—told of old trees so covered with pigeon droppings that "when we climbed them, we never got our clothes clean again."

An Audubon description in 1844 is worth noting. "The approach of the mighty feathered army produced a loud rushing roar and a steady breeze, attended by sudden darkness that might be mistaken for a fearful tornado about to overwhelm the face of Nature. For several hours the vast host, extending some miles in breadth, still continues to pass in flocks without diminution. The whole air is filled with birds; they shut out the light as if it were an eclipse."

That Western Canada was in the flight path and birds were often numerous, there can be little doubt. Explorers and travellers shot and ate the thick breast meat and pronounced it better than duck and other wild fowl. Milton and Cheadle, travelling westward from Fort Edmonton in 1863, saw the beautiful birds in their abundance and registered their pleasure at the delicacy of the meat. "Pigeons and wood partridge," the journal tells, "became very plentiful and we shot them at first in great numbers."

Henry Y. Hind, professor of chemistry and geology at Trinity College in Toronto, when leaving Fort Garry to conduct a prairie survey for the confused government in 1857, noted the pigeon traps constructed from nets and set out by Red River settlers who relished pigeon pie.

Netting offered an easy method of catching pigeons and was employed in the East as well as the West. One side of an expansive cord net was pegged to the ground while the other side was suspended on poles in such manner that it could be made to fall on an unsuspecting flock enticed to the spot by means of grain or decoys. Although many settlers obtained their winter supplies by means of the nets, there is no reason to believe that guns were not the chief means of slaughter leading to annihilation.

And Rev. George Grant, writing about his journey across the West with the Sanford Fleming expedition in 1872, was attracted by the abundance of game and made special mention of the pigeons and the excellent eating qualities of "pigeon with rice and curry for breakfast."

Herein was the principal reason for the passenger pigeon disaster: the birds were good to eat. Breasts were thick and the flavour was unsurpassed. The slaughter gathered momentum. The birds being easy to shoot and easy to lure into nets, a professional hunter could fill three or four barrels in one day. Thus from a day's kill, the sale of a thousand to twelve hundred birds at fifty cents a dozen—going price in Eastern cities like Montreal, Toronto and New York—could mean an unusually high return, considering the values of that period. Even the backcountry price of one cent per bird gave better than an average wage at the midpoint of the century.

There is record of shipments of three carloads of pigeons daily for forty days from the Town of Hartford, Michigan, in 1869. The estimated total was close to twelve million birds while the shipments from another Michigan point were placed at fifteen million birds in two years. And a district in Wisconsin saw a hundred barrels a day being packed and sold during the nesting season in 1871. Unquestionably, it was profitable and scarcely anybody objected.

One observer who saw five hundred hunters getting twenty thousand birds each by netting in Michigan did have something to say about probable consequences. "At this rate," he wrote with more than the usual amount of understanding, "the pigeon will soon join the buffalo on the list so disgraceful to humanity—the extinct species." It was a prophecy to be fulfilled in a shockingly short space of time.

It must have been easy, however, to follow the crowd and enter into the spirit of the slaughter. Ambitious people enquired if there were not other uses to which the "unlimited" bird resources could be put to human profit. Farmers in some parts tried smoking and stupefying the nesting birds with sulphur fumes, then clubbing the victims and gathering them for use as fertilizer on their fields. Of course, it was sinful trespass upon Nature's preserves but the few admonitions and warnings continued to fall upon deaf ears. The subscribers to free enterprise were out for profit. Even after the bird population began to decline, it was easy to rationalize that the flocks had simply gone elsewhere or were in the trough of a natural cycle. "The pigeons will be back," they said blithely.

But the lovely birds were not coming back. When numbers were plainly decimated, local laws to protect them against commercial hunters were passed in some parts of the continent. But it was too late. The population had been shattered and normal propagation seemed to be disrupted.

During the first decade of the present century, scientists and bird lovers made frantic efforts to save the passenger pigeons but they were in vain. The last one was seen in Manitoba in 1898 and one was shot in the Province of Quebec in 1907. By 1909, only two birds of the species were known to remain, a female called Martha and her mate, both in the Zoological Gardens in Cincinnati, both twenty-four years of age, one or both by that time sterile from old age.

In a spirit of desperation, ornithologists offered attractive cash rewards to anyone who could find living pigeons such as would bring new hope for survival of the race. But there was no response. The wild birds, so recently numerous enough to blacken the skies, had disappeared. The unhappy end was approaching.

The male bird in the Cincinnati Zoo died, and, finally, on 1 September 1914, the twenty-nine-year-old Martha—last of a great race which had known incredible numbers—died, too. It marked the end of a race which successfully withstood glaciers, winter cold, summer heat, food famines, natural enemies and disease but could not withstand those new predator arrivals on the North American continent—men who conducted their killings on a grand scale, men who would sell birds by the barrel.

From *Entrusted To My Care* (1966)

Storms Without Shelter

Reveille, the 6:30 AM bugle call that reverberated through the barracks like thunder in a mountain valley, was a first-class effort by the youthful Fred Bagley, now known as the kid cop. He smiled broadly and appeared to gain at once the two additional inches he so dearly wanted for his boyish stature. Then, above the blurred chatter of men dressing hurriedly, came another clear but unexpected call from an exuberant soul who might have been a strong contender for the first hog calling contest: "Hey, you whiskey-trading devils at Whoop-Up, oil your muskets and hang on. We're coming!" It sounded like Irish Frank Norman.

Nobody had to be reminded that it was Saturday, 6 June 1874, a day with a special significance: the bugle that called the Mounties to a new day called them also to a new life pregnant with adventure, danger, and opportunity for service in faraway parts. It was the day the young men of a still-untested force had been looking forward to with such excitement.

Sub-Inspector James Walker was up and around a long hour before the bugle call. He was to be responsible for all the police horses during the journey to Fort Dufferin—244 of them leaving Toronto and thirty-four more to be added at Detroit.[1] On this momentous morning, with the June sunrise coming too early for sleepy humans to enjoy, Walker wanted to make a final check of the stables and their occupants and then write a letter to his mother and father.

As he had discovered on the home farm, the stable at an early hour is always a pleasant experience. There are no sounds more honest and cheering than the first whinnies from friendly horses hungry for their morning ration of oats. To those first greetings from the stalls, Walker responded with words of reassurance. All was well in the stables on this morning, and he turned to writing the letter.

As soon as breakfast at the barracks ended, all hands were turned to stable chores—feeding, watering, and exercising the horses and ministering to special needs like swollen fetlocks—and then to loading personal belongings on the two trains. Next, horse feed and equipment were loaded. The horses were loaded last. Most had never been close to a train and were frightened. The hazards were multiplied because the men handling them had little or no practical experience with horses. There were, indeed, moments of pandemonium, but by one o'clock, all the horses had been loaded and crowds of well-wishers had assembled for a friendly farewell.

The gathering crowd was disappointed. They came expecting to see the men of the new force wearing their new uniforms, reported by the press as beautiful. But instead of scarlet Norfolk jackets, grey riding breeches, black-top boots and spurs, and pillbox forage caps, the men were wearing street clothes, and not always good ones either. What a letdown for the ladies!

The 1874 contingent of Mounties was to travel much of the way on American railroads, going by Chicago, St. Paul, and Fargo, North Dakota. There, they would leave the railroad and follow a twisting trail to Fort Dufferin on the Manitoba side of the border.

American permission was required to move a semimilitary body like the NWMP over United States territory. The American authorities agreed to the request but specified that uniforms could not be worn and guns and ammunition could not be exposed during the journey through United States territory. Accordingly, uniforms and weapons were boxed and sealed.

At 1:30 PM, the first of two marching bands arrived on the scene to enliven the farewell. Sharp at two o'clock, the conductor mounted to the lower step of a coach and shouted: "All aboard for the Firewater Frontier."

The spectators cheered as the two fifteen-car trains drew away from the Grand Trunk depot. Before the first train was out of sight, though, it was forced to stop abruptly to eject a stowaway seeking a free ride to adventure.

The commissioner and the second half of the force were on their way. Bugler Fred Bagley spoke for everybody when he wrote later: "A feeling of intense elation buoyed us up as our trains pulled out of the station and we started on our way west, bound for the Great Adventure."[2]

Early the following morning, the 278 horses were unloaded at the Chicago stockyards. It had rained heavily all night and the pens were afloat with water and muck. It was a dismal pause for both the horses and the two officers and thirty men assigned to guard them.[3]

The constant raiding by hungry rats made the Chicago stockyards an even more unpleasant memory. They emerged from every nook and cranny, driving the horses from their feed boxes until the recruits on duty stepped in with clubs.

Twenty-four hours later, the trains set out for St. Paul, where still more supplies and equipment would be added to the freight. The commissioner had decided that the force should be encouraged to become self-supporting as quickly as possible and had asked Walker to purchase mowing machines and hay rakes there, as well as a year's supply of flour and bacon. Hence, their stay in the Minnesota city was prolonged, but the force, with an extra car of freight, entrained again on the Northern Pacific Railway on 11 June and arrived on the day following in Fargo, the nearest railway point to Fort Dufferin.

Leaving the train, the men had the feeling that they were severing their ties with civilization. The days of cozy living were over. They'd have to become accustomed to sleeping on the ground and taking their food from an outdoor kitchen. The first bread baked in the outdoor ovens was said to resemble "nothing more than dough with a crust on it."

"Here," said James Walker, "the real work of the expedition commenced. . . . Our wagons were all in the knock-down state and the harness and saddles were just so many boxes of straps. All of these had to be put together before we could make a start for the Canadian boundary."[4]

Among those who left written records of that part of the journey was Sub-Constable E.H. Maunsell from Ireland. At Fargo he would have been classified as one of the greenest of the recruits, but in later years, after taking his discharge from the force, he became one of the best-known and most successful ranchers in southern Alberta. Recalling Fargo, he wrote:

We started to unload the wagons, which were in pieces. Now a wagon does not seem a complicated vehicle when the parts are together, but many of us did not know the tongue from the reach or whether the large wheels went on the front or back axles. We then started a more complicated job—putting the harness together. The harness was not all of the same kind, which made the job more difficult. Of course, we had the saddle major, but he could not be everywhere at once. The officers seemed as helpless as the men and the remarks made about them more than reconciled me to the humble rank I held. There was one exception, Sub-Inspector Walker. He was everywhere, helping and imparting knowledge.

Having got through these labors, we pitched the tents, and were each served with two blankets and a waterproof sheet. All then had supper—very different from what we enjoyed the night before—very fat boiled pork, hard tack, and well boiled tea without milk. Some men were told to drive who had never harnessed or driven a team before. Some horses were put in teams which never had harness on them before—result, several runaways . . ."[5]

These were days when more farm-raised recruits like James Walker would have proven their worth. Unfortunately, most of the amusing experiences arising from city-raised recruits trying to master the techniques of horsemanship were not written into the main story. A story that survived concerned two young constables raised on town streets who were trying to harness a team for the trip to Dufferin. After much delay, all harness appeared to be in place and secured, except for one bridle for a horse that refused to co-operate by opening its mouth to take the bit. The men tried to pry the animal's mouth open with a piece of wood, but without success. Finally, one of the exasperated horsemen said to the other: "We'll just have to wait."

"Wait for what?" his companion asked.

"We'll just have to wait till the beggar yawns."

~

"When our eighty wagons were loaded," Walker wrote, "the fun really began. Most of the horses had been bought on appearance. Some now objected to the harness; others refused to draw the wagons. Some started kicking and some fiery teams with inexperienced drivers started across the prairie with loaded wagons, out of control, and had to be rounded up by men on horseback. The circus was repeated every morning during the 160-mile march to Fort Dufferin."

At Dufferin, located approximately where the Manitoba town of Emerson later arose, the newly arrived officers and men of D, E, and F troops were welcomed by Assistant Commissioner James F. Macleod and troops A, B, and C, who had come west late in the previous autumn and wintered at the Old Stone Fort north of Winnipeg. For most of the recent arrivals, it was their first meeting with the assistant commissioner; there was some whispered speculation about how the Irish-born commissioner from England and the Scottish-born assistant commissioner from the Isle of Skye would get along. One thing was certain: the immediate tasks of reorganizing the troops and planning for the long trek into the unknown or little-known would be enough to keep leaders fully occupied.

For the commissioner, arriving at Dufferin on the evening of 19 June was, in his words, like the removal "of a great load of responsibility from my shoulders." He was relieved to have all the members of his force back on Canadian soil and to have taken them this far without a major mishap. But for near-mishap, he didn't have much longer to wait. What could have been more humiliating than the loss of all the horses? What could have been more embarrassing than having to explain why the much-publicized Riders of the Plains were left suddenly with nothing to ride?

Walker was so much a part of the story, he deserves the privilege of telling it in his own words. But first the commissioner's appraisal of the night: "On the night after our arrival, one of the most dreadful thunderstorms ever witnessed in this country—and they have had some bad ones—burst over us," the commissioner wrote in his first annual report. There was apparently one incessant sheet of lightning from 10:00 PM to 6:00 AM. "About midnight," the commissioner explained, "250 of our horses stampeded after breaking halter and picket ropes and even knocking over some of the wagons which encircled them. It was a fearful sight. Some of our men had the hardihood to attempt to stop the horses but it only resulted in their being knocked over and trampled and in this manner six of our pluckiest men got hurt, one of them being seriously injured about the head."[6]

At least one of those who had the "hardihood" to intervene had success. James Walker emerged as the hero of that awful night. Exactly fifty years later, when facing the Alberta Military Institute, he recalled the dangerous experience. The midnight stampede, he said, was a memory sure to stay with all members of the force of that time:

> It wasn't the tame kind of stampede we are accustomed to seeing nowadays, but three hundred horses going perfectly wild, breaking their fastenings where they were tied to wagons at the beginning of the terrific thunder storm of rain and hail in the middle of the night.
>
> Our camp was arranged in a square, the wagons lined up on three sides and the tents on the fourth. The horses were tied to the wagons inside the square. Our wagons had canvas coverings. The wind tore these loose and they struck the

heads of the horses, driving them wild and sending them through the tents like a cyclone. Quite a number of the men were injured and tents were knocked down. I had not undressed when this happened and ran out of the tent to see what the trouble was and was able to catch a horse going past and put my saddle on it, and went after the herd into the storm. The night was pitch dark except during the flashes of lightning. Fortunately, there were no fences in those days. The horses took the trail back over the boundary line that we had just crossed and I followed their tracks by the light of the lightning flashes until daylight. When I got to the Pembina River, the round poles that covered the bridge had got shifted and some of the horses had fallen through. It took me some time in the dark to repair the bridge and get my horse over. After daylight dawned, I began to find stray horses feeding along the road and to make sure I got ahead of all the horses, I rode into Grand Forks [on the border between North Dakota and Minnesota], some 60 miles from our camp. I then turned and started driving the runaway horses back to camp. Later, I was met by a sergeant and party who had left camp at daylight to assist me. We arrived back at camp with the horses about eleven o'clock that night—just twenty-four hours after they left. During that time I caught and rode five different horses, was wet through and dried three times and had ridden 120 miles by trail, besides many extra miles rounding up horses along the way. The horses did not get over their fright all that summer and had to be watched closely as an unusual noise would stampede them again.[7]

In total miles travelled with horse and saddle in 1874, Walker's performance would have surpassed that of any other person in the force. Two or three days after the stampede, the commissioner received a telegram from Grand Forks. It reported that two Mounted Police horses had been captured and would be held until someone came for them. Walker, as the officer still in charge of the police horses, knew that two of the horses from the midnight stampede were still unaccounted for and supposed they had been drowned or killed when they fell through the broken bridge at Pembina. He left for Grand Forks at once and on arrival there found "a team of very fine horses with the broad arrow brand. Our horses were all branded 'MP.' The two in question must have got away from the Boundary Survey camp at Wood Mountain about two weeks before and had gone across country to Grand Forks, over four hundred miles. I commandeered them for my troop and they made the round trip of 1874, back to Dufferin."[8]

Extensive and complex preparations were being made at Dufferin for the trip west. The commissioner had engaged about a hundred Red River carts with oxen and Métis drivers for transport purposes. He had decided to take a herd of beef cattle as a source of meat for rations and to furnish animals for breeding purposes at one or another of the proposed Mounted Police regional posts or stations. Steps would now have to be taken to locate and purchase the cattle.

Just before they were to leave Dufferin, Walker reported to the commissioner that an American dealer had called at the camp. He had a herd of a hundred head of oxen and mixed cattle for sale a short distance south of the border. Walker was instructed to ride south to inspect and purchase the cattle.

The herd may have been seen by some observers as an additional burden on the long march, but as time was to tell, some of the animals furnished much-needed food, and the work oxen proved invaluable in taking the places of the many draft horses that were exhausted on the trail.

While the force was still in camp at Dufferin and preparing for the long tramp, frightening reports were coming in about the warlike conduct of the Sioux Indians in the United States. One report warned that a war party had attacked the village of St. Joe, North Dakota, about thirty miles west of Dufferin, and had murdered the members of one family. The same Indians were reported to be crossing the boundary and riding toward Dufferin. The commissioner felt compelled to act and ordered all available men to parade, mounted and armed, to intercept the approaching Indians. It was the first occasion on which all members of the force paraded together. The troop took to the trail and was absent for eight hours without as much as seeing Indians.

Understandably, news of the massacre made many people nervous and jittery. Some of the untested men in the camp had second thoughts about their own safety, and there were a few desertions. The commissioners would have been quite within their rights if they had attempted to bring the deserters back and punish them, but they reasoned that deserters were not worth the time and effort likely to be spent pursuing them.

Instead of trying to win back the men who lacked the natural courage to go on, the commissioners made it easy for any who entertained doubts about facing the uncertainties of the West to quit before going farther. Explaining his policy in his first annual report, French wrote:

> I had endeavored before leaving Toronto to get rid of any who were not willing to 'rough it.' On two distinct occasions, I assembled all ranks and plainly told them that . . . they must expect plenty of hardship, that they might be wet day after day and have to lie in wet clothes [at night], that they might be a day or two without food and, I feared, they would be often without water. I called on any present who were not prepared to take the chance of these privations to fallout and they could have their discharges, there being plenty of good men ready to take their places. A few did accept discharges and one feels they acted properly in that matter.

Some of the men quickly tired of the food from the outdoor kitchen, and some allowed the savagery of the Red River mosquitoes to discourage them. It was, however, the slaughter of St. Joe that inspired the greatest rash of withdrawals, so "by the time the Force left Dufferin, the comparatively large number of thirty-one men were absent without leave . . . Fortunately, we brought twenty spare men, so that the Force was not as short-handed as some supposed."[9]

From *Colonel James Walker: Man of the Western Frontier* (1989)

The Inglorious Return

It was the most difficult decision Sitting Bull had ever been obliged to make. No doubt he repeated the unhappy sentiment communicated to relations at Standing Rock some time earlier: "Once I was strong and brave, and my people had hearts of iron, but now I am a coward and will fight no more forever. My people are cold and hungry. My women are sick and my children freezing. I will do as the Great Father wishes. I will give my guns and ponies into his hands. My arrows are broken and my war paint thrown to the wind."[1]

With no hope of obtaining a reserve in Canada, he attempted to negotiate for some much-needed supplies for his destitute followers. Inspector A.R. Macdonell, who took over the Mounted Police command at Wood Mountain from Inspector Crozier in June, showed an inherited parsimony and was no more helpful than his predecessor. Sitting Bull's own body was emaciated and even the horses and dogs were weakened from hunger. Called to the Police headquarters a few days after his return from Qu'Appelle, Bull was as stubborn as ever and Inspector Macdonell, not knowing what was in the Chief's mind, became impatient and ordered him to leave.

Jean Louis Legaré, the tall, friendly and courteous French-Canadian trader—"one of the finest men I have ever known," according to Marie Albina Hamilton[2]—had befriended the Sioux from the day the first band crossed the Boundary to pitch tipis in Canada, almost five years earlier. After Major James Walsh, Legaré ranked as the white man in whom the Indians had the greatest confidence. Most traders placed profits far ahead of a reputation for honest dealing and cared but little for Indian welfare. Earlier in the summer, Legaré had provisioned a group of local Sioux and had accompanied them to Fort Buford. He was ready to go again, this time with a bigger prize, Sitting Bull. But he knew the necessity of caution and diplomacy; the Americans had hinted at a reward for anyone who succeeded in bringing Sitting Bull to surrender and if the Chief was given reason to suspect that the trader was using him for personal gain, he would certainly have shown how obstinate he would be.

Sitting Bull gave Legaré the opportunity to repeat the oft-sounded advice about returning and then surprised the trader by saying he would consider going back if assured of sufficient provisions for his immediate needs as well as for the long trip. One writer contended that Sitting Bull demanded money—three hundred dollars—in addition to ten bags of flour and other supplies.[3] It seems doubtful, however, that cash, with which the Chief was quite unfamiliar, would be one of his demands. Jean Louis agreed to supply the necessities. He promised to furnish the wagons, carts, horses, and helpers needed and to escort the Indians personally to see that they were properly received at the American post.

Having received Bull's word, Jean Louis became the man of the hour and the Police recognized the magnitude of the task he was undertaking. Moving about two hundred men, women and children with their tipis and belongings would require considerable equipment and Jean Louis, understanding from Major Brotherton that the United States would reimburse him for expenses, was prepared to back the operation with all the resources he could command. Since the freetraders had no business dealings with the Hudson's Bay Company, it was necessary to cart supplies over the long trail from St. Paul in Minnesota and costs were high. Jean Louis took stock of his reserves and furnished ten bags of flour as an advance payment and agreed to have ten more for the journey. But as the day for departure drew near, the Chief protested that Legaré was loading nine bags, not ten. Sitting Bull could not read but he could count.

When Legaré's cavalcade of wagons and carts was ready, the Chief announced that he would require another ten days to reconsider. Legaré was exasperated but he did not dare offend the Chief and run the risk of inviting refusal to go through with the plan. He accepted, with the understanding of a definite deadline, 11 July 1881. In the meantime, Legaré was feeding the Indians, and as a means of sustaining their confidence even provided a feast with gifts of tobacco.

It was not a joyful departure. Minutes before Jean Louis gave the signal to start, several families withdrew, determined to remain in Canada, whatever it might hold for them. The cavalcade was the biggest seen in those parts since the Mounted Police trek of seven years earlier. Thirty-five wagons, three carts, and undetermined number of horse-drawn travois and sixty or more horses with riders moved away in disorderly array. Wagons were piled high with supplies and tipis. Women and children rode on top or walked behind and kept company with the numerous dogs. There were still Indians, particularly men, who refused to ride on the white man's wagon wheels—which they saw as symbols of evil. To guide the carts and wagons, Jean Louis employed his Métis friends, among them, Jean Chartrand who lived long and often related the experiences of the trip. He recalled Sitting Bull's insistence that his own mounted warriors act as advance and rear guards for the expedition. The man who showed no fear on the battlefield was now fearful that his enemies would take advantage of his weakened position and swoop down to kill.

The travellers were ten miles along the way when they pitched tipis for the first night. Legaré ordered one of his Métis helpers to make the first distribution of supplies: flour, bacon, tea, and sugar. Even then there was argument about the rations being too small. One excited Indian drew his revolver and blasted a bag of the flour until the contents were lost. Legaré was most anxious to avoid trouble and submissively replaced the damaged bag. But at this point he realized that his total stock of one ton of flour would not be enough to feed the 200 or 225 people until they reached Buford and knew he must make other arrangements. After the Indians had settled down for the night, he instructed two of his most reliable Métis to ride through the darkness and advise Major Brotherton at Fort Buford that he was on the way with Sitting Bull but faced a serious food shortage which could wreck the entire plan. He requested a wagonload of meat and flour to be sent forward with all possible haste—but without a military escort which might alarm the Indians.

Major Brotherton was as anxious as Legaré to see this mission completed. On his instructions, Captain Walter Clifford and a small staff proceeded with two loaded wagons to meet Legaré. The Major understood Legaré's worry about creating needless alarm and he took a further precaution. There existed a danger that an American force in the area might confront Sitting Bull's Sioux and spoil the plan by trying to effect a capture in the field. To guard against this, Captain Clifford carried specific orders to take immediate command of any troops in the area to ensure against any action likely to alarm the Indians or interfere with their voluntary surrender. Clifford accompanied the wagons while the Métis made a wide detour, rejoining Sitting Bull's party from the rear, thereby avoiding any appearance of collusion.[4]

As Legaré expected, Sitting Bull was disturbed by the approach of the American officer and wagons but when informed that the loads were made up exclusively of food supplies—flour and pemmican—and were intended for his people, he acceded. The supplies had arrived none too soon. Legaré's stocks were becoming dangerously low and now, in the best Indian tradition, the arrival of fresh provisions called for a celebration before going on.

Captain Clifford had a pleasant personality and his smile alone was enough to set the Chief at ease. He was able to answer certain questions which seemed to be bothering the Chief; one concerned the Chief's daughter who eloped with a young buck from Wood Mountain and then surrendered at Fort Buford. A rumour had reached her father that she was held prisoner in chains at Fort Yates. Clifford was able to tell the old man that the girl was well and free. Pleased with the good news, the Chief seemed almost ready to forgive Clifford for wearing the uniform of the United States army.

Two days later, 19 July, Legaré's wagons reached Fort Buford and the Indians were apprehensive. Lined up imposingly were the United States troops with their guns ready. In the background was the fort, the symbol of the new authority in their lives. Major Brotherton advanced to greet Legaré and smiled at Sitting Bull who continued to sit stoically on his old cream-coloured horse. His blanket was drawn to hide his face and he was in no hurry to dismount or to indulge in handshaking. A sign of a smile came only when he recognized Inspector A.R. Macdonell who had ridden in from Wood Mountain to be present for this occasion. Sitting Bull had not known Macdonell long. He knew this Inspector could be firm and tough but he bore a resemblance to Major James Walsh and the Chief liked him much better than the efficient and rather overbearing Crozier.

Macdonell greeted the Chief and told him what Major Brotherton had planned. The Sioux would give up their guns and some of their horses and could then pitch tipis beside the fort and prepare to eat all they wanted of United States government food. "And when you're ready," Macdonell added, "we'll have a meeting in Major Brotherton's office—Brotherton and Legaré and you and I will talk about the plans they have for you."

The Indians dismounted, dutifully deposited their guns, and then gathered in small groups or strolled aimlessly beside the river. Bull alone sat motionless on his horse until Macdonell signalled to him to come to Major Brotherton's office. The Chief responded slowly, his reluctance showing in every step. He took with him one of his young sons, the one named Crowfoot because of his admiration for the Blackfoot Chief. The officer was wise enough to know that the presence of Macdonell and Legaré would make it easier for him to give the impression of good faith on the part of the Government. Brotherton explained that as soon as possible, Bull and his followers would be transported down river to Fort Yates and Standing Rock Reservation where most of the Sioux from Wood Mountain were already located. There, the Major was sure, Sitting Bull could live peacefully and comfortably. As long as he refrained from hostile acts, he would not be molested by soldiers.

Sitting Bull sat as motionless as a marble statue—and just as silent.

He knew it would be his last chance to speak in the presence of the Canadians. Finally, he broke the silence. He was now convinced that surrender on his part was the proper decision, distasteful as it might be. He hoped that he and his people would still be allowed some liberties. He hoped he would be allowed to hunt and even tramp back to visit Wood Mountain. He wished those of his tribe who remained at Wood Mountain would now decide to join him here. Turning to Inspector Macdonell and his friend, the trader, he said: "Tell them to come. Tell them I said so. They'll be all right here."

Then he lifted his old rifle from under his blanket, handed it to his seven-year-old son and said: "You take your father's gun. I surrender it through you. You must learn the ways of the whites and how to live with them. I'm too old to learn much. And remember, your father was the last Sioux to surrender his gun."

With the least possible delay, river-boats were requisitioned and Sitting Bull and all the disarmed Sioux were on their way to the Indian agency at Standing Rock, downstream on the Missouri. Captain Clifford, the officer in charge, had twenty soldiers with him but said he did not feel the need for any. The Indians were perfectly orderly. The dispatch from Fort Buford, dated 29 July 1881, reporting Sitting Bull and one hundred and eighty-seven of his band leaving by steamer for Standing Rock that day added only: "Bull was silent and reserved."[5]

Along the way, the Chief became the object of great interest. Crowds turned out at stopping places to gaze at this man whose name had for so long filled North Americans with terror. He returned their stares with fixed defiance. With him were five other chiefs: White Dog, Scarlet Thunder, High-As-The-Clouds, Four Horns, and Bone Tomahawk. With him, also, were his two wives, children, sisters, and his aged father.

As the boat splashed its way downstream, nobody in the Indian party was finding more entertainment from passing scenes than Sitting Bull's father. Having made very few contacts with the new race except in warfare, much that the old man saw was strange and new to him. For the first time in his life he saw the white man's villages and towns, and even more amazing, a railroad track with a train on it. He had seen wagons on the trails and steamboats on the rivers and felt quite reconciled to these but steam engines running on rails frightened him. The old man was not alone in his disdain for rails and the locomotives which thundered over them. The feeling seemed to be shared by most Indians and Métis that those "iron horses" and "singing wires" were frightening the wild game away and inviting settlers to enter the land. Surely, they were among the most disturbing features of the new civilization, generally "bad medicine."

Even Sitting Bull failed to hide his fear, as a news report from Bismarck, dated 1 August 1881, noted:

> Sitting Bull arrived here yesterday. . . . He arrives at Standing Rock today. . . . He has great fear of locomotives. The terror of the North, the hero of a hundred battles, the Indian brave who never quailed before the arrow, the tomahawk or the rifle, is afraid of a locomotive. It evinces a power quite beyond his comprehension, and for once he feels himself awed into realization of his utter inability to cope with the forces of civilization. Wherever the locomotive penetrates, the savage is subdued.[6]

Bull's arrival at Standing Rock, without arms, without horses, marked the end of one of the most important chapters in North American history. The United States military beheld it with the sense of relief. The Indian Wars which plagued the West for so many years appeared to have ended.

From *Sitting Bull: The Years in Canada* (1973)

The Changing West 1881–1910

~

The Great Clarence and His Generation of Big Steers

He was just a big white steer with no interest in romance and no hope of posterity, but Clarence Kirklevington was smooth and beautiful and soon became the pride of members of the Shorthorn community and the talk of admiring cattlemen everywhere. As a Canadian steer who won championships at the highest fat stock court on the continent, he did more for the Shorthorn breed in this country than anything that happened since the Russells of Richmond Hill captured the cow championship at the World's Fair in 1876.

Unusual size is always capable of catching human attention. Large gentlemen and fat ladies have unfailing value as circus attractions, and extremely heavy steers—especially if they combined quality with weight—were their equals in novelty. But values are relative and it took a much bigger steer to be seen as a novelty in 1880 than in 1980. Like hobble skirts and button boots in their time, heavy steers had their years of popularity. Men might argue endlessly about type and quality in cattle but the scales settled questions of weight and, fortunately, the weights of many of the big steers of yesterday are on record.

The craze for size in steers in early Canada came in part from the big appetites of people performing heavy work and in part from British traditions. The exact weight of the "Herefordshire Ox" that won the sweepstakes award at the first Smithfield Show in London in 1799 is not known but his immense form can be imagined from his height of six feet and seven inches at the withers or, in the language of the horsemen, nineteen hands and three inches.

In the years that followed, the English breeders of Shorthorns were winning attention with animals like Durham Ox and White Heifer That Travelled, the former said to weigh 3,024 pounds at five years. But the average steer weights at the English shows of a century ago were probably no higher than those reported from early American shows. At the first American Fat Stock Show, held under the auspices of the Illinois State Board of Agriculture, the class for steers "four years and over" had twelve entries, all Shorthorns except for one Hereford. The lightest weight in the class was 1,980 pounds and the heaviest, 3,155 pounds. The average weight for the twelve head was 2,491 pounds. If the two lightest entries were omitted from calculation, the remaining ten steers would have averaged 2,594 pounds. The class would have been something to see and remember. And the grand champion steer of that show weighed 2,185 pounds.

Similar ideals prevailed in Canada. The steer spectaculars might be seen in show rings, in Christmas beef displays and at public stock yards. The champion fat steer at the Winnipeg Industrial Exhibition as late as 1898 was reported to outweigh the winning aged Clydesdale stallion at the same show by two hundred pounds.

The steer that earned the right to be remembered as the most famous in Canadian cattle history—perhaps in North American history—was the white and glamorous Clarence Kirklevington, bred and owned by Canada West Farm Stock Association, Brantford, and fed under the discerning eye of John Hope, the farm manager.

The beautiful farm in the loop of the Grand River at Brantford was the dream of Hon. George Brown whose tragic death had occurred so recently. But the farm and herd of English Shorthorns would be maintained by Brown's brother-in-law Thomas Nelson, and John Hope was continuing in management. Hope and others watched with eager interest for the calf from the royally bred Bates Duchess cow, the imported Kirklevington Duchess of Horton, carried from the service of Fourth Duke of Clarence, probably the most famous English Shorthorn bull in Canada at that time.

John Clay, who had a counselling responsibility at the farm, related the general disappointment on the day of the calf's birth. Clay and Hope had driven out from Brantford to the farm on the evening of 8 February 1881. It was a cold, clear night and after warming themselves beside the stove, Clay and Hope retired to the office which adjoined the house. "We had commenced on some work when James Smith [the herdsman] came in with a very solemn face and informed us that Kirklevington Duchess of Horton had just dropped a bull calf and, awful to think of, it was a white one. He had the red craze bad as any of us. So we went out to see this unwelcome arrival and when we got to the box he was born in, he was just getting up on his forelegs seeking for food. He was a lusty chap and white as the snow outside. Poor Hope was terribly disappointed as the mating of the above cow and the Fourth Duke of Clarence was made with great expectations. We went back to the office and smoked in silence for a bit. Then I plucked up courage and said to Hope: 'Now is our chance to train a well bred steer for the Fat Stock Show.'"[1]

Because of his colour, Clarence became a show steer instead of a show bull. But as noted by John Clay, he had his sire's vigour and gentle nature and proved to be an excellent feeder. During the next three years he made three appearances at the Chicago Fat Stock Show and bettered his record each time. At his first visit to the show, he weighed 1,620 pounds at 645 days of age, a rate of growth of almost two and a half pounds per day.[2] And in competition with twenty-six of the best yearlings on the continent, Clarence was the winner.

Interbreed rivalry was growing keen, and one of the results of Clarence Kirklevington's success in 1882 was an order from Geary Brothers of Bothwell, Ontario for the best Aberdeen-Angus steer available in Scotland. The steer purchased was Black Prince, which on leaving Scotland weighed well over a ton. The journey was slow and was followed by a long quarantine period in Canada, at the end of which Black Prince was down in weight and in danger of being late for the Kansas City Show. In order to ensure his appearance, the owners shipped him by express to Kansas City at a cost of four hundred dollars; they were rewarded by the Prince winning his class but not the supreme championship. From Kansas City, the black steer was forwarded to Chicago where Clarence

Kirklevington was making his second appearance. Public interest mounted but there was no clear victor because two championships were awarded in those years, one by breeder and feeder judges and one by butcher judges. As it turned out, Clarence Kirklevington won the championship awarded by the breeders and feeders and Black Prince won the other.

The outcome of the Chicago show looked like a draw, but there would be another year and both steers were taken back to Ontario. Farmers up and down the concessions talked and argued about the relative merits of these two bovine giants and hoped they would meet again. They did meet again, at the Chicago show of 1884. Clarence by this time was three years and seven months old and weighed twenty-four hundred pounds. Black Prince was probably older and may have been heavier. This would be the final and crucial test because both steers were entered in the carcass class which would follow the tanbark competitions. On foot, both steers won their respective classes until they came to the championships. Clarence, in addition to cash prizes, won a hay cutter, a supply of commercial feed and a sewing machine, none of which he would be able to use. Finally, Clarence won the sweepstakes for the best Shorthorn steer of any age, the grand sweepstakes for the best steer, cow or heifer in the show, and then the grand sweepstakes for the best carcass, any age or breed. No entry could do better than that. It was a Clarence Kirklevington year and friends of the Shorthorns were elated.

There was a sad side to it. As John Clay explained the scene: "When the steer was slaughtered, Sandie Thompson, the herdsman, wept like a child and I fancy John Hope kept out of the way. I took care to be away from the building."[3] The reporter for the *Canadian Live Stock Journal* added that the herdsman's last glance at his pet steer was not very clear because of his wet eyes and "he went his way musing on the mysterious necessity that calls for the slaughter of dumb dependents to supply the wants of men."[4]

From *Highlights of Shorthorn History* (1982)

Trader Burns

Of course Pat Burns liked the girls and liked to dance, even awkwardly, but he was practical more than romantic and business purposes came first. One of the ladies who remembered said, "His mind was full of schemes and even when we danced he made me think he was judging me for weight and market value."

After securing the quarter section adjacent to his as a pre-emption, his intention was to bring a big part of it under cultivation for grains with the least possible delay. He would raise a few pigs and as many cattle as his grass would support and be a mixed farmer just like most other people operating half-section farms. But for this aggressive fellow, farming did not work that way. He could not help seeing opportunities in trading livestock, and as he seized them, he was left with less and less time for the homestead.

Whether or not he was motivated by the challenge of public service, the frontier community needed somebody of his kind. Neighbours needed a person from whom they could buy soon-to-freshen milk cows and ready-to-use oxen, also someone to whom they could sell surplus livestock when they needed the money, and they encouraged his growing involvement in dealing. But there was that conflict between dealing and farming and gradually the former was gaining over the latter.

The homestead inspector shook his head and said in a warning tone; "You know you just meet the minimum cultivation requirement with nothing to spare and your house can't be approved until you get it chinked. But what is more serious, you fall short in time spent in residence on the homestead. Why don't you spend more time living on this place, at least until you get your patent? You know you can't get homestead credit for this place when you're working in the lumber woods more than fifty miles away, no matter how much money you're making there."

It was told, probably quite erroneously, that Burns and a neighbour fellow built a two-room cabin on the boundary line between their respective quarters, with each homesteader sleeping and claiming residence at opposite ends of the house. Technically, each resident would be on or over his own land. Such a prank might have been employed by some unscrupulous homesteaders but there is no evidence whatever that it was tried or even considered by Burns and his friends. Pat, to be sure, had his own cabin and its location was not even close to a fence line. Nevertheless, there were delays in qualifying for the title and instead of getting it at the end of the prescribed three years, the official transfer of deed from the Crown to "Patrick Byrne" for both homestead and preemption quarters was registered on 11 March 1885.[1]

Some of Pat Burns's absences from the farm were short, some were long. After the rather long period of employment in the lumber woods at Totogan, there were various freighting assignments taking him and his oxen over the tortuous trails to Portage la Prairie, Brandon, and Winnipeg which brought more in grocery money than he could have made by staying on the homestead. The freighting undertakings, in turn, revealed still more business opportunities.

Opportunity, as Burns was discovering, was where you found it, sometimes where you did not expect to find it, often where you simply made it. In the following summer, 1882, native grasses grew profusely and Burns, who could never be comfortable when seeing something useful going to waste, took to cutting hay and stacking far beyond the anticipated needs of his oxen, while many homesteaders were languishing in midsummer idleness. But how was he to turn the surplus hay to profit? There was only a negligible local sale for something that most people could have for the cutting but, according to rumour, there was a market for hay at Brandon.

W.G. Sanderson, whose Ontario ploughshares before coming to the West were sharpened by the author's blacksmith grandsire, George

McEwan, settled beside the trail about three and a half miles south of Burns and was an observer of Burns's methods in marketing hay, the same techniques that carried him far in the world of industry. In anticipation of his plan, Burns bought thin oxen in the autumn when prices were deflated almost to give-away levels, then saw them grow fat on the good prairie wool. Late in the winter he borrowed sleighs from his neighbours and made hayracks from dry poplar poles, of which he had great resources. Finally, he loaded the racks from hay remaining in the stacks, hitched a pair of the oxen to each sleigh, and with oxen tied to racks ahead, creating a formidable train of loaded sleighs, he drove over the snow toward Brandon, normally a journey requiring two long days.

At Brandon's market square, Burns first sold the hay, getting seven dollars per load, then dismantled the empty hayracks and sold the poplar poles for firewood at six dollars per cord. Finally, he piled the empty sleighs on a single set of runners and sold all the oxen except one team which was reserved to pull the load of sleighs and the operator, with a rewarding roll of bills in his pocket, back to Clanwilliam Municipality.[2]

What might have been Burns's first Manitoba purchase of breeding stock for resale comprised two cows, a brindle and a red, bought from a farmer at Westbourne, at a time when he knew he could facilitate delivery as far as Minnedosa by throwing them in with a herd of cattle that John Wake was driving from Winnipeg. The two-cow transaction marked a new chapter in trading.

The two young cows sold readily although one, according to local lore, produced a brief spell of embarrassment. It was like this: the homesteader who bought the brindle led her home and tied her in his new log stable, pleased with the prospect of having a family milk cow. Days later, when neighbouring wives came together to knit and consume tea and review all local events, the new cow came up for discussion and then inspection. The comment was altogether favourable until one lady, more observant than the others, noticed the total absence of incisor teeth on the cow's upper jaw and concluded that, contrary to the seller's claim, the animal was not a young cow at all but probably an aged one already losing teeth and in decline. The man who would sell her as a young cow was surely being deceptive and Pat Burns's reputation was in serious danger until he was able to convince the sceptical ladies that upper incisors were never part of a cow's natural equipment.

After selling the two cows and counting a moderate profit, Burns went again to the Westbourne man, Stewart by name, with the intention of buying four cows to be brought on with John Wake's next drive from Winnipeg. As the negotiations were related by William J. Wilde of Red Deer and Calgary, a long-time friend of Pat Burns, the Clanwilliam man told the Westbourne farmer that he was prepared to buy four or six cows and added with a sigh of regret that only the lack of money would prevent him from taking fifteen.

"That's all right," Stewart said, "take them and give me a promissory note."

Pat was agreeable and the cattle were selected, but just before the animals were to be driven away, there had to be that moment of accounting and settlement. Pat paid some cash and Stewart instructed him to go ahead and make out the promissory note for the balance.

At this point, Burns was obliged to confess something, saying, according to Wilde, "You had better make it out, Mr. Stewart. I don't know how."

"Neither do I," said Stewart, "so to hell with the note; take the cattle and pay me when you have sold them."

"That," Wilde added, "was the spirit of the West. That was the way business was done." Certainly it was the way that most of Pat Burns's early trading was conducted.

Westbourne proved to be good trading ground and Burns went there rather often. He liked to call at the farm of Walter Lynch, a pioneer who had come to Manitoba in 1870, bringing the first purebred Shorthorn cows in the West. Both Burns and Lynch spoke with an Ontario-Irish accent and both would rather trade than answer a call to dinner, and on one visit when Lynch was hard pressed to find something to sell, Burns protested that to meet without making some kind of a deal would invite bad luck. Lynch agreed and Pat finally bought a clucking hen and a setting of eggs to be taken back to his homestead farm. But the transaction failed to generate the luck expected; the hen in transit lost her urge to cover eggs and mother chicks and Burns, to salvage something, cooked the eggs and dressed the unwilling hen for his table.

Another Burns customer living in the direction of Westbourne, Keith MacDonald, was said to have been raised on haggis and whisky. When Burns and MacDonald traded, it was as if the honour of Ireland and Scotland were at stake. In the course of one lengthy struggle over the sale of a three-year-old steer, contention arose over the estimates of the animal's weight. Burns said the steer weighed 1,280 pounds and his offer was three and one-half cents per pound.

Burns was not a gambler, but he was not above backing his judgment with his money. The deal in this instance was concluded with a side bet about the weight. If the steer proved to weigh more than 1,280 pounds, Burns would buy MacDonald a new hat, and if the weight was less than that figure, MacDonald would buy a hat for Burns. When the steer finally came to the scales, its weight was shown to be 1,270 pounds, and in due course, Pat was presented with a new hat. But the hat did not fit and when Burns complained that it was too small, the Scot was ready with his reply: "I know it is too small; so was the price I got for my steer."

As of 21 March 1881, Manitoba's boundaries were extended westward and northward to give the province the impressive size known today. Suddenly, on that date, Pat Burns and his neighbours were in the province of Manitoba rather than in the Northwest Territories. Some homesteaders objected to being placed in Manitoba, presuming the change would result in higher taxes. To Burns, the change was of no special consequence. What with freighting, trading, and farming, his life was already full and he was spending about as much time in the province as in the Territories.

As time passed, he was finding less time for farming and then less time for freighting. Dealing in livestock could keep him busy at all seasons. He was away from the farm so much that neighbours wondered if the homestead would escape cancellation. The danger was real. It was fair criticism, both before and after receiving title for the land in 1885, that Burns was becoming slightly out of touch with his farm. It would come to him as a shock when, in 1885, his attention was directed to the local newspaper which showed a list of farms in the Municipality of Clanwilliam about to be sold for taxes. The notice read, brutally, that unless the tax arrears were paid in the meantime, "I shall on Monday, the 19th day of October, at two o'clock, sell by public auction . . ."[3]

Listed among the properties to be sold was the "north half of the NW1/4 of 18-16-17-Wl," which was part of the Burns farm. The amount of arrears was small, only $8.61, and his failure to pay could have been explained as an oversight. Nevertheless, the owner had not paid his taxes in full and it suggested something more than an oversight.

Like any other businessman, Burns was giving his best attention to the more profitable of his enterprises and that was in droving. He was becoming well known all the way from Minnedosa to Winnipeg, and before long, the local editor was treating him as a visitor when he appeared in town. Late in 1885, the news read that: "Mr. P. Burns of Winnipeg was in town this week,"[4] and days later, "Mr. P. Burns, the cattle buyer, is in town visiting old friends and doing a little business at the same time."

The Minnedosa region was becoming an important producer of cattle and other livestock and the editor of the weekly *Tribune* gave credit to the shippers, John Wake, Pat Burns, and Sewell and Proven. "Six years ago," the editor wrote, "there were only three cows in the settlements north of Minnedosa. Now many settlers have herds ranging up to one hundred head. The first shipment out of the district was made in 1883, not quite three years ago, when about twenty head were shipped by J. Wake to Winnipeg."[5] From this beginning, the editor noted boastfully, shipments in the recent year, March of 1885 to March of 1886, made by the three leading dealers had risen in value to $35,200.

Then there was a new trend. Pat Burns was giving more of his attention to the shipping of pigs, really pioneering in this aspect of the business. Pigs could not be driven overland to market like cattle in pre-rail years, and consequently they were not marketed far from home. But now, in 1886, the pork producers saw hope in rail shipments and Burns was the one to test it.

On 19 February 1886, he was reported as shipping a carload of pigs from Minnedosa to Winnipeg. A similar shipment was reported on 14 May and then, on 6 August, the news told that "Mr. P. Burns, the cattle dealer, was in town this week purchasing hogs for the Montreal market. He was making up six carloads."[6]

Obviously, he now had bank credit and this was the first shipment of its kind from the West to the East. Indeed, it was being made so soon after the completion of the transcontinental railway the shipping company did not have a freight tariff for pigs being moved that far. But Burns talked to the railway officials and gained their approval for an experimental shipment with tentative freight rates. It was clearly understood that in the event of a loss by the shipper—meaning Burns—he would be entitled to apply for a refund up to the total cost of freight.

The pigs were shipped, six carloads, and about three weeks later, Burns paid a call at the freight offices to report succinctly that no refund would be requested. He was on his way west to recruit another shipment of pigs for the Eastern trade and the movement grew.

Pat's withdrawal from the Clanwilliam farm was gradual at first, and then when the meat contracts took him far away, it was complete. He loved that farm and loved the community but it became ever clearer that neither the district nor the farm could contain him. Still, he was reluctant to part with the land holding so many rich memories, and he resolutely refused all offers from prospective purchasers until years after he was established in Alberta. Moreover, he resolved firmly that he would be discriminating in the person permitted to purchase. The buyer, as it turned out, was a MacPherson.

Pete MacPherson from Lorneville, Ontario, cousin of Pat's former neighbours, Jim and Hugh MacPherson, came to Manitoba in 1889 and ten years later bought the Burns land. The Land Titles Office records show the transfer of title on both quarters being registered on 16 June 1899, from Patrick Byrne to Peter R.A. MacPherson, at a price of one thousand dollars for each quarter.

From *Pat Burns: Cattle King* (1979)

First Fair at Hub City

It was with the aid of an exhibition that Saskatoon was founded. The Ontario folk who conceived the idea of a temperance colony adequately removed from John Barleycorn and all his sinful relations applied to the Dominion Government for a tract of land and then advertised the plan at the Toronto Exhibition in 1881.

The tract comprising a couple of million acres obtained by the founders was on the South Saskatchewan River and the response to the idea of a booze-proof colony exceeded expectations. The Temperance Colonization Society was organized and in June of 1882, J.N. Lake, W.S. Hill, and George W. Grant left Toronto with a survey party to inspect the property. First they had to find it, but that was one reason for the surveyors.

The reports sent back were favourable. The soil was all right and the 150 miles between the chosen site and the nearest railroad at Moose Jaw represented a satisfactory margin of safety for those who sought assurance of isolation from all the foul odours of alcohol. Thus though conceived in the iniquitous and gin-soaked East, Saskatoon was born amid the virgin purity of a remote spot on the prairies; or so abstemious leaders chose to believe.

A few settlers arrived in the fall of 1882, but the main body came over the trail from Moose Jaw in the following year. The *Nor'-West Farmer* of July 1883 undertook to introduce the new community to the world:

> Saskatoon is the name of the metropolis of the Temperance Colonization Company. It is said to be one of the prettiest townsites in the North-West.

Everyone who had seen it agreed that it was an attractive site, but monotonously difficult to reach. Only those with iron in their wills as well as in their blood would venture that far from rails and relations. The Temperance Colony was being seeded with stock of a screened and selected kind.

In 1884, newcomers scarcely settled in their adopted surroundings organized the temperance Colony Pioneer Society. The new organization was many things but chiefly an agricultural society. James Hamilton was the first president, taking office following an organization meeting on 1 March. From the beginning, it was a vigorous society. It arranged about starting the first school, passed the hat around the colony, and collected $271.64 with which to pay teacher J.W. Powers. From the constitution drawn up on 15 March, the reader will see evidence of enterprise:

> The objects of this society shall be the discussion of matters pertaining to the welfare of the settlers, useful counsel, the dissemination of useful knowledge, and social intercourse.

The constitution provided that "the Chaplain shall assist at the opening and closing of the meetings," and that

> any member who has been guilty of immoral conduct or violated the constitution . . . may be expelled or fined.

Strange it must seem that moral irregularities would be considered a possibility among the members of a Saskatoon Exhibition organization. But times have changed and the directors of recent years have appeared so virtuous that all provision for disciplining has been removed from the constitution.

The Society worked for a ferry across the river, a co-operative store and a grist mill. It fixed the price of custom threshing at seven cents a bushel in 1885 and placed a ceiling of $3.10 per hundred pounds on flour in 1886. It investigated the possibilities of removing some of the twists in the trail to Moose Jaw for the purpose of shortening it, and it agitated for a Police Station.

Academic and cultural progress was not overlooked. On 9 February 1885, Thomas Copland was presenting a paper with the scholarly title "Application of Theory to Practical Farming."

The Society slumped in 1886 but not for long. From the same roots there arose a new branch with a new name, the Central Saskatchewan Agricultural Society. Much as it must have irritated the founders of the colony, non-temperance as well as temperance members were admitted, and the Police Station was seen as a bigger need than ever. James P. Lake became president, and Thomas Copland secretary. Some of Copland's land afterwards became the campus of the University of Saskatchewan and in one of its reverend halls there hangs today a portrait of the old man holding an impressive scroll which, until the artist did a "Houdini" transformation on it, had been the handle of a curling broom.

The new executive announced a fair for the second Wednesday in October 1886. That first fair was held on the east side of the river, about where Nutana Collegiate stands today. There were no gates on the grounds, no grandstand and no sports other than races, but according to Joseph Caswell, every settler brought something to exhibit.

The prize list offered more of interest than monetary reward, but nobody exhibited to get rich. For the best herd of Durham cattle, the first prize was a dollar and a diploma; for the best in Ayrshires, the reward was the same. Joseph Caswell and his brother had brought some Shorthorn cattle (Durhams in the prize list) from Ontario that spring, driven the cows from Moose Jaw to Saskatoon on foot, and then returned to the railroad to transport the new bull to Saskatoon by wagon. The bull was too fat to walk that distance with the cows. Anyway, the herd was ready for exhibition at the Fall Fair and the fat bull received as much admiration as Babe Ruth at a youth rally.

Attending the Golden Jubilee of the Saskatoon Exhibition was Mrs. B.E. Anderson of Sutherland who recalled walking to Saskatoon and driving two cows, two heifers, and a heifer calf for that first fair. Nancy, the calf, was stubborn and wanted to go home and when they arrived at the scene of the fair, both the little girl and the calf were tired. To make matters worse, it was learned that there was no class for Nancy. But there were other calves in similar position and sympathetic directors made a special class and Nancy won first prize and fifty cents.

In the class for oxen, there was bigger prize money: for a yoke of working oxen, the first prize was two dollars and the second, one dollar. H. Donavon offered a special prize of a dollar for the best trotting ox hitched to a buckboard. A trotting ox and a hefty buckboard represented the most dependable transportation, at least until the mosquitoes and warble flies tormented the critter to the point where he struck off to plunge into the nearest slough, taking buckboard and passengers with him. Mr. Kusch was the proud owner of the best trotting ox.

There is no evidence of inferiority among those who drove and exhibited oxen on the streets of Saskatoon at that first fair. Joseph Caswell, who was a director and an exhibitor on that occasion and had the distinction of being an exhibitor in the livestock classes at Saskatoon Exhibition exactly fifty years later, told the writer that when the class for the "Best Walking Team" was called, Stanley King entered with his oxen. The horsemen protested. (They have accounted for most of the exhibition protests since that time.) But the committee took a stand against racial discrimination and ruled that two oxen made a legitimate team. King won the competition.

Robert Caswell, who later owned the internationally famous Shorthorn bull, Gainford Marquis, won a dollar for the best pen of fowl and H. Bowman had the winning trotting horse, an Indian pony, blind in one eye, but the fastest trotter seen around Saskatoon in those years. Racing purses at that show would never induce inflation on a national scale. First prize in the one-mile trot was one dollar, and first in the two-mile trot was two dollars. It appeared to be computed on the basis of a dollar a mile which would not entirely satisfy the Prairie Thoroughbred Breeders of the present generation.

In the wheat section there were three classes, one for Red Fife, one for White Russian and one for "any other variety." In each there were two prizes, two dollars and one dollar. Special prizes provided by public spirited citizens were intended to meet the special needs of the community, and had a distinctive character about them. W.H. Trounce, one of the directors, thought he understood something of the agony that went with bachelorhood, and here he is offering the tempting reward of one pound of the best tea for the "best loaf of bread, two pounds or over, made by anyone keeping bach." Trounce was an advocate of big loaves. He would have no patience with a modern one-pound loaf that practically disappears when a hungry man has taken a couple of meals from it.

Director Trounce was anxious that the settlers be clothed as well as full of two-pounder loaves, and a minute dated 6 September 1887, reads:

> Moved by Smith, seconded by Garrison that Mr. Trounce's offer of fifty cents for prize for best darned stockings and fifty cents for the best patched pants be accepted. Motion carried.

The settlers had neither a University, an Experimental Farm, nor a handy Department of Agriculture to which to turn for guidance and therefore a Fall Fair offered about the only experience in Adult Education. There was something bigger and better than the prize money about it.

The Exhibition helped to give character to the Hub City, and no city had more. Its founders from Ontario intended that it should be a dry city. It is still dry but not in the way the pioneer Methodists thought about it. In spite of drought, however, Saskatoon is the City Beautiful, with landscaped riverbanks, well groomed boulevards and plenty of trees. Though it be an island in a sea of waving grain, the setting of the Bessborough Hotel, once a city dump for cans, ashes and amputated branches, is one of the topmost beauty spots of Western Canada. And the spirit of which Sid Johns, director of the Saskatoon Exhibition from 1922 until his death in 1943, never ceased to boast is still there. A visitor from abroad said about Saskatoon, as he discovered it in the winter season, "coldest weather and warmest hospitality I have ever known."

From *Agriculture on Parade* (1950)

Meet Sir Frederick

Two long days of jolting stagecoach travel immersed the passengers in the powerful language of Frank "Polly" Pollinger who guided his four-horse team of ever-nervous broncos over the hundred-mile trail from Calgary to Fort Macleod. After his endurance had reached its limit twenty-seven-year-old Frederick Haultain, mumbling with an English accent that betrayed his place of birth, said he would rather walk than ride any farther.

He stepped to the plank sidewalk in front of Harry "Kamoose" Taylor's famous hotel, stretched, and made a glancing survey of the town. The shabby structures and the hodgepodge arrangement were not what he expected to see. Disappointed, he turned to Pollinger, who was unloading trunks, and asked, "Are you sure this is Fort Macleod?" Luckily, Pollinger didn't hear him.

Of course there was nobody present to greet him. He could not expect a personal welcome where he was not even known. He looked in vain for the Mounted Policemen striding about in bright uniforms. The only local people within view were the few idlers leaning heavily against the hotel as if to furnish a prop for the front wall. These fellows, with nothing better to do, were being entertained by the stranger's good clothes and polished shoes. "Another city slicker," they seemed to be saying. "Here from the East, no doubt. But he won't stay long. The Toronto men never do."

Haultain was inclined to agree; he wouldn't be staying long in a town with no trees except for the ribbon of willows and poplars growing in the damp soil close to the Oldman River. And so far he had not seen one painted house. But the deepest wound of all came when his eyes fell upon a sign in a store window: WORKMEN WANTED. GOOD WAGES. NO ENGLISHMEN NEED APPLY. Why had he allowed himself to be carried away by the romantic idea of opening a law office at Fort Macleod? Surely he had reached the end of the world.

There would be no stagecoach returning to Calgary until the next day and he would be obliged to spend at least one night at Taylor's hotel. He would find out if Taylor really charged extra for clean sheets. Counting his remaining cash he found it less than enough to pay for a few days of accommodation at the hotel and stagecoach fare back as far as Calgary. But regardless of the major decision about returning to Peterborough, he needed a bed for the night and turned in where Old Kamoose was standing in the doorway.

Looking the young man over in the manner of a cowboy studying a horse he thought of buying, Kamoose asked, "You a clergyman or a professional poker player? They're the only ones we see here with good clothes like yours."

Explaining that he was neither of these, Haultain admitted his purpose was to open a law office but that he was not sure about staying. Taylor replied, "You know there's one lawyer here now, McCaul by name, but don't let that stop you. The men around here are always getting charged with stealing cattle or trading whiskey and they're constantly looking for lawyers to defend them. You'd better try it for a month. There's a log cabin—you can see it from here—that you could rent for ten dollars a month, big enough for a desk and a bed and you'd be in business."

After twenty-four hours at Fort Macleod, the absence of trees and house paint was not nearly as obvious and Haultain believed he could like the place. Instead of returning to Calgary and the East, he rented the log cabin and made a small sign to inform the public that F.W.G. Haultain was a lawyer ready for business. It was a decision he never regretted. What had looked at first as the end of the world was really the beginning of a new one, a world offering unusually rich opportunities for public service, a political world in which he would be the foremost performer. At the end of the first month he had fully accepted Fort

Macleod and Fort Macleod had accepted him. He distinguished himself in and out of the courtroom. He sang in the church choir, played soccer with the Mounted Police, and bought a forty-dollar horse from Jerry Potts and took to riding with a stock saddle.

Three years after the unspectacular arrival, Haultain was elected to represent his area in the legislative council of the Northwest Territories. For the rest of his long life he served in positions of high authority and influence, and nobody made a finer record. For twenty-five unbroken years he sat as a member of the legislature, first in the territorial legislature and then in the Saskatchewan legislature. For the eight years prior to the formation of the two new provinces, he was the premier of the Northwest Territories—for all practical purposes the only premier in territorial years. Following his quarter century in the legislatures, there was another twenty-five-year stint of distinguished service as the chief justice for Saskatchewan, to say nothing of twenty-two years as chancellor of the University of Saskatchewan. Like every public servant, he had his setbacks, but took comfort from the words he loved to quote from Sir James Barrie's address at St. Andrews University:

> Fight on my men, says Sir Andrew Barton,
> I am hurt, but I am not slain;
> I'll lie me down and bleed awhile,
> And then I'll rise and fight again.[1]

It is difficult to think of anybody in public life in western Canada who displayed more of the qualities of statesmanship than the many-titled Frederick Haultain.

As he experienced political reverses, so, in early years, he had his political enemies, but when he celebrated his eightieth birthday in 1937, there was no one who wasn't ready to sing his praise. A friend who knew him well said he wasn't always easy to comprehend but he was always easy to love. He had a boyish shyness that never left him. He was quiet until the appropriate moment to speak out and then he was fluent. In the opinion of those who could judge objectively he was the greatest parliamentary debater of his time. The Honorable Walter Scott, premier of Saskatchewan, believed Haultain's only rival in parliamentary debate in Canada was Sir Richard Cartwright. He may have enjoyed the thrust and parry of formal debate, but what he loved more was good conversation, the quiet, relaxed conversation with friends. He would have been distressed to see, in later years, how the art of conversation, the best of all pastimes, had deteriorated as television came to dominate home life.

He had the body and muscle to be a great athlete. Tennis, soccer, and cricket were his favorite sports, but after acquiring his own horse he became one of Fort Macleod's most enthusiastic polo players and was prominent in organizing the local polo club.

Inevitably, his political fortunes rose and fell but his principles were steadfast. C.W. Peterson, who could recall working and even living with him, pronounced him "absolutely incorruptible." There are few other public figures who served as long without a single charge of graft or political patronage or irregularity of any kind. Such a record is the more remarkable when seen in the light of the breadth of his activities and contributions. No student of public affairs in western Canada can review the Haultain years without realizing that the advent of responsible government in the prairie region was mainly his accomplishment. He was also the leading architect in planning for the transformation from Territories to provinces.

Qualifications for the distinction of statesmanship were never very clear but whatever they were, Haultain seemed to have them. Bob Edwards of the Calgary *Eye Opener*, after attending the funeral of a man who served in the provincial legislature and listening to the extravagant eulogy, said he had finally discovered the definition of a statesman. " A statesman," said he, "is a dead politician." What the country needed, the editor implied, was more statesmen—that is, more dead politicians. But even that caustic editor, who maintained a constant attack on political pomposity, contended that the innuendo did not apply to Frederick Haultain, whom he admired as "a very great statesman." But Bob Edwards was not alone in extolling Haultain's statesmanship as unsurpassed in his generation. James Clinkskill who, as the legislative representative for Battleford, sat with him in the territorial assembly from 1888 to 1898, testified many years later: "He stands to this day head and shoulders over any man who has taken part in political life in the West. The fact is that he was too much the statesman and too little the politician to suit Canadian ideas in that period."[2]

Much of his advice about the creation of Saskatchewan and Alberta was wasted because it was rejected by the federal government. But that did not mean Haultain was wrong. He had the best of constitutional reasons for believing that the senior government should not interfere in educational matters in the provinces. His insistence that natural resources should be turned over to the new provinces in 1905 was vindicated when they were later transferred. And even at the beginning of the present century, he sensed the danger of too much government in Canada. If he had had his way, the geography of western Canada would have been quite different; for better or worse, there would have been one province instead of two between Manitoba and British Columbia. He suggested calling the big province by the name Buffalo. His friends would have called it the Province of Haultain. But regardless of the name, the case for one big province has remained debatable to the present time, and students have continued to enquire if the one-province concept would have given the West a stronger voice in the councils of the nation. What city would have been named to be the capital? Which political party would be in power in the big province eighty years later? More important, to what extent would the big provincial area inherit the political ideals of the man who fashioned it—ideals such as pay-as-you-go financing, no-party government at the provincial level, strict adherence to democratic principles, and the exercise of thrift in government with the same diligence as citizens must practice in their private lives?

There was no secret about Haultain's leaning toward the Conservative Party in federal politics but his territorial cabinets were as nearly nonpartisan as he could make them. His staunchest cabinet colleague was James Ross, a Liberal from Moose Jaw. In a federal campaign, Haultain and Ross might be found speaking for different sides—sometimes from the same platform—and then returning to their territorial responsibilities with no loss of loyalty toward each other. If Haultain had had his way, the same nonpartisanship would have prevailed in the new provinces.

Admirers of Haultain have always found it difficult to forgive the intensely partisan government at Ottawa in 1905 for denying what seemed Haultain's clear right to be named as the first premier of one of the two new provinces. If appointed the provisional premier of either province, he would, in all likelihood, have formed successive governments. Students of political history have presumed that as an extremely able Western premier, he would have been invited to join the Borden government at Ottawa. In due course he would likely have been a candidate for national leadership of the Conservative Party and probably prime minister at some time during the twenties. It is, at least, a fascinating topic for speculation. There could be no doubt that he had the capacity to be a great prime minister.

It was not that he sought high honours or a place for himself in history. On the contrary, he was one of the most modest and self-effacing persons. He had no pretense. His normal expression was serious but not severe, and roguish smiles would break through intermittently, like sunshine piercing broken clouds. He might have gained substantial wealth from the practice of law, but personal fortune held no attraction for him. There were more important goals than money. It is sad, he reasoned, when people become so engrossed in the pursuit of wealth that they miss the rudiments of good living. When he took time for relaxation, he would find the greatest of delights—regardless of money and cost—in a comfortable fireside chair, a glass of whiskey, and congenial company for an evening of conversation and stories about territorial politics.

It seemed that everything Haultain did was carried out with distinction. It leads one to speculate about the outcome if Sir Frederick's fate had brought him to act his part on a bigger parliamentary stage like that of the dominion. What would have been the result if Haultain's destiny was to become the prime minister of Canada and John A.

Macdonald's was to serve as the premier of the Northwest Territories? Nobody can be sure of the answer, but it is safe to say that neither office would have suffered and Haultain would have been assured a place in history and a fairer measure of lasting gratitude—and Macdonald, not Haultain, would have been in danger of being forgotten.

Canadians, busy converting a wilderness to a land of prosperity, found history as something they thought they could live without. They would remember prime ministers with names like Macdonald and Laurier and forget many leaders with no less ability. Haultain, whose story might hold high inspirational value for young and old, was one of those to be largely forgotten. True, a few schools were given Haultain's name, but from enquiries made in 1955 when Saskatchewan and Alberta were celebrating their fiftieth anniversaries, most people living near those places of learning didn't know why the name was chosen. At one big city school it was found in the course of a visit that fifty per cent of the teachers and nearly all of the pupils questioned had no idea why their school bore the Haultain name. One teacher believed that Haultain was a parliamentarian in England and another was under the impression that he was the first mayor of Calgary. One grade eight boy at the same school presented a blank expression when asked about the man, and then beamed satisfaction when he thought the answer came to him: "I think he was a hockey player with the Boston Bruins."

If Frederick Haultain was too soon forgotten, he was not alone in suffering the slight. That failure may be related to the shortage of great and dedicated leaders of which Canadians have complained in recent years. A more generous recognition of the outstanding leaders of other years, and a better familiarity with the men and women who shaped our history might induce more able and unselfish people to become candidates for the high calling of public service.

From *Frederick Haultain: Frontier Statesman of the Canadian Northwest* (1985)

Bedson's Buffalo

Samuel Lawrence Bedson, with his birthplace in England, said he was born in a soldier's uniform. In keeping with family tradition, he was, in 1885, a forty-three-year-old officer with the rank of quartermaster sergeant, marching west under the command of Col. Garnet Wolsley, for the suppression of the Red River Insurrection, and seeing Western Canada for the first time. When his battalion was disbanded in the next year, he was appointed warden of the recently created jail being set up at Lower Fort Garry where his battalion had been quartered. He was in Manitoba to stay and forge an essential link in the chain of events that would do much to rescue the prairie buffalo from threatened oblivion by helping to create a North American "stockpile" of breeding animals that would, ultimately, be brought back in triumph to buffalo country in Canada.

In pursuing a purpose, Nature can be devious. In Bedson's first year in Manitoba, the Government of Canada acknowledged the need for a penitentiary for the area and asked Bedson to conduct a study and recommend a site. His advice to build on Stony Mountain was accepted and construction began in 1874, at about which time Bedson was appointed warden of the institution. He became one of the best-known and most popular citizens in Manitoba. His personality and his involvement with buffalo, needless to say, contributed more to his popularity than his association with the penitentiary.

Settlers in the district, less than twenty miles north of Winnipeg, watched with interest as the "pen" was built, describing it as "the castle," a term which, in the light of its appearance on the commanding eminence, was not inappropriate. It ensured that the warden received the added appellation of nursery rhyme fame, "The King of the Castle."

Years later, when Bedson was referred to as "The King of the Castle," one of his admirers interjected saying, "Call him what you like but don't forget that in all likelihood, Canada would not have had Wainwright Buffalo Park and the best collection of park buffalo in the world if it hadn't been for Col. Bedson in the years after 1880."

The penitentiary was still incomplete when Governor General and Lady Dufferin paid an official visit in August 1877 and it was still two-and-one-half years before Bedson had his herd of buffalo but it was significant that the two key men in directing the vice-regal reception and entertainment—Col. Bedson and Hon. James McKay—were the two who deserved the highest praise in the Manitoba struggle to save the buffalo. The same two men took much pride in their farms, especially in their horses and then in their buffalo. As Norm Gorman, who researched Bedson's characteristics with special care, pointed out, the Colonel had a sympathetic feeling for all animals. "He was no hunter," Gorman wrote. "He would rather catch and tame a coyote or a bear than shoot it." Well remembered was his team of young moose orphans which he and his stockman, Joe Daniels, hitched to a toboggan for a cross-country winter tour.

Starting with thirteen head, Bedson's herd grew rapidly, leading somebody to observe—probably as intended humour—that the high rate of increase in Bedson's herd was an indication that the owner had to be a most efficient operator or possess some of the traits of a successful rustler. But the suggestion of theft had to be intended as a joke because there was no other herd of buffalo in the country from which to steal and Benson had never been suspected of stealing anything, not even an opinion or a kiss. His success, however, might have been explained, in part, by his well-known feeling of kindness for animals, wild or domesticated. He was known to carry an orphan moose home rather than desert it to starvation. His barnyard had known some strange tenants, and visitors who made the mistake of wandering around Bedson's yard after dark knew exactly what it was like to stumble over a tethered bear or a half-grown buffalo bull.

James McKay died in December, 1879, and an auction sale of his farm and household effects, including thirteen buffalo, was announced for 20 January 1880. Warden Bedson entertained a secret desire to buy a small breeding foundation of the species but was sure he could not pay for more than four or five head. And he was discouraged to learn that there were buyers for the animals from as far away as Scotland.

The sale started at noon on 20 January and ended late on 22 January, and the buffalo that were expected to be offered individually were presented as a herd. Bedson was sure the plan would eliminate him as a buyer, but he had visited Sir Donald Smith and secured a loan for up to a thousand dollars. When the bidding ended, probably nobody was more surprised than Bedson to find himself the owner of the last surviving herd of prairie buffalo in Canada for the unbelievable total of one thousand dollars. He was happy with the purchase but now he was worried about how he would get them home to Stony Mountain.

He told himself it could be done. He would have two of his own hired workers on good horses and borrow two riders from the McKay farm who were familiar with the buffalo. The plans for the morning drive, though, were complicated by the nighttime birth of a bison calf. Bedson felt the cow and calf should remain behind but one of the cowboys believed that the calf could survive the twenty-one-mile walk. The calf passed its first test with distinction. Then, after walking over the wintry trail from Deer Lodge to Stony Mountain and bedding down in the snow beside its mother at the end of the day, the little fellow followed the thirteen older buffalo which broke out of their new paddock during the night and returned to Deer Lodge.

The cowboys agreed that the buffalo did not appear to be overly tired and favoured an immediate repetition of the drive. Before nightfall, the buffalo were again at Stony Mountain and more securely enclosed. And the calf of forty-eight-hours—seen taking a reviving swig of mother's milk—was none the worse from its walk of at least sixty-three miles in thirty-six hours. Bedson was impressed by the obvious stamina that he hoped to see incorporated in the genetic constitution of a hybrid strain or breed emerging from Canada's domestic cattle and the buffalo.

Bedson's buffalo were picturesque and exciting if not always congenial and cooperative. He must have realized that with a paddock full of buffalo and a penitentiary full of prisoners, there would be no dull moments for him. As time passed, he discovered that the species was more amenable to domestication than he and many others had expected. Increasingly, his bison were being allowed to roam about the community although some neighbours said they were a nuisance. Joe Daniels, the cowboy in charge, was satisfied most of the time to let the animals choose their directions but "keep in touch with them" and know where they were at all times. Bedson was convinced that animals allowed to wander away at will were more likely to wander back to the barnyard that offered hay, water, and salt.

It may have been a natural springtime urge that induced five of Bedson's buffalo to stray westward farther than usual in April, 1889, and encounter trouble with hunters. Bedson had sold the herd almost a year earlier but only part of it had been delivered. Regardless of who would bear the loss, Bedson was upset about it and public indignation was intense.

The five animals had been missing for a few days before Bedson sent one of his experienced men to find them. Following clues, Sam McCormack rode toward Portage la Prairie and at High Bluff he learned that the five animals were there until a family of traditional hunters surrendered to the temptation to pursue and shoot. Three of the five were killed and a fourth was wounded. McCormack, at that point, turned his attention to the recovery of the hides and heads, and the giving of all possible assistance to the police working on the case. The shooting of four buffalo was seen as a heavy loss and there was nothing of benefit from the affair except a clear call from the press and public for laws that "will punish severely anyone destroying one of these now almost extinct animals."[1]

Bedson did not become tired of the buffalo but larger numbers and circumstances were producing more problems. From the thirteen original head the herd had grown to eighty-five head of breeding animals and enough hybrids to make a total of 118, nine years later. The increasing density of farm settlement was forcing a retreat from the practice of allowing his animals to run more or less at large and, finally, the warden was about to retire shortly and keeping the herd would be difficult if not impossible. There would be no problem in finding a buyer and, so, he cut out enough buffalo and hybrids to be given to Sir Donald Smith to liquidate his debt of one thousand dollars used to buy the buffalo, and then sold the remainder to C.J. "Buffalo" Jones of Garden City, Kansas, USA— eighty-three head for a total reported to be between fifteen and fifty thousand dollars—the lower figure considered most plausible.

The animals in the Jones purchase were to be shipped from the Winnipeg Stockyard, roughly half in late 1888 and the balance in 1889. Nobody seemed to anticipate the difficulties in bringing the herds into the stockyard at Winnipeg and loading them on freight cars. "Buffalo" Jones sent some of his best cowboys to Manitoba to assist in the movement and loading, but it is doubtful if the American rodeo performers among them had ever seen anything more spectacular or hazardous than what awaited them at the loading chutes in Winnipeg.

The first task was to gather all the Bedson buffalo, including the ones that enjoyed the freedom to roam, and deliver them inside the massive stone walls, five feet high and a foot and one-half in thickness, that surrounded the stableyard at Stony Mountain. Though it was a wall to halt an army tank it didn't impress Bedson's buffalo.

The buffalo had seen the barnyard setting many times before and with memories of good hay, they had no hesitation in entering the open gate again. But when the heavy gate was closed behind them, their wild superstition was instantly fired. With the old "boss bull" taking the lead, the herd began to mill or circle, looking for a way of escape. It looked like the start of a stampede, certainly no place for human loiterers, and observers immediately climbed to the top of the fence. But one man, wiser in the ways of buffalo, left the fence to find a safer observation point, farther away. He did it just as the old bull who seemed to be in command led "the buffalo brigade" in a charge that opened the wall and allowed every member of the herd to follow, on the run to the grassland beyond.

The wall was patched up with loose stones and when the herd was again rounded up in the morning, the six riders who were to direct the drive to the Winnipeg Stockyard, about fifteen miles across country, made a quick division and cut out thirty-three head for the Winnipeg delivery. With luck, they would be at the stockyard in five or six hours and have the buffalo loaded and billed to "Buffalo" Jones by sundown.

No doubt the cowboys were glad to be on their way before the buffalo wrecked more Stony Mountain property. They were walking and running quietly, like homestead country oxen. But as the herd approached the entrance to the stockyard, and another gate, the "boss bull" gave a warning. Thirty-three short buffalo tails went up like banners at a political convention and the herd broke into a gallop, straight for Stony Mountain. It took an hour but the herd was finally turned and travelling again toward the stockyard. Common sense told the riders that the buffalo would be getting tired and ready to forget their silly caprice. But the buffalo were not familiar with that reasoning and when the gate was opened, there was another coordinated dash.

The riders decided to pause for lunch, let the horses cool off and the buffalo graze for a while. "We'll try again at one o'clock," the cowboy foreman announced, and so it was. Men and horses were tired, buffalo and horses wanted water and buffalo needed time to consume a stomachful of dry Manitoba grass, still pretty good stuff when frozen. At one o'clock, cowboys and horses were again in motion, pressing the contrary brutes toward the entrance. Each time they tried the result was the same until late in the afternoon when a wall of human spectators so blurred the outline of the gate that the buffalo were inside without appearing to be aware of it and the big gate was finally closed.

Next morning, 14 December, men on horses and men on foot tried to force the thirty-three unyielding critters into the loading chutes leading upward to the freight cars. But as might have been expected by this time, the buffalo were having nothing to do with the little compartments with gates, and more hours were spent and lost coaxing, threatening, goading and trying trickery. Then the unexpected happened.

A *Winnipeg Free Press* reporter gave the credit for the success to the old buffalo bull, who presumably had decided that the resistance had gone far enough. Cowboy frustration was reaching its limit when, in the words of the reporter, "a tremendous old bull which had been making trouble all day by breaking away and hooking the younger cattle, undertook to run the show himself and where the men failed, he succeeded. He got behind the herd and began making it exceedingly lively for the buffalo ahead, prodding them, bellowing at them, and driving the laggards forward with vigorous prods of his horns. The old fellow was trying in the manner which buffalo have followed from time immemorial to work up a stampede.

"When his dream of a stampede wasn't materializing, he would try something else. Tossing his head scornfully, he wheeled about and ran back into the compartment he had just left, jumped into the next one, clearing a fence ten feet high. Not liking the looks of the new quarters he jumped back again and then struck out wildly for Stony Mountain. He cleared every obstacle until he reached the board fence which bound the west side of the stockyards. This paling is fourteen feet high but he jumped at it, struck it near the top, went through it with a crash, and struck out for home across the prairies, a very much disturbed and agitated buffalo."[2]

The display of buffalo determination won admiration. According to a Winnipeg resident who had been watching, every time the buffalo broke away from the mounted riders, there were at least a few cheers from spectators who wished all the animals could remain in Manitoba. The train carrying the buffalo was to stop for feeding and watering of the animals at Grand Forks, St. Paul, and Minneapolis. At each point, city crowds of adults and school children came to enjoy, study, and mourn the shattered remnant of a once-mighty race. One of the town's newspaper editors wrote appreciatively, "Two carloads of live buffalo en route from Winnipeg to Kansas via the M. and M., unloading to feed at this point and a concourse of spectators were present to look on. One little calf was the sole juvenile of the party and he seemed lost in the crowd of adult buffalo. These creatures were the property of Major Bedson, warden of the penitentiary of Stony Mountain, Manitoba, and are the lone representatives of the nearly extinct race . . ."[3]

The calf that drew so much admiration at Grand Forks was one of the victims of the rough journey by freight. Several buffalo were trampled to death on the trip and the calf would be the most likely to suffer. It is easy to speculate and say the cars were overcrowded. But the journey was completed and to prove that the wild brutes were not becoming more gentle, the hazards and losses were just as high when the second shipment was made to "Buffalo" Jones's ranch a year later. Indeed, the most frightening experience was in the second year's shipment when thirteen of the wildest buffalo escaped right in an occupied section of Kansas City and were completely out of control. It was said that pandemonium prevailed for a few hours but, miraculously, the demonic big beasts were all captured in the wooded area beside the Missouri River and there were no injuries.

It is a wonder that Bedson, working closely with the bison for a decade, escaped serious injury. The stories about his narrow escapes were numerous. One told many times by his daughter, Menotah, had a Christmas afternoon setting. Guests were showing about as much interest in a buffalo-powered sleigh ride as in the promise of roast turkey. The fun-loving Colonel ordered that a certain two-year-old bull be harnessed and hitched to a toboggan. Everybody present wanted a reserved seat on the toboggan. The harnessed buffalo was brought out, restrained by half a dozen prisoners on stable duty, by holding back on a stout rope around the bull's neck.

The guests probably made the bull nervous and his patience was wearing thin. Riders were seated when the bull, without warning, leaped forward, upsetting the toboggan and scattering the attendants holding the rope. The angered animal headed for an open gate and was soon out of sight. Mr. Bedson thought the bull would return to its stable shelter when darkness came. There was no point in pursuing until there was some indication of the direction chosen. Nothing more was seen of toboggan or bull for many days.

Months passed without a clue but spring brought a letter from North Dakota, enquiring if a stray buffalo with a heavy rope knotted around his neck might belong in Manitoba. A Bedson employee was sent to Dakota where he readily identified the bull with a rope around his neck that had left home in a huff on Christmas day. He was now a famous bull and Mr. Bedson wondered if the animal was worth the high cost of bringing him back. What the owner decided is not clear.

After the sale to "Buffalo" Jones and the delivery, Mr. Bedson was down to one aging buffalo bull and the Winnipeg press noted: "But one buffalo remains out at Stony Mountain of the fine herd that recently roamed the plains in that locality and he is old, lame and evidently lonesome."[4] His friends probably said that if the old bull is lonely, so is Sam Bedson. He didn't want to sell his buffalo herd but the warden was still a man with broad interests, including lifelong loyalties to his early military years. When rebellion broke on the south Saskatchewan River in 1885, he quickly offered his services and General Middleton asked him to accept the post of Chief Transport Officer. He accepted and saw service on the trails and on the Steamship Northcote when it came under fire near Batoche.

"Buffalo" Jones, being a showman and dealer, saw that members of Bedson's former herd visited many lands. Some were taken to the World's Fair at Paris, some to the World's Fair at Chicago and others were sold to remote parts of the world.

What would prove of lasting interest to Canadians was the sale of the herd to Allard and Pablo of western Montana. After Allard's death in 1896, his share of buffalo was taken over by Pablo who came to have the biggest herd in the world and with whom the Government of Canada negotiated to buy and bring back to Canada in 1907. It is easy to believe that most of the herd purchased by the Government of Canada at that time traced in one line or another to Bedson stock.

From *Buffalo: Sacred and Sacrificed* (1995)

The Plains "Noblemen"

Two settlements of French plutocrats—one at Trochu, northeast of Calgary, and the other south of Whitewood in Saskatchewan—furnished the makings for one of the most romantic chapters in the history of western colonization. Neither survived as planned, but the more westerly one provided the foundation upon which the Alberta village of Trochu was built, and both left records of pioneer imagination, courage, and mistakes.

At the time, colonial and foreign agriculture held an unusual attraction for men of rank and capital. Some of the Old World investors acquired ranching interests in Texas and Wyoming, then in the Canadian foothills. A few, like Sir John Lister Kaye, believed they could win fame and fortune by bold and large-scale farming on the frontier. Most of those overseas operators won the fame but missed the fortune. But it was only a small step to the idea of a frontier farming program that would allow the wealthy proprietors to live on the land, enjoying frontier freedom plus a measure of Old World comforts they might bring with them. They could still hope for dividends.

What became known as the Settlement of the French Counts of Whitewood was some years ahead of the Trochu experiment. Otherwise, the two projects were very similar. Granted, both were French more than French-Canadian, and both were novel rather than typical of any large influx of settlers to the new West. But that point could also be made of the English settlement at nearby Cannington Manor and to an extent of the bigger settlement known as the Barr Colony on the Fourth Meridian where Lloydminster arose. The Barr Colony, however, did survive and then flourished.

The English gentry who followed Captain Edward Pierce to build Cannington Manor, just a year or so before the French came to Whitewood, set about to build and live the way Englishmen like to live, with comfortable homes and time for hunting, cricket, music, and tea at four o'clock. They were moderately successful for awhile—until the "money from home" began to diminish. Their conduct provided an entertaining spectacle on the otherwise unostentatious homestead frontier, but it seemed even more unusual and entertaining to find French Counts and noblemen attempting to farm far back from civilization and railways.

The fact that the two settlements happened to be in the same area, south of the main line of the Canadian Pacific Railway, at about the same time, was purely coincidental. There was no communication between the two groups before they arrived and not much after. In their pursuit of ways of life that suited them, both displayed a desire to be self-sufficient without adhering rigidly or needlessly to convention.

The Frenchmen, commonly called "the Counts," were not all counts, but all were high-bred citizens of the land to which they continued to give their loyalty, and the term "count" was probably close enough. Large scale colonization, or an attempt at French occupation of the Northwest, did not seem to have been in their thoughts. This was their own adventure and neither French power on the prairies nor church expansion was important to them. Their roots were in France and would remain there, notwithstanding the adventure in Canada. They knew what they wanted in farm settings and demanded good soil, attractive scenery, and native trees. In settling upon the Pipestone Valley they chose well, obtaining excellent grazing for cattle and some native trees.

The first homesteads and farms were staked out in 1885, just two years after Captain Pierce and family led the way for the English "invasion" of the Cannington Manor district. Strangely enough it was a French-speaking German, Dr. Rudolph Meyer, who preceded the Counts to the area, to appraise the district and make some land selection. His obvious aim, no doubt in keeping with his instructions, was to create an "island" retreat far enough from the constraints of civilization to afford new freedom, but close enough to be within range of comforts and pleasures an Assiniboia farm community could not be expected to furnish.

The Count and Countess of Roffignac were among the first to arrive. They settled on a picturesque valley farm which became widely known as Rolandrie Ranch. They were followed by Count Joumillhac, whose farm, called Richelieu, on the north side of the valley rivalled the Roffignac ranch for elegance. Count de Langle's ranch, also on the north side, became a showplace because of its good horses, and Count de Sora's holdings gained the same kind of recognition for the high quality of sheep bred there.

In hoping to live in ease on the quiet homestead frontier, the Counts certainly did not leave their imagination and vigour behind. Most of them chose to specialize in something and they had lots of bright ideas. Wheat and coarse grains were the most reliable crops, but they experimented boldly and tried new crops like chicory and sugar beets. The sugar beets grew well enough, but manufacturing sugar was a problem. And, although the chicory did well on the Pipestone soil, the market did not materialize as the Counts expected.

Some of them specialized in dairy farming and built a cheese factory near Moose Mountain; the exotic Gruyère cheese was attempted, but there were flaws in the technique and it was not a success. The most encouraging results came in the breeding of Thoroughbred horses, for many of the Counts, once officers in the French cavalry, brought useful experience and horsemanship.

If the French community had a business and social centre, it was the Roffignac ranch, Rolandrie. The proprietor appeared to have plenty of capital and he was most enterprising in trying new farming practices. The leader in trying sugar beets, he deserved credit even though the project did not prosper. It seemed like a good idea in a country where sugar prices were constantly high, and in 1890 he obtained and distributed a large quantity of sugar beet seed. Hopefully, capital would be forthcoming for the purchase of machinery and equipment to recover sugar from the beets. It did not come and not much sugar was obtained. The idea was abandoned.

The Rolandrie Ranch also maintained some of the best Thoroughbred horses in Canada, horses which rivalled the best blood stock kept by the high-living Beckton Brothers over at Cannington Manor. Rolandrie sponsored its own racing program too, and for superior horses, close races, and fine French racecourse etiquette, nothing on the Prairies was likely to surpass it.

Whitewood, on the main line of the CPR about one hundred miles east of Regina, was the nearest market town for the Counts and it prospered with French spending. Most of the Counts lived on their farms, where they built expensive houses and kept servants, gardeners, grooms and, butlers, but a few preferred to live in Whitewood and drive back and forth between the town and their farms. The citizens of the town watched with interest and sometimes amusement, especially when the Frenchmen staged their annual ball at the Whitewood Hotel. Elegant coaches driven four-in-hand by coachmen in full livery, brought them to the ball, and good manners, fine clothes in the latest Paris style, classical music, the best of French wines and ballroom decor made this the social event of all Assiniboia. The Counts were making social history as well as agricultural history and doing it in the most unlikely place.

The Counts and their ladies were charming people and gave no offence. But, as with the charmers at Cannington Manor, where lack of practical experience was a handicap and expenditures exceeded revenues rather too consistently, problems mounted. Gradually, the gentlemen and their families moved back to Paris where civilization seemed less offensive after five years of reality on the Western Canadian frontier. They left behind some fine farmsteads and numerous memories for the homesteaders in the area.

What happened in the Alberta community of Trochu was similar in many ways. Nothing else in the story of French-speaking settlements in that province was like it; nothing else was as glamorous. And, strange as the settlement by the French counts of Whitewood must appear, it is even more astonishing that another would rise in Alberta. One difference: most of those in the Trochu group were former cavalry officers. The simple result was fewer Counts and more colonels. A visitor having trouble with the French names discovered an easy solution to his problem—just address every male as "Colonel." Apparently, no one's feelings were hurt.

There was practically no connection between the settlement at Whitewood and the later one at Trochu except through one man, Count Paul de Beaudrap, who had settled at Whitewood and, anxious to repeat the experiment, joined Armand Trochu in the new scheme in 1905, just as Alberta was formed.

Armand Trochu from whom the prairie town obtained its name, came from Brittany. He was forty-six when he was attracted in 1903 by the grassy valley along the Red Deer River east of Olds. Sheilagh Jamieson, writing in *The History Of Trochu and District*, says he came to Calgary the year before and spent several months visiting the Sheep Creek Ranch owned by fellow Frenchman Raymond de Malherbe at Millarville.

Millarville, it should be noted, had a sizeable group of French-speaking people at the time and the Malherbe ranch, known in the community as "Frenchman's Place," was a favourite retreat for French visitors. Malherbe's main interest was in Thoroughbred horses.

Trochu may have had no plans when he arrived in Calgary in 1902, but after his stay at Millarville and, perhaps a visit with some French-Canadian friends at Pincher Creek, he wanted to take up ranching himself. In the meantime, he met in Calgary a Mrs. de Chauny, who offered shelter and guidance to French travellers, and discovered that her son Louis was also interested in finding land suitable for ranching.

The two young men decided to seek ranch land together. Setting out in the spring of 1903 with saddle horses and pack horses and using the Malherbe ranch at Millarville as their base, they followed the foothills north as far as Rocky Mountain House. They saw beautiful country, but not the ranch setting they wanted, and returned to Millarville. With fresh horses and supplies, they started again, this time travelling northeast from Calgary. In the vicinity of Three Hills, it seems, they met a Métis who advised them to inspect a nearby valley, not far back from the Red Deer River.

Trochu liked what he saw and after determining the exact location of a certain parcel of land, he returned to Calgary and bought from the Hudson's Bay Company N1/2 8-33-23 W4. Later, when land in the area was thrown open for homesteading, he filed on the southwest quarter of Section Sixteen in the same township. Now, unknown to him, his farm touched on two sides of the land on which the town of Trochu would rise.

Like any other settler, he had ground to break and cultivate, fences to make and buildings to construct. Lumber for his house was hauled from Didsbury. Progress was slow and Trochu was impatient. He took a partner, but the relationship did not last. Trochu went back to France, hoping to raise capital for a bigger farming program, and, while he was absent in 1904, Count Paul de Beaudrap and his family drove out from Calgary, having heard about his efforts. As one of the Counts in the Whitewood settlement, Beaudrap had lasted longer than most but had finally returned to France. Now, after finding it difficult to settle down in his native land, he was back in Canada, ready to begin the pioneering all over again.

Without waiting for Trochu's return from France, Beaudrap began looking for a farm. He finally bought a one-thousand-dollar property furnished with log buildings fourteen miles east of Trochu's place and a couple of miles south. He called his new home Jeanne d'Arc Ranch.

There, in the grassy ravines leading down to the Red Deer River badlands, the courageous Mrs. Paul de Beaudrap became the first resident white woman in a big area. The location was much more remote and conditions more primitive than at Whitewood, but the family was resourceful and adapted quickly. More Beaudrap relatives and friends came from France and bought land or homesteaded.

The Jeanne d'Arc Ranch was expanded by both homesteading and purchase and gained prominence for its production of good livestock— cattle, sheep, pigs and especially Percheron horses, which found a ready market in new areas where farmer settlers needed power. The breed, which originated in the district of La Perche in northwestern France, was a logical choice and Beaudrap imported high-class stallions for his breeding and improvement program. He also brought in a few Belgian stallions which must have made him the breed founder in central Alberta.

The blue blood of France did not spare Beaudrap and his family from pioneer hardship. They knew what it was to have sickness in the home when the nearest medical aid was a hundred miles away; they felt the bitter experience of being lost in prairie blizzards, and they could not forget the cruel prairie fire that swept down on ranch and buildings with disastrous results in 1906, soon after they arrived. But in spite of all, the Beaudraps persevered nobly.

In the meantime, Armand Trochu found two partners for his enterprise, first Joseph Devilder, who was apparently well supplied with the needed funds, and then Leon Charles Eckenfelder, originally from Alsace-Lorraine. Devilder filed on the northwest of Section Sixteen, which happened to be one of the quarters on which Trochu would be built. Together, these three made a strong partnership. Trochu moved at once to form the Ste. Anne Ranching and Trading Company, soon to be the most important business enterprise in the settlement.

More men of rank were attracted—Edgar Popillard, Marc de Cathelineau, François de Torquard, D. Louis Schulier and others, most of them with cavalry backgrounds in the French army. It is not surprising that horsemanship in the Trochu valley was of a high order.

By 1906 the settlement was changing greatly, for better or for worse. Trochu obtained his own post office which he called Ste. Anne of the

Prairies. It was used briefly, but before the end of that year, the post office became Trochu, Northwest Territories, and Armand Trochu became the first postmaster. About the same time more wives and families arrived from France, subduing the gay days at Bachelors' Hall on the Ste. Anne Ranch.

It was still an intensely French atmosphere—French language, French music, French flag and, when occasion demanded, the French national anthem. As at the periodic arrival of the priest for the celebration of mass at Jeanne d'Arc Ranch, the selection was the Marseillaise.

More changes! More progress! The railway was constructed. The village to be known as Trochu was laid out. People of other ethnic origins began moving in. But the French influence remained strong. The annual sports days started in 1907 retained a French character, and the Trochu agricultural society formed in 1910, named Armand Trochu, president and Leon Charles Eckenfelder, secretary. The first fairs brought out the best displays of French cavalry uniforms the country has known.

The First World War marked the end of the French settlement for all practical purposes. French loyalty was never in doubt, and all who could qualify for service including Eckenfelder, returned home. Most did not come back to Alberta. However, Paul de Beaudrap's son, Xavier, returned and remained to farm. Eckenfelder returned but died soon after the war ended. Trochu, who was considered too old for war, had a heart attack in 1917 and went home to France. Much of the land held by the Ste. Anne Company was ultimately surrendered to the village and only a few French names remained.

It was exciting and colourful while it lasted, but it did not last long. It was like the "ships that pass in the night," and memories came to constitute the principal remaining link with the gallant effort to create a lush French oasis in what might have been seen as a frontier desert.

From *French in the West* (1984)

Trails and Rails to the North

Progress and all its civilizing changes were on the march. On 21 July 1890, Calgary was the scene of an epic sod-turning. Two thousand eager citizens, a brass band, the local fire brigade, and a highlander with bagpipes were present for the moment when the Hon. Edgar Dewdney, Minister of the Interior, lifted the first sod in the construction of the Calgary–Edmonton railroad.

After the shovelful of soil was duly turned and somebody expressed well-chosen words about coming prosperity, the Calgary people and their guests turned their attention to a carcass of ox, roasted whole and waiting to be consumed. Big appetites were then the rule and no part of the ox remained except bones and a few sinews. As far as a student can judge, the only discordant note in an otherwise happy program was a public objection from one Thomas Smith, of Edmonton, to a remark that the Calgary area was equal to the best. It wasn't, the man from the North insisted; Edmonton's soil was superior and so were the products grown there. But the Calgary crowd was in a benevolent mood that day and there was no violence.

What should not have been overlooked, however, was that the events of the day signalled the end of the historic Calgary–Edmonton Trail: a rutted lifeline of two hundred miles which had witnessed freight and transportation vehicles of almost every conceivable size and shape. Every adult munching barbecued beef on that midsummer day knew something about the romance and hardships associated with the "North Trail."

The Edmonton-bound trail traffic differed distinctly from that going south. For one thing, Red River carts—those two-wheeled, all-wood contraptions with dry axles screaming to be heard for miles—were quite conspicuous. The *Calgary Herald* might note in a commonplace manner that a freight train "composed of sixteen carts went north to Edmonton today," and just as often, the *Edmonton Bulletin* would report something of the kind: "Seventeen carts of Ad McPherson's in charge of J. Westway arrived on the south side on Sunday, nineteen days out from Calgary. The roads are very bad for cattle, wearing their feet out rapidly and making quick travel impossible."

With a freight rate of eight to ten cents a pound, operators on the Calgary–Edmonton route found their business fairly attractive and the more progressive ones were seeking ways of enlarging their carrying capacity. The carts were inherited from the older trails, but bigger freight wagons began to gain popularity—two-horse wagons, four-horse wagons and six-horse outfits. Edmonton people were said to be rejoicing when, in December, 1884, "Two four-horse and two six-horse teams belonging to Ad McPherson" were expected to arrive in good time "with loads of green apples, fresh oysters, whiskey, and other Christmas groceries" for the festive season.

The trail south of Calgary was famous for its huge ox-drawn freight wagons or bull-team outfits, but only a very few of those went over the softer ground northward. The first of their kind seen on the northerly route arrived at Edmonton in June 1885, an I.G. Baker Company outfit comprising nine units. Each unit carried seven thousand pounds of freight on two wagons hooked together and was drawn by twelve oxen. Thus, there were 108 oxen furnishing power for this particular "freight train." Seeing such a freight-moving outfit was a new experience for the people of Edmonton, but for the owners the result was not entirely satisfactory; owing to the soft ground the time was slow and the experts concluded that the Red River carts and small wagons were still best for this particular trail. One of the mongrel outfits adding distinction to the trail went out of Calgary on 1 September 1886, propelled by "three teams of horses, five pairs of oxen and one span of mules on the lead," all hitched together and all working like one big unhappy family.

The one-way trip to Edmonton with freight took anywhere from two to three weeks, although the stagecoaches carrying passengers and mail did it in five days. In the mid-'80s the travelling public enjoyed the convenience of a weekly service on the route—two Concord coaches drawn by four-horse teams. One would leave Calgary and the other leave Edmonton at the same time, pass at the crossing two or three miles above the present city of Red Deer and arrive at their respective destinations at the same time—if they were fortunate. Each coach could accommodate four passengers in the back part and one riding with the driver.

While Calgary was still without a newspaper, the *Edmonton Bulletin* carried the stagecoach schedule: "Edmonton and Calgary stage making weekly trips between said points leaves Jasper House, Edmonton, Monday at nine, and the steamboat dock at 9:30, stopping at Peace Hills, Battle River, Red Deer Crossing and Willow Creek, arriving at Calgary on Friday. Returning leaves Calgary Monday, stopping at same places and arrives Edmonton on Friday. Fare each way, $25.00. One hundred pounds of baggage allowed. Express matter 10 cents per pound."

Strangely enough, the two regular drivers over the route, although unrelated, had exactly the same names; both were Pete Campbell. For purposes of convenience one was "Little Pete" and the other "Big Pete"; or one was "Northbound Pete," and the other "Southbound Pete." They were courageous drivers and often they were on time. Delays could be expected, however, and sometimes mishaps. Storms resulted in loss of time and occasionally there were accidents. Indeed, anything could happen along that two-hundred-mile route and over the years nearly everything did happen—broken wheels, upsets, sick horses, and even highway robbery on a storybook scale.

The encounter with brigands occurred in the summer of 1886, just four years before the sod was turned for the new railway. The stage coach, with full complement of passengers and "Little Pete" Campbell driving, was eighteen miles out of Calgary when two bandits stepped out on the trail and took complete command. The men were armed with carbines and revolvers and wore masks made from a Union Jack flag. They had been hiding in the long grass close to the roadside and sprang up suddenly when the stage horses were within ten or twelve feet from them. The stage stopped at once.

Driver and passengers were rudely ordered to come down and march to a coulee. In the sheltered spot chosen by the gunmen the victims were searched and their money taken. A newspaper report told that "The driver, P. Campbell, lost $200; J. Burns, Jr., travelling for Ashdown of Winnipeg, $70 but another seventy he had on him was overlooked; J. Clockey, representing the Massey Manufacturing Co., $30, and Mr. Gautier who had been working all last winter for Lamoureux Bros., $125." Any way one viewed it, the total represented a tidy haul. After pocketing the money the robbers returned to the stage and went through the mail bags and luggage. Evidently they got nothing of value in the baggage and, somehow, overlooked the sacks of registered mail.

After completing their searches they unhitched the horses, mounted them and rode away, leaving driver and penniless passengers stranded helplessly on the prairie, somewhere north of where Balzac stands today. The two highwaymen, with pockets bulging and good horses under them, rode north while within view of their victims and probably reversed the direction of flight as soon as they considered it safe to do so. As for Campbell and his stage passengers, they started southward toward Calgary on foot, dejected and totally unimpressed by the bit of glamour added that day to the story of the Calgary–Edmonton Trail.

Passenger Burns was the first to make his way to Calgary where he reported the costly experience. Mounted Police took to the trail at once. Fresh in their memories was a recent robbery on the Elbow River, and they suspected a connection between the two crimes. At the scene of the holdup the police picked up the tracks of the fleeing robbers and followed until they came upon parts of the flag used for masks. The police net was extended in all directions but not with much encouragement. No suspects were encountered—unless there had been reason to be suspicious of two strangers seen at "Clinker" Scott's cabin beside the

Bow, west of Calgary. But Scott, who figured prominently in the Silver City mining debacle, assured the police the two strangers were his friends and had been there for days.

A day or two later, however, "Clinker" Scott was murdered in his cabin and the two strangers had disappeared. Speculation was rife. Was it that Scott couldn't be trusted with the secret of a holdup on the Calgary–Edmonton Trail or was there a quarrel about the division of the loot? In any case, police pursuit continued as far as Denver, Colorado, but without success.

But the interruption to passenger transportation on the trail was brief. On the morning after the robbery "Little Pete" was hitching for the journey to Edmonton—just twenty-four hours late.

Over the same twisty route went soldiers ordered to suppress rebellion in the year 1885; land-seekers like Stephan Gudmundsson Stephansson who became the great Icelandic poet of Markerville; nation-builders like Reverend Leo Gaetz who stopped at the Red Deer River in 1884; and people bound for the Far North country, like Sheridan Lawrence's family making the nine-hundred-mile trip to Fort Vermilion in 1886. The cart and wagon wheels turned slowly and perchance monotonously, but for nearly two decades that north–south trail was "Highway Number One" to the people living and travelling between the Bow and North Saskatchewan rivers.

Now, things were changing. A month after the ceremonial sod was turned, a railroad grade being built by use of wheelbarrows and horse-drawn scrapers reached a point forty miles north of Calgary. And in the meantime, railroad construction was bringing its boom-type prosperity to the community beside the Bow River. Men who chose to be track-layers commanded $1.75 a day and those who could qualify as "spikers," $2.00 a day.

Until August, 1891, when the railroad was completed for operation, the Calgary–Edmonton Trail lost none of its lifeline character; but then, abruptly, most of the carts and wagons were abandoned at one end or the other—many to remain in obscure places until they rotted. Too late it was realized that the creaking carts and heavy wagons held sentiment and memories and some of them should have been preserved.

Calgary and Edmonton felt the advantages immediately. For the cart and wagon drivers, however, those hardy and distinctive men who liked to sleep in their blankets beside the trail, the adjustments were difficult. Many of the men were half-breeds with French names and no other form of livelihood invited them. As the rails advanced they became displaced persons, in many cases going into semi-retirement in northern settlements where they would feel only a minimum of irritation from advancing civilization.

For the eyes of any who might be able to peer into the future there were still bigger changes to be made along "The Trail." Not only would engineers produce a railroad, but they'd build a graded highway and then a super-highway for speeding traffic—right where cart and wagon wheels had cut their deepest ruts. And if such were not enough, planes would fly back and forth many times daily to add to the story.

Perhaps the Hon. Edgar Dewdney had a vision that day in 1890. He said it was not an ordinary sod-turning and insisted upon filling a big wheelbarrow with sod. Or perhaps he was just working up an appetite for the barbecued beef.

From *Calgary Cavalcade* (1958)

Trail to Disaster

Norman Lee of the British Columbia Chilcotin was a good loser. For him the "Trail of '98" was a cattleman's tragedy, returning nothing but costly experience. He lost everything: the beef from one hundred and seventy-five cattle, supplies, equipment, and laborious effort.

By the time he arrived back at Vancouver months later, his chattels were reduced to "a blanket, a dog and a dollar." It could be added, however, that he still had his sense of humour and the will to go back to cattle ranching on the inter-mountain grass.

Lee first set foot upon British Columbia soil in 1882, after making the journey from his native England by way of New York, Salt Lake City, and San Francisco. In the Nicola Valley he learned the art of cowpunching and then worked with crews building the CPR in the mountains. The year 1887 found him in the Chilcotin, west of the Fraser River. In that vast land of grass and trees and scenery, he indulged in trading and started with cattle.

Early in the spring of '98, when talk of Klondike gold was on every tongue, Lee resolved to take his herd of cattle to Dawson City by an all-Canadian route and on 17 May of that year the great drive began from his place at Hanceville. Two hundred cattle made up the herd and with it were the necessary helpers, five cowboys, a horse wrangler, and cook.

Lee divided the herd, allowing each man to drive a small band of thirty or forty head; the cattle travelled better that way, especially in forest country—and for much of the way they would be in forests. At first the drive went forward at ten or twelve miles a day. The cattle were fresh and they might have covered more distance were it not for the fallen timbers blocking many parts of the trail.

Each day's program called for the cattle to start soon after sunrise, leaving the pack horses to move as soon as they were loaded. Spare saddle horses were driven on ahead of the cattle, and the wrangler was expected to stop about noon when he identified good feeding ground. There he would build a fire and prepare lunch for the oncoming cattlemen. After the midday meal, the pack train and cook would move ahead of the cattle to select a suitable campsite for the night. The idea was good but sometimes the man in charge misjudged a normal day's travel for the cattle and made camp too far away.

Along the Blackwater River there were good places to camp but while the cattle were still fresh and keen to return to home pastures, night herding was necessary. A note in Lee's diary, easy to understand, tells that night herding "in pouring rain is the reverse of pleasantness."

Lee was not the only cattleman on the trail; in that diary loaned most graciously by his sister, Miss Grace Lee of Starcross, England, he says, "Of the cattle that started from Chilcotin, Jim Cornell was about a week ahead of us with seventy-five head, Jerry Gravelle about three days with one hundred and we heard that Johnny Harris with two hundred was trying hard to catch us."

Although not acknowledged, there was unmistakable competition between those in charge of the several drives. And the Harris outfit did overtake and pass the Lee cattle.

Early in June they were on the Telegraph Trail, about fifty miles from Quesnel. Now, for a limited distance, there was more traffic, "all kinds and varieties of horses, all sorts and conditions of men," all headed northward to the land of easy fortunes.

"At the end of the first day on this trail," wrote Lee, "we camped at Mud River, a small river which seemed to be deep enough to require swimming. An Indian had built a raft and was busily engaged ferrying people, horses and goods across. He must have coined money as his charges were pretty stiff. I made a bargain with him to cross my stuff and then I made a discovery. A little way down stream was a trail leading to the river which I followed and found that I could ford the cattle and pack animals easily which was duly done, and our example was followed by all the other pilgrims who were about to cross with the help of the Indian. The ferryman saw that his business was at an end so climbed into his raft . . . vanished down the creek."

Lee then made a further discovery, that the ferryman had actually placed a dam on the stream to make the need for his transportation service appear convincing.

The Nechaco River was crossed and at the Hudson's Bay post beside Fraser Lake the cattlemen replenished dwindling supplies. Lee asked the company officer how often he received mail and the reply was, "We never get mail here."

From Fraser Lake to Hazelton the route was largely through heavy timber but it afforded fairly good grazing. A danger to cattle was in poisonous plants; one steer in Lee's herd died as a consequence and Harris lost a dozen or more animals. The treatment for steers suffering from poison, according to local advice, was to "bleed them by chopping off pieces of their tails and feed them with much bacon grease." Evidently the recommendation was not taken seriously.

At Hazelton there was to be a three-day rest stop; the cattle needed it and the cattlemen welcomed it. But there was added delay; Hudson's Bay rum proved to be such an attraction that three more days elapsed before all cowboys were ready for the trail. And to settle accounts with the Bay company officer, a few steers had to be left behind.

Out of Hazelton, they had to swim the Skeena River. Then there was the quaint Indian Village of Kispiox and more rivers as cattle, horses and men moved toward Telegraph Creek.

The Telegraph Trail was gay with native flowers and wildlife, but hazards were increasing. Stinking horse carcasses beside the paths made it clear. Feed problems became increasingly serious; cattle were passing through heavy timber and over mud flats with only occasional swamps offering grass. Horses suffered more than the cattle; according to information furnished by E.D. Sheringham who accompanied Lee on the expedition, the horses became the victims of "mud fever" and began to lose their hooves. In order to spare the weakened animals, all but necessities were discarded from packs, and cowboys even took to herding on foot. But in spite of all the relief offered in this way, the horses became weaker and most of them died on the trail.

By the end of August, after travelling close to the snow line, picking their precarious way over the summit of Groundhog Mountain and sometimes skirting dangerous mountain precipices, the cattlemen were some two hundred and sixty miles beyond Hazelton. Worst of all, human food reserves were diminishing all too quickly. Lee walked on ahead to Telegraph Creek and along the way bought flour and bacon wherever possible and "cached it in the woods, blazing a tree with my cow brand so that the boys would know where to find the stuff."

Lee arrived at Telegraph Creek on 2 September, a few days ahead of his cattle, and discovered that Jim Cornell who had made good time with his smaller herd, was there and having decided against going beyond that place, was already operating a butcher shop and getting rid of his beef.

To Lee, however, the only plan offering hope of success was to drive to Teslin, there slaughter the cattle and raft the dressed beef over the lake and rivers to Dawson City. A man called McIntosh was sent on to Teslin with instructions to commence building the rafts.

Having forced his cattle across the Stikine River on 6 September and seen them heading toward Teslin, Lee repaired to Glenora to secure another pack train. Three weeks later he overtook his herd, forty miles from Teslin. Then, going on ahead, he rode into Teslin in company with Johnny Harris and Jerry Gravelle and their herds.

McIntosh had the necessary logs ready for scow construction but it remained for Lee to make arrangements for corrals and slaughtering facilities.

Lee's cattle, having completed the first major part of the projected journey, were at Teslin on 3 October. Attendants had reason to believe the worst of the undertaking was behind them. The slaughtering began and men moved with an air of triumph. An experienced butcher hired on the site was able to dress twenty cattle per day while Lee's regular helpers handled another twenty. Hence, the work went forward briskly and slaughter of the last steer coincided precisely with completion of the two scows, each forty feet by sixteen feet in size.

The beef was not all choice, not by any means; the long and hard journey had robbed the animals of any fat they might have had at the start of the trip but Dawson City miners were not fastidious and red meat would be more important than quality.

A fair wind was needed to conduct the loaded rafts for one hundred miles across the lake and on the morning of 17 October, the breeze seemed perfect. Lee and his men had two days of good sailing but northern weather can be tricky and treacherous. On the third day the wind became strong, then violent. It seemed as though the scows would break. Men attempted to guide them to some sheltered cove along the shore but there was no such haven. Finally, the rafts were heaved against the shoreline rocks. For two days, gales continued and frustrated men were powerless to do more than watch one scow and then the other being wrecked.

The storm ended but what was left for the cattlemen? The beef—much of it submerged—was utterly valueless in that unpopulated part of the North and it was too late in the season to consider the construction of other scows, even if the meat could be salvaged.

There was nothing for it but to accept defeat and abandon the beef. Some of the men accepted Lee's offer of the little boat they brought along and departed toward Dawson City. Lee and Will Copeland said they were returning to Teslin—sixty miles back. Food supplies were divided and men went their different ways.

From Teslin a small party went out to inspect the wrecked cargo of beef and returned with thirty quarters considered possibly fit for food. Of these Lee claimed a percentage but there was practically no local sale for it because of the large number of crippled oxen slaughtered there at the end of the trail. The fact was pretty obvious; the undertaking had ended in complete loss for Lee.

As for the other men who came over the trail with cattle, Harris with a raft of beef was four days ahead of Lee and escaped the fateful storm on the lake but word was received later that his outfit became "frozen in" about two hundred miles above Dawson City and the beef, like Lee's, was a complete loss.

There was nothing more to hold Norman Lee in the North. He and Copeland constructed a hand sleigh on which to carry their few belongings and, with their faithful dog, began the long trek to the coast. Their hope had been to get down the Stikine before it was frozen over but winter came in with a vengeance and the snow was already deep. At Glenora the report was that navigation had ended. So deep was the snow that even the hand sleigh had to be abandoned. Leaving Glenora on 2 December, the two men tramped over ice and snow, making their own trail for one hundred miles, and arrived at the Alaskan boundary on Christmas day. After some delay they managed to get across to Wrangel and there catch a boat going south.

It took a stout heart to undertake such a twelve-hundred-mile drive through unsettled wilderness and it took a stout heart to accept the loss and return cheerfully to raise more cattle in the Chilcotin. All honour to the memory of Norman Lee.

From *Blazing the Old Cattle Trail* (1962)

The Alberta Hotel

Seventy-five thousand dollars for a hotel! It did seem fantastic, yet that was what Norman Jackson paid for the Alberta just at the time Bob Edwards moved to Calgary. But the buyer got more than a fourteen-year-old structure; he got traditions, memories, and sentiment, because no building in Calgary had such a story as the old sandstone hotel, started in 1888 and opened for business in 1890.

It was the crossroads at which businessmen, cattlemen, and salty characters met; and for Bob Edwards it exerted a magnetic pull soon after he took up residence on Stephen Avenue. If a person looking for the editor didn't find him in his Cameron Block offices the place to look was the smoke-filled rotunda, the noisy bar or the excellent dining room, just two blocks to the west. There at the hotel much of the copy for the pages of the *Eye Opener* was written.

The Alberta's bar was the longest between Winnipeg and Vancouver, and the most famous; its hours were 7:00 AM to 11:30 PM and drinks were two for a quarter. Behind the 125-foot-long bar were ten busy men, among them well-known early Calgarians like Fred Adams, Tom Pierce, and George Rutley, who became about as much a part of the place as the swinging doors. Fred Adams, "the eminent mixologist," was Bob Edwards's nomination for the office of committee chairman to see the fictional Bertie Buzzard-Cholomondeley elected to the House of Commons for Calgary constituency. And when Pierce retired, his total dispensations, according to Bob Edwards, were enough liquid to fill all the horse troughs in the province and sufficient left over to float the two boats which made up the Canadian navy.

Everything, it seemed, started at the Alberta Hotel: business deals, fights, and fun—even gunplay now and then. With Mother Fulham calling daily for garbage, things could be lively at the back of the hotel as well as the front. Calgary's A.A. Gray, who came to the city in the same year as Bob Edwards, could recall one of those occasions when the back of the hotel became a centre of interest. At that time he had a job painting the hotel rooms at a dollar a day. As usual, Mother Fulham tied her horse in the lane and entered the hotel kitchen, hoping to qualify for a piece of left-over pie or a cookie. Gray's painting partner whispered to the chef to detain the lady with an extra morsel of food while he attended to a self-assigned task. He slipped out, unhitched Fulham's pony, shoved the shafts of the democrat through the CPR wire fence and re-hitched with democrat on one side of the fence and horse on the other.

In her own good time Mother Fulham left the kitchen, and like a princess ascending a throne, mounted her democrat without suspecting any felonious act. She hesitated, took the old clay pipe from her mouth, and ran her grimy fingers through her hair, wondering momentarily if she was really sober. Then it dawned upon her that she was the victim of a vile Protestant trick. By this time she had an audience and shouted her curses, making it very clear what she would do if she could get her powerful hands on the responsible miscreant.

And gunplay? The Alberta didn't escape. Tom Pierce was the hero in humbling one gunman at the bar. When Pierce wasn't pouring, he was polishing glassware or something else, a habit ingrained by years of practice. Bob Edwards always regretted being absent that day when a stranger with a criminal glint in his eye stepped up to the bar as Pierce was polishing. The man took a revolver from his hip pocket and placed it on the counter-top with the muzzle only inches from the bartender's navel. Pierce, however, had not tended bar all those years without developing a certain callousness. He continued to polish the soda siphon in his hands but raised it slightly until the nozzle was in line with the gunman's face; then he pumped a big charge of fluid into the bad man's eyes, and casually picked up the gun.

E.A. Shelley, night clerk when Bob Edwards first stopped there, recalled that guns went off rather frequently around the hotel. As one who started as a twelve-year-old bellboy the very day the hotel opened and finished as manager when it closed its doors in the face of prohibition twenty-six years later, he should know. Vivid in his memory was the day when the barroom seemed to be full of bullets. Into the bar rode an Englishman on his black horse. Without dismounting, he began shooting wildly. Customers and workers ducked and cleared out, but the shooting continued until every mirror and most of the bottles were shattered. Next day, when confronted with a bill for damages amounting to $2800, the gunman settled cheerfully by writing a cheque, then went away searching for some new form of amusement.

Of course, the fellow was one of those remittance men with lots of money for a few days each month. The Alberta Hotel had a special attraction for them, and for other Old Country travellers who came to launch a hunting expedition into the mountains. They admired the stuffed heads of bighorn sheep and bears in store windows, bought the best guns and often did not get nearer the mountains than the end of Stephen Avenue.

But striking as were the long bar and the amusing fellows with money and monocles, the Alberta had something far more unique—a collection of acclimatized foothills personalities giving patronage to one part or another of the hotel. Here was a personality cross-section without parallel.

Bob Edwards could enjoy unusual outdoor people like the volatile firefighter, Cappie Smart, and the unschooled garbage queen, Mother Fulham; but for steady fare he needed more men like Paddy Nolan with whom he could engage in relaxed and varied conversation. Indeed, it was one of life's sweetest prizes—conversation. More and more he was becoming conscious of a need for that mental exercise afforded by discussion and intelligent repartee. At Wetaskiwin he had tried to starve the intellectual part of himself, and at High River to feed it with half rations. Now, in the associations of the old Alberta Hotel, Bob Edwards found something for which his need was increasingly clear—men with ideas and the capacity and will to share them. Here was a community within a community, one made attractive by brilliant individuality. More and more he was drawn into that labyrinth of Alberta Hotel life, surroundings from which he gained many of his richest experiences.

Of the friends he made around the hotel, many will be forever nameless; but now and then one springs from obscurity to say, "Dear Old Bob— many were the snorts and the good hours I had at the Alberta with him." At the same time, a most significant percentage of the Makers of Southern Alberta were thereabout. Ramrod-straight Colonel James Walker might be found there at almost any time—the old Colonel who was a member of the first troop of Mounted Police that trekked across the plains to build Fort Macleod, chairman of Calgary's first administrative committee, president of the Agricultural Society when the first Calgary fair was held, and a man who, according to General Sir Arthur Currie, "breaks out every fifty years and goes to war." Fred Stimson, first manager of the Bar U Ranch, kept a room there for years; and so did cattle kings Pat Burns and George Lane. R.B. Bennett lived there for awhile and made his noon meal at the Alberta a long-time practice.

Here were the aristocrats of the new country, and Bob Edwards's delight at the end of a day was to draw a chair close to one of them and talk through a cloud of smoke from cigars "made in Calgary." George Lane, whose cowboy frame suggested that it might have been pieced together by a committee, could tell about long cattle drives, rustling and bad winters—hardships to discourage all but the stout of spirit. And yet he could say that since coming to the Foothills as a "mail order" cowhand at thirty-five dollars a month in 1884, the good years which followed bad ones invariably wiped out losses. Now his biggest worry was settlers and their damnable barbed wire. More feathers would be ruffled before this mounting conflict between ranchers and grain growers would be settled.

But George Lane was cheerful. His last trainload of steers had sold at Winnipeg to net him close to four cents a pound. Why, "this very day" he had seen John Ware, that massive Negro rancher with massive heart, driving out of Calgary with a brand new buggy. And markets couldn't be very bad when George Emerson, who released the first cattle west of High River in 1879, could lose a Gordon, Ironside and Fares cheque in payment for steers sold in the previous year and not even miss it until Billy Fares enquired why it had never been cashed.

"Yes sir, Fares sent his son-in-law out to Emerson's ranch to find out why that cheque issued ten months before had never gone through the bank in the customary way. Old George couldn't recall what had happened to it, supposing only that it was deposited to his account. He said he would look in his pockets, however, and sure enough, in an old vest hanging abandoned in the woodshed, he found the cheque where he had stuffed it away months before."

For Bob Edwards, no lobby party was complete until his kindred spirit, Paddy Nolan, joined it; and then it was perfect only if it did not exceed a total of three or four people at a time. In one respect, Bob and his incisive friend were not alike; a large audience inspired Paddy's natural gifts of oratory but tended to silence the relatively bashful Edwards. And so it was at a lunch table, or where a few chairs were pushed together in a cluster, that Bob was at his best. Then he would lead with bold verbal thrusts to invite equal boldness from the big and affable lawyer.

Paddy's appearance there would make Rancher George Lane wish again that the man had not quit a special assignment from the Western Stock Growers' Association to assist with the prosecutions of all suspected cattle rustlers. Nolan could be pardoned for favouring defence, in which his success was phenomenal; but when he was arguing for alleged cattle thieves, ranchers found it doubly difficult to get the convictions necessary to stamp out the menace of rustling. Bob recounted that after one of Paddy's clients was cleared of a charge of horse stealing, the lawyer asked: "Honour bright, now, Bill, you did steal that horse, didn't you?"

"Now look here, Mr. Nolan," was the reply, "I always did think I stole that horse, but since I heard your speech to that 'ere jury, I'll be doggoned if I ain't got my doubts about it."

For others, Paddy's arrival would suggest some recent gossip—perhaps the lawyer's proposal to change the name of his law firm from Nolan and Eaton to the more meaningful one of "Drinkin' and Eaton;" or it might be the story Bob published about his friends' misfortune on a trip to Fort Macleod to defend a case when the journey had to be made by stage coach. When fording the river close to the Fort, the stage upset and the passengers received a ducking. The town had no dry clothes big enough for Paddy and the court wouldn't wait for wet clothes to dry.

The anxious client bought a Hudson Bay blanket, the biggest one in the stores, wrapped it around the unclothed frame, and made sure his high-priced advocate was present for the moment of his great need. The spectacle was one never before seen in court, with the lawyer assuring the judge, quite cheerfully, that everything was all right; "I'm here, Your Lordship, to present the naked truth."

Paddy protested that the story as it came out of the South was exaggerated, and added the comment that "Fort Macleod is an outlying district and the men I've met down there can outlie any encountered this side of Edmonton."

With Paddy drawing a chair into the little circle, the stage was being set for repartee. Bob could be expected to offer a learned question about Ancient Greece or Canadian law; or it might be pure mirth—a definition of a lawyer, for example.

"A lawyer," said Bob, pointing to the recognized wellspring of Irish humour, "is a man who induces two others to remove their coats for a fight and then runs away with the coats."

"Yes," responded Paddy, "but if he stole an editor's coat, he wouldn't get much—some buttons and a corkscrew from the pockets."

"Never mind, Paddy," Bob would reply, "You with your big income and me with my buttons and booze bills, we'll all be on the same dead level a hundred years from now."

It was during one of those lobby sessions at which Colonel Porter was present that Western Canada heard the first proposal for a pipeline to carry anything except water. Alberta's oil resources were still among nature's most closely guarded secrets, but with thirsty people in the Herald Building directly across the avenue from the Alberta Hotel, Bob Edwards proposed:

> A pipe-line across the street and under the road-way to accommodate the staff and save their valuable time. Mr. Perley, proprietor of the Alberta, was willing to lay a half-inch pipe to convey whiskey across to the office but Mr. Young (managing director of the *Daily Herald*) insisted upon an additional two-inch pipe for beer. The negotiations fell through.[1]

Even stockily built Jimmy Reilly, former mayor of Calgary, would come over to the Alberta when he had time to leave his own Royal Hotel, hoping to find Bob and Paddy occupying their big chairs near the entrance to the bar. And Calgary's architect, "Deafie" J.J. Wilson, often joined the group though he missed all parts of the conversation except the periodic suggestions about visits to the bar. To all questions directed at "Deafie," his answer was the same: "Don't mind if I do."

Clearly, the Edwards-Nolan combination was giving both the Alberta rotunda and the City of Calgary a bit of special lustre at that time. "Old Man" Simpson, editor of the *Cranbrook Herald*, said: "The three sights of the place are Paddy Nolan, Bob Edwards and the City Hall."[2] He was reporting on the Western Newspapermen's Convention at Calgary in January, 1905, at which Nolan gave a paper on the Law of Libel. Continuing with Simpson's report: "Those who have not met either of the gentlemen named have lived in vain. The Lord never created a better entertainer than Paddy Nolan. As an after dinner speaker he is par excellence and compared with him, Chauncey Depew looks like a newspaperman's promise to pay a note of a million dollars. It is said that for years when a man contemplated the act of appropriating another man's steer or horse, he first retained the services of Paddy

Nolan. Bob Edwards is a modest individual who is editing a Sunday School publication known as the *Eye Opener* with the laudable ambition of bringing the recreant souls of Calgary to their milk."

Indeed, most men thereabout who knew the Edwards-Nolan team made no attempt to resist the attraction. There was just one notable exception. Thirty-five-year-old R.B. Bennett, with an expression of grave responsibility, would leave the Alberta dining room where he took meals quite regularly, and walk briskly past the lighthearted group in which Bob Edwards sat, without either pause or recognition.

Bob had his enemies—many of them; but in that colourful Alberta Hotel community there was only this one man with whom he was not on friendly terms. For that there was a reason, however; perhaps a chain of reasons.

And so an evening would wear on. As their friends retired, Bob and Paddy would be left alone. Both were "night hawks." But they liked each other's company at any time and liked to have a while alone, not to rib each other but to talk quietly, philosophically, about their friends and themselves.

"Some great friends we've got, Bob," Paddy observed on one of these late nights. "They're people who have found their joy in their tasks. Do you ever feel that you want to ask the people around you where they find or hope to find their greatest satisfaction?"

Bob's eyes twinkled at the challenge. "I suppose Cappie Smart would be happiest refereeing a big boxing battle at Madison Square Garden; and Chief Cuddy would dream of a land where the wicked cease to make trouble; Commissioner Samis would hang the editor of the *Eye Opener* and Bennett would wind up his estate."

"All right Bob. Without any levity, tell me where you find the best satisfactions. I know you don't expect such a question but I'm serious."

"Come, Paddy, do you expect me to have the answer ready? Well, these hours with you and George Lane and Colonel Porter and the others are priceless, and writing copy for the old paper is one of my pleasures; but what a question to ask a man when he's sitting a few feet from a barroom door! Hang it, Paddy; I guess the Saturday morning hour when I meet the boys who sell the paper and pass out their copies for street trade is the best one in my week."

"Tell me this, then: how many kids get papers without payment?"

Bob looked puzzled. "Why do you ask that? I've never discussed it. . . . The mothers of three of those lads are widows, you know, and another. . . . "

"That's what I thought."

"There are other things too, Paddy. I live with a sort of secret hope that between drunks I'm doing something to give this new West an individuality—social and political individuality."

"And give its people reason to be proud they turned their backs on the security and comforts of the old communities in the East and else-where?"

"Yes."

"And make the CPR and Bennett rue their mistakes?"

"Yes."

From *Eye Opener Bob* (1957)

Ernest Cashel: Nolan's Most Infamous Client

"Poor Ernest! He was a damned fool but most everybody who knew him liked the kid," Nolan said of his most notorious client and the West's most famous criminal during the Nolan years. "But don't call him a common criminal," Paddy pleaded. "He had a good mother and a good home. He just played the fool by taking up with the wrong company and yielding to bad habits. But he's smart—too smart for the police he out-witted and embarrassed—and he's got a first-class sense of humour. And in case it escaped your notice, Cashel is a good Irish name. Isn't it the name of a charming small city of history in County Tipperary, a short dis-tance from my own Limerick?"

Nobody knew Ernest Cashel as well as Nolan and his sympathy for him grew steadily. The "kid" was of medium height, lean, dark, person-able, and almost twenty-one years of age when he appeared on the Canadian scene. He didn't look like a criminal and didn't talk like one. He was a good conversationalist and had a fondness for laughter, of which a Calgary reporter took note, saying: "He never for a moment lost his nerve. His conduct was at all times good. He gave no trouble what-ever to his jailers [except in making his escapes] and he was always ready to enjoy a laugh at anything which seemed amusing"[1]

These lines were written when Cashel was awaiting his appoint-ment with the executioner. Shortly afterwards a stranger in the Mounted Police jail peered through the bars of Cashel's cell and awk-wardly asked: "How long you in here for?"

To which Cashel replied: "How long am I in for? Seven days—and then I get hung."

Cashel's troubles with the law began soon after he left home in Wyoming at the age of fourteen. Twice, he was sentenced to jail terms and twice he escaped. Coming to Canada as a fugitive from justice, he worked on the Cochrane Ranch and next on a farm at Shepard on Calgary's east side where he was suspected of passing forged cheques. Such a cheque appeared in Calgary and the city's chief of police, Thomas English, claimed the right to pursue the suspect. Periodically, the chief had an urge to make a public display of his skill and authority and prove to the city and the world that a city policeman was as good as a Mounted Policeman. Nor was he overlooking the fact that a percentage of money from fines from arrests made by city officers belonged to the city.

The bad-cheque artist was believed to be working at the Coleman farm at Ponoka and Chief English sallied north by train to arrest and return his man. At Ponoka, on 15 October 1902, he invited the Mounted Police to furnish the necessary transportation to the farm and back but wanted it understood that the prisoner was the responsibility of the chief. The wanted man was located and while the Mounted Policeman, who would have been well able to make the arrest, simply held the driving horses, English arrested the man who offered no resistance. He made him secure with leg irons and loaded him in the sleigh for the drive back to Ponoka where he would be loaded like so much freight on the southbound train.

The chief with his prisoner in tow enjoyed the gaze of passengers on the train. Then, as the train rumbled on, the prisoner got the chief's permission to visit the men's washroom. The chief accompanied him to the washroom door and instructed in a loud voice: "Don't be long in there."

But the prisoner was longer than he should have been and was not responding to the chief's calls. English was worried. With the help of the train conductor, the door was forced open and the washroom was empty. The prisoner had opened the window and dropped from the moving train. The train was stopped and the chief made a cursory search in the evening darkness without any success and the deflated city officer returned to Calgary to ask the Mounted Police to find his man.

Cashel, with no coat or other warm clothes, faced a cold night but wandered on to stop at a farmhouse five and a half miles north of Lacombe after all members of the home had gone to bed. He knocked loudly at the door and Amasa Driggs opened to see a half-frozen man in shirt sleeves. "Come in before you perish," Driggs instructed. "I'll light the fire and make you some tea." Mrs. Driggs joined her husband and fussed with the teapot and bread and butter while listening to Cashel's story of mishap. He was on his way home, he said, when the untrained pony he was riding bucked him off and dashed away to freedom, taking his coat and mitts that were tied to the saddlehorn. There he was, without a horse; without proper clothing and food, and lost. Motherly Mrs. Driggs could not wait longer to announce her hastily drawn plan: "As soon as you have had your tea and bread and butter, I'll move our two boys from their bed to sleep on the floor and you can get into their already warm bed and spend the rest of the night."

The young stranger who said his name was Ellsworth, Bert Ellsworth, seemed very grateful. He wouldn't sleep late because he should be on his way but if it was all right with the Driggs, he'd like to borrow a horse and saddle in the morning so he could find and recover his wild horse. "Of course you can," Mr. and Mrs. Driggs said at once.

The Driggs were sorry to see the Ellsworth boy leaving in the morning but had his promise that he would see them within a day or two when he returned their horse and saddle. But the days passed and the horse and saddle were not returned. Driggs reported the loss to the Mounted Police at Lacombe who said the description of the man was very much like that of another man for whom they were looking. But the wanted man was not easy to overtake and was leaving behind a trail of crimes: thefts of horses, saddles, guns, clothing, a two-wheel cart, money and, at Morley, a diamond ring.

The police were humiliated until 24 January 1903, more than three months after the dramatic escape from Chief English, when Constable Blyth of the Mounted arrested Cashel at Anthracite in the Banff area.

Cashel was brought to preliminary trial at Calgary on 2 February 1903, although the Mounted Police were in no hurry to proceed; they would have preferred to hold their prisoner until they had more evidence about the mysterious disappearance of Isaac Rufus Belt from his cabin on the Red Deer River, downstream from the town of Red Deer. As the police discovered, Cashel's trail after leaving the Driggs home went by way of Belt's place. They had their suspicions but needed to find either Belt or his body before laying charges.

Nolan put up the best possible case for Cashel's defence but the evidence of the thefts was quite positive: Glen Healy's stolen horse was identified, as were the stolen diamond ring and the American fifty dollar bill that Belt was known to have in his possession. Almost every item seemed to speak against the young man. A conviction seemed certain and Nolan made a plea for leniency but Chief Justice Sifton wasn't impressed and sentenced Cashel to three years in penitentiary.

The search for Belt's body was intensified and on 20 July, a Red Deer River farmer, John Watson, looking over his cattle, saw something suspiciously like a human body floating in quiet water close to the shore, about thirty miles downstream from Belt's cabin. The farmer galloped to a neighbour's and together they returned to make the body secure with a rope and stake driven into the mud. The police were notified and in a day or so they arrived with an official coroner and various other people, including Belt's nephew, Henry Thomas.

Seeing the advanced state of decomposition, the coroner shook his head. One hand and the dead man's head were missing and flesh was falling from the bones. Some ribs were broken and the body was naked except for boots and socks. But something had to be done and the first task was to take the remains from the water without allowing it to fall apart. With the aid of ropes the body was eased out onto the shore where it was possible to clear soil, moss, and slime from it. The operation revealed what suggested a bullet wound on the thoracic wall. The opening was cleared and from it fell a lead bullet.

An on-the-spot jury was sworn in and the coroner, Dr. E.M. Sharpe, took and recorded some testimony, including the belief of Henry Thomas that the dead man was his uncle, Isaac Rufus Belt. The coroner's report concluded with the observation that Belt was murdered in October, 1902, on or close to the river and one Ernest Cashel should be questioned. The inquest ended and the remains were placed in a rough box and buried nearby.

The remains were exhumed later for further study of the path taken by the bullet and of unusual features such as the toe deformity the old man was known to have on his left foot. The police believed they had enough to warrant a murder charge against Cashel and a preliminary hearing at Calgary—not Red Deer—was conducted in September, 1903, with James Short appearing for the crown and P.J. Nolan for the defence. The preliminary was long and drawn out—eleven days—and Superintendent Sanders of the Mounted Police became impatient with Nolan for taking so much time. In giving an impression that he was telling Nolan how to conduct the defence, however, he was making a big mistake and had to listen to the lawyer declaring in angry terms that if a man's life was at stake, he was prepared to talk until Christmas, if necessary, to ensure a fair trial for his client.

Instead of exercising restraint in the preliminary, Nolan cross-examined every crown witness and warned the prosecution to have its case in good order because he intended to bombard it on its failure to identify the murdered man convincingly.

Cashel, however, was formally committed for trial at the next sitting of the Supreme Court and the police spent endless time in building their case and did it well. Nolan, representing the prisoner, did not have much to work on and may have known he was fighting a losing battle but believed that there remained a reasonable doubt about Cashel's guilt and worked hard, coming to his final speech to the jury with typical earnestness. He told the jury that the police start commonly with a theory that a certain man is guilty and then work to prove the theory is correct. He urged members of the jury that before they convict, they must satisfy themselves that the body taken from the river in a highly decomposed state, more than nine months after the estimated time of death, was positively that of Isaac Rufus Belt—certainly not an easy thing to do. Secondly, if the body was that of Belt, how did death occur? Thirdly, if it was the body of Belt and he was murdered, can you with such little evidence and all of it circumstantial, be satisfied that it was Cashel who killed him?

"True, Cashel was at Belt's home on 27 October 1902," Nolan conceded. "A few days later, they found Cashel with some of the man's things and later Belt disappeared. That," Mr. Nolan said, "is the whole case for the Crown. Suspicion is not proof and Belt may have given all those things to Cashel."[2]

Nolan spoke pleadingly for two hours, repeating again and again: "Suspicion is not proof." But Paddy Nolan's magic didn't work this time and the jury found Cashel guilty, but added a recommendation for mercy. He was sentenced to die by hanging with the execution set for 15 December 1903.

In the middle of November, Ernest's brother John arrived from his home in Wyoming and received permission from the chief justice to visit the prisoner. A special cell was constructed for the condemned man in order to keep him separated from other prisoners and ensure against escape, and an electric bell alarm was installed between the guard room and the barracks so that all residents could be called out at once in the event of an attack or anything of unusual or serious nature.[3]

John Cashel could visit his brother but was not to go within five feet of the cell. The various precautions were properly considered but they were not as good as planned. On the afternoon of 10 December John Cashel paid one of his usual visits to his brother. Rev. George Kerby, the prisoner's spiritual adviser, was the only other visitor that day. There was apparently some confusion about Mr. Kerby's departure and John Cashel broke the rule that was to prevent him from coming within five feet of the cell and was afterwards believed to have passed something through the bars. Then, at 6:30 PM when the guard duty was being changed from day to night staff, the prisoner seized the best moment for a break and pulled two revolvers from his pockets and effectively covered three guards, only one of whom was armed. The single armed constable was ordered to unbuckle his holster belt and drop his gun to the floor. The three constables were then herded into Cashel's cell and locked up. Cashel calmly took the keys from the provost's desk, unlocked his shackles and the door and walked out into the night. It wasn't for some ten minutes that the arriving night guards discovered the prisoner's escape and his jailers behind bars. The alarm was sounded and every available man was pressed into the pursuit.

Within a few minutes, John Cashel was arrested on the street, carrying a parcel of warm clothing and a pocket full of revolver cartridges. And Paddy Nolan, who was already in Ottawa pleading for a new trial for his client, heard about the escape in the office of the minister of justice next day. Paying a brief farewell to the minister, he said as he walked out: "We may not need a new trial."

The whole country from Banff to Maple Creek was blanketed with policemen and a reward of one thousand dollars was posted for information leading to the capture. Actually, the fugitive did not go far. He was seen at various points but not by the police. The date fixed for his hanging was postponed again and again as rumours were heard about him surfacing in strange places. Significantly, the young fellow had friends and doors were opened to him. Time and again the police knew where he was but once they got there, he was elsewhere in the area. Why he didn't flee to the United States was explained by his hope to be near enough to help his brother John who was quickly imprisoned for assisting his escape.

Ernest's presence was reported from Shepard, on Calgary's east side. The police invited volunteers to help them to thoroughly comb the area. Forty men took to the fields and trails after being instructed that if burning a house or haystack where he was known to be in hiding would save human lives, they were not to hesitate. Finally, while searching the Pitman farm just six miles from the city, a shot was fired from the cellar of an old building and the police knew they were close to their quarry. Inspector Duffus managed to speak to Cashel and advised him to surrender before the building was set ablaze. It was only when smoke began to fill the cellar that Cashel agreed to come out without his guns. He was immediately arrested and hustled away to the death cell that was kept for him.

He talked freely about using an excavation in a nearby haystack for sleeping quarters and the cellar for use during the day. The farm was occupied by two brothers who apparently knew of Cashel's presence. They were arrested and one was sent to jail for six months.[4]

On this January day of recapture, Cashel was taken before the chief justice who set a new date, 2 February 1904—nine days later—for the execution and Cashel's sad but dramatic career ended on that date.

The *Calgary Herald*, on the day of execution, carried a general synopsis of Cashel's sensational years and did it mercifully, recognizing that the young man had made serious mistakes but was not all bad, stating:

> The circumstances surrounding Cashel's recapture are such as to convey the idea that he is not by any means the desperado which the yellow journalists would have the public believe. There is no doubt whatever but that he could very easily have shot two at least of the party which surrounded the shack in the cellar of which he was hiding. As a matter of fact, he deliberately refrained from shooting Constable Biggs, who owes his life today to Cashel's generosity.
>
> That he should not have availed himself of his liberty to get out of the country is not at all puzzling to those who know him. Cashel was a man of no great intelligence and had little if any education and the predominating idea in his mind was to remain in the neighbourhood in the preposterous hope of being of some assistance to his brother John, whom he knew to be in prison in the guard room.
>
> The most extraordinary fact in connection with his

escape was that he should for such a length of time—forty-five days—have successfully eluded his pursuers and still remained within a few miles of the city. Had it not been for his recklessness in visiting different farmhouses and disclosing his identity, it is safe to say that he might still be at large. The recklessness so frequently displayed by Cashel was due in a great measure to his thorough belief in his own ability in outwitting his pursuers even at close range. The letter in his own handwriting left at Higby's on the Saturday following his escape in which he mentioned the $1,000 reward for his capture, his letter to the Rev. Leitch mailed in Calgary on 24 December and enclosed in a Dominion hotel envelope, his frequent visits to farmhouses within easy reach of the city, all go to show that Cashel was the victim of his own vanity.

A criminal who has throughout displayed so much sincere affection for his mother cannot be altogether bad and the manner in which he responded to Rev. Mr. Kerby's efforts to prepare him for his end would show that under different circumstances, Cashel might have been a useful member of society.[5]

It was a generous farewell and it left some people wondering who wrote it. It was never confirmed but it was easy to believe that the author was the great lawyer, friend of the friendless, who had a writing connection with the *Herald* at that time, Paddy Nolan.

If Paddy Nolan knew Cashel better than any other Canadian, it might be added that Bob Edwards knew Nolan better than anybody outside Paddy's family and his words are worth noting here: "The supreme characteristic of P.J. Nolan, the barrister, was loyalty to his client. No matter how obviously guilty his client might be, Paddy seemed to have the faculty of hypnotizing himself into the firm belief that the murderer, horse thief or whatever it might be, was perfectly innocent. To this very human trait may be; attributed, in a measure, his astonishing success at the bar.

"For example, he always believed and stoutly maintained in conversation with his intimates, that Cashel was innocent of the murder for which he was hanged. He made a trip to Ottawa at his own expense to try and induce the Minister of Justice to commute the sentence. Not only that, but he would not permit Cashel's body to be buried in the jail precincts. Again at his own expense—for he got no fees in this case— he had the body removed to a cemetery and given a Christian burial. No man had a more tender heart than old Paddy and he loved to take the part of the underdog."[6]

From *He Left Them Laughing When He Said Good-bye:*
The Life and Times of Frontier Lawyer Paddy Nolan (1987)

"To Hell With Ottawa: We'll Do it Ourselves"

After being returned to power in the general election of 1908, one of the first questions Prime Minister Sir Wilfrid Laurier heard was: "When will the railway to Hudson Bay be finished?"

His promise to build the road was made in good faith but nobody had properly assessed the problem of delivering five hundred miles of railway across the unsurveyed rocks and muskegs of Northern Canada to an undetermined port terminal. In spite of all the debates and studies and expeditions, most of the pertinent questions concerning construction remained unanswered, and fortunately for the Prime Minister, he had never actually named a completion date. His immediate concern was to silence the objectors and make a start. There was general agreement among his followers that the road would be built from the Saskatchewan River at The Pas but nobody was sure where it should terminate on the northern shore.

At the time of publicly committing the Government of Canada to the building, Sir Wilfrid could say that engineers with transits and levels and knee-high boots were already on the ground to make the necessary surveys. But when a year passed and then two years without any tangible signs of progress, the project was again caught up in political controversy. Eastern editors and critics succeeded in casting grave doubt upon the scheme. Some of the criticism may have been pure invention, like editorial comment aired in the House of Commons on 10 April 1910. As Hansard recorded it, Thomas MacNutt, Member for Saltcoats, directed Parliament's attention to a Montreal *Gazette* report that survey engineers were forced to discontinue operations because of an "impassable obstacle in the shape of an extensive muskeg which cannot be bridged." The editor, seizing upon it as fresh evidence of national folly, added: "The country may have cause for satisfaction if a physical muskeg keeps it out of a financial muskeg into which the construction of a railway threatens to plunge it."[1]

When the same story was carried in the *Toronto Globe* a short time later, the muskeg had grown to become "a bottomless bog," but in reply to the member's question, Hon. G.P. Graham, Minister of Railways and Canals, said he had conferred with his chief engineer, John Armstrong, and was assured that no great obstacle had been encountered and the muskeg was not a serious barrier to construction. "The government," he added, "had no intention of abandoning but, rather, intended to proceed with all possible speed."

The declaration to proceed with "speed" brought some laughs. A year and a half had passed since the Prime Minister reported survey engineers working in the field, yet no tenders had been called and no decision made about the northern terminal. The Pas community at the end of the Canadian Northern branch line would be the starting point but where would it go from there? Would the new line terminate at the mouth of the Churchill River or that of the Nelson? Nobody knew.

How would the decision about a terminal be decided? As the cynics said they expected, there would be another government-appointed investigation, this one to be conducted by the staff of the Department of Marine and Fisheries. But it would not be necessary to delay the beginning of construction because the work would start at the southern end where, for the first 150 miles, the grade could be built without regard to the northern terminal.

Of necessity, the first structure to be built had to be a bridge across the Saskatchewan River at The Pas. If the government was serious about building the railway, there was no apparent reason why the bridge should not be undertaken at once. Western people said so. On 27 April 1910, spending estimates brought down in the House of Commons contained an item of five hundred thousand dollars for "immediate construction" of the road to Hudson Bay. This was interpreted to mean a start on the bridge.

But Western people were finding more and more reason to wonder what the word "immediate" meant in Ottawa. Before the summer passed, however, the government gestured by awarding a contract for the construction of a steel bridge across the river. For very good reason, the Ottawa officials were worried about growing rifts between East and West over the Hudson Bay Railway issue, also about a continuing deterioration of government support in the West. Something new and better in public relations was needed. More publicity was attempted. Ottawa news writers began embellishing the program for the railroad and announced that the bridge would be ready for use "next winter." Grading would be hastened and steel was expected to reach the Bay by the end of 1911. The biggest news of all: "Four Transcontinental Railways Building Lines To Le Pas Junction."[2] It was great to think of big railroading corporations being so eager to gain a connection with the Bay. It made an excellent story but the various transcontinentals never reached The Pas.

It may have been the Prime Minister's idea to elevate Eastern Canadian interest in and respect for the Bay by having the Governor General, Earl Grey, pay a visit there in 1910. Whether His Excellency really liked the idea or not, he agreed to go. Following the traditional Hudson's Bay Company canoe route, he visited York Factory and then Churchill, returning by way of Hudson Strait and the St. Lawrence. If he was travelling to generate a better reception for the Hudson Bay Route, at which many Eastern people were still directing jibes, he was doing it dutifully and well by making all the right comments. It was a delightful cruise, he reported, and as for ice in the Bay and Strait, he did not see sufficient of it "to cool a glass of champagne."[3]

The year 1910 ended with a sod-turning, the only act of moving earth in connection with the railway grade. No contracts except the one for a bridge had been awarded. "That railway will never be built by speeches," Western farm leaders were saying, with obvious impatience and disgust. "This road has been promised to the people of the West for the past twenty years. When are we going to see actual construction? Our people are tired of having promises and no fulfilment."

Just as the unhappy marketing circumstances of 1923 and 1924 brought forth the Western Wheat Pool, so government inaction and vacillation in building the railway to the Bay gave self-reliant agrarians of the West the idea of building their own road and operating it themselves. "To Hell with Ottawa; we'll do it ourselves," some were shouting defiantly. Why not? Their own leaders assured them that there were no physical, financial or political barriers they could not surmount. Government engineers had shown how a railway could be built to either Nelson or Churchill at a moderate cost per mile, so "let's build it. We can pay for it while we're waiting for the Government to act."

Presented most effectively by an article in the *Grain Growers' Guide*, the official organ of the pioneer Grain Growers' Associations, and one which was ever ready to champion co-operative endeavours, the idea was debated in livery stables and general stores across the wheat country and gained support. Even the estimated cost running to many millions did not frighten the enraged farmers. If one hundred thousand Western people would subscribe one hundred dollars each, the total would go at least halfway in building the railway, the writer of the article appearing in the *Guide* submitted. The balance of the needed capital could be raised by a loan from the government fund of twenty million dollars accumulated from sale of Western land set aside expressly to help in building to the Bay. Failing all else, the Peoples' Joint Stock Company might raise the balance of needed money by the sale of bonds. And with the rails laid close to a succession of waterfalls, these could be developed to "furnish all the power necessary to operate the road by electricity."

The writer did not overlook the possibility that if Western people organized to construct and operate the northern railway, the Government of Canada might then be moved to advance its plans and begin building without further delay. In that event, the Co-operative would let the government finish the building and then offer to take over the operation. In view of Eastern antagonisms toward the railway, it would be better if such a railway utility were operated by a Western body such as the one proposed. The railway would benefit all of Canada but its primary purpose was to serve the West where people "have been and are still exploited without mercy by the great transportation companies . . . and they now have come to the conclusion that the best safeguard and assurance of an escape from the transportation monopoly that has long oppressed them, lies in building a road and operating it for themselves."[4]

The plan now under discussion across the West was put together by a delegation of farmers travelling to Ottawa late in 1910. Perhaps it was E.A. Partridge, fighting farmer from Sintaluta, who made the clearest call for direct action in forming a company to build, own, and operate a railway to the Bay. An organization committee consisting of David Railton, Sr., of Sintaluta, T.W. Knowles, of Emerson, and E.A. Partridge, was struck at once and subscriptions for members and shares were invited. Before the delegates completed their return to the West by train, many of them subscribed to the plan by signing applications in the following form:

> We the undersigned, in the event of the federal government failing to undertake the speedy construction of the Hudson's Bay Railway and its operation through the medium of an independent commission, and from the viewpoint of the interests of our western population in the matter of efficient and cheap service provided throughout the year, desire to express our faith in the feasibility and desirability of the western people, with suitable government assistance, building and operating the road for themselves as a popular joint stock company enterprise, by placing a subscription of $10 each at the disposal of an organizing committee, and agreeing when at least five hundred signatures be obtained, to sign, if requested, the memorandum of association and take at least $100.00 stock in the proposed company.

In launching the campaign to obtain subscriptions, the committee appealed not only to farmers but to Western people in all professions to write applications and send their subscription money to the Home Bank of Canada at Sintaluta for deposit in the Hudson Bay Subscription Fund. In signing an application and paying ten dollars, the subscriber was taking the first step toward becoming a shareholder to the extent of at least one share with value of one hundred dollars. The committee would be permitted to draw upon the funds to meet organizing expenses and if the public response was sufficiently favourable, the Company would be formed and subscribing members asked to pay the balance of one hundred dollars for each share of stock. In the event of failure to accomplish the purpose, however, the unspent money would be returned to subscribers.

Application forms were forwarded to secretaries of Grain Growers' Associations, Boards of Trade, and other bodies expected to display interest. With the forms went a public appeal over the names of members of the organizing committee:

> People of the West, if the creation of a cheap, efficient and independent avenue of transportation to and from the world's markets by a short route appeals to you as being highly desirable, lose no opportunity in doing your part in making it an accomplished fact. The method adopted to launch the enterprise may seem crude in form owing to the necessity for dispatch, but it is hoped that the auspices under which the movement originated and the personnel of the committee, will be sufficient guarantee of good faith and the likelihood that any reasonable support from the general public will be followed by vigorous and capable action on the part of the committee.

People to whom the appeal was directed were assured that as soon as the organization of the company was consummated, the Government of Canada would be petitioned for a charter and some financial assistance in building. It was proposed, then, that if and when the government decided to nationalize the railroads of the country, the company would be ready and willing to hand over its Hudson Bay Railway; but any attempt by private capitalists to buy out the peoples' railway would be met with a fine and firm refusal.

Just one week after the first general call to action in support of the proposed railway enterprise, the *Grain Growers' Guide* carried a rousing challenge directly from that middle-aged and discomposing campaigner, E.A. Partridge, now signing as Chairman of the Provisional Organizing Committee.[5] It was a "To Whom It May Concern" message, meant to be directed at everybody who might benefit from cheap transportation and find an interest.

"Everybody pays freight charges, express charges and railway fares," he wrote, "and everybody in Canada who does so pays at least double what the service would cost if the railways were capitalized at their physical value and operated at cost, including fair interest on money invested."

Some people called this forty-eight-year-old homesteader-farmer from Sintaluta an agitator and troublemaker. He was an emotional fellow but he was intensely serious and could become greatly upset by evidence of injustice. And he could be devastating in his denunciation of wrong-doers in big business. Obviously, he was no friend of either the Winnipeg Grain Exchange or the CPR. Now, he was making a plea for a monster co-operative and speaking bluntly: "Never again," he wrote, "will be present so favourable an opportunity to smash the tribute-levying powers of the great Transcontinental roads with their allies, the Beef Trust and the Grain Combine, as that which we, the burden bearers of the western plains, can seize if we have the courage, by co-operatively building and operating a railroad to Hudson's Bay supplied with all the necessary adjuncts for the cheap exportation of the products of the ranch and farm, before the capitalistic interests gain possession or a railway-owned Government boggles the enterprise."

In other words, "those who use the railways should run them" and in so doing confuse those "insolent, cattle-killing, claim-evading, stock-watered, tax-exempted, subsidy-fattened, privilege-drunken corporations that have long dominated parliaments and robbed the people in the guise of common carriers, but in the practical role of highwaymen."

Clearly, the man could be vitriolic but he was also thoughtful and responsible, extremely eager to see his fellow farmers rising to this, the biggest challenge to confront them in their adopted land.

The public response was fairly good but far from being overwhelming. It wasn't every farmer, of course, who could spare ten dollars, even for a good cause, and certainly not many of the rural people of the time could anticipate one hundred dollars of surplus money with which to pay for a share of stock when it became necessary. But some were enthusiastic—like the one writing from Pincher Creek, signing as Bunchgrass, who urged building the road all the way from Hudson Bay to the Rocky Mountains where it would connect with the Crow's Nest Railway and become an outlet to the Pacific, thus giving the co-operative company "the finest transcontinental railway in America, resting on the best harbour on the Pacific Coast and upon the only port of consequence on the Atlantic side."[6]

Whether it was owing to the initiative of the Western farm group or merely the approaching general election, the Government of Canada responded with a fresh display of good intentions. Hon. George P. Graham, in speaking to his annual railway budget on 11 March 1911, announced a government decision to definitely construct the Hudson Bay Railway itself and make arrangements for the construction of terminal facilities and elevators, and for a steamship service between the Bay terminal and the British Isles. The government would "proceed with this work." The first stretch of grade, from The Pas northward, would be undertaken at once.

Was this just another pretty speech or did the government really mean business? A serious intent was indicated by the calling of tenders for the first section of the road. About mid-summer—10 August 1911—

as politicians were getting into another general election campaign, mainly on the issue of Reciprocity, it was announced loudly and clearly that by a cabinet decision, the contract for construction of the first section of the line—185 miles from The Pas to Thicket Portage—was awarded to J.D. McArthur of Winnipeg, whose tender was just less than three million dollars. The contractor was said to be ready to begin work at once, hoping to have a big part of the grading finished before the onset of winter. The party in power, appealing for voter support, hoped also that the work of construction would advance enough to be conspicuous before election day, 21 September 1911.

Having started to build, the government—whichever party happened to form it—could not stop now. E.A. Partridge's drive for the "People's Hudson Bay Railway Company" lost its momentum and before very long was nothing more than a memory.

From *Battle for the Bay: The Story of the Hudson Bay Railroad* (1975)

Culture and Agriculture 1910–1946

～

Education, Experiment,
and an Unlikely Champion

"Agriculture," declared Sir Wilfrid Laurier, "is not only a work of the hands but a work of brain. It is an art which should take a foremost rank in the curriculum. It is the finest of all studies and sciences." It did not take long for the farmers of the Western wheat and cattle empires to recognize the truth of this. At first a homesteader with a degree or a library was likely to come in for a good deal of livery-stable ridicule. It seemed fairly clear that hard work and bull-dog determination paid bigger practical dividends than could be expected from a college diploma, and a man couldn't live on culture any more than he could breakfast on love. But changes in soil, machines, parasites, climate, and merchandising methods began to call for skill. Agriculture began to demand workers who were trained and educated along broad lines. There came a realization that farming people required a working knowledge of science and that a broad education, embracing cultural subjects as well as technical, was as much needed by farmers as by lawyers and dentists.

Science and farmers are destined to be partners in the world's principal business, that of producing human food. The man on the land needs all the educational preparation possible if he is to protect the soil, which is the greatest of all natural resources, maintain its productivity, avoid loss by erosion, control plant diseases, out-guess the parasites that attack plants and animals, prevent malnutrition and breeding failures in livestock, understand and repair all the mechanical aids and electrical gadgets on a modern farm, meet a hundred commercial and operational problems which arise daily, and take a philosophical and Christian view of the golf-playing insurance agent who does less work, drives a bigger car, and drops in unannounced for Sunday dinner.

The first formal education for agriculture on the continent was given at Michigan State College; in Canada, at the Ontario Agricultural College in Guelph, beginning in 1874. A farm bought at Mimico, close to Toronto, for this purpose was abandoned following an election and a change of government.

Reasons given were thistles and closeness to a big city. Something might have been done to destroy the thistles but legislators, even in that period, realized that nothing could be done about Toronto, and the temptations and evils to which it would expose young and untarnished men from the farms. Besides, a stand against thistles and sin would be well received by voters in rural Ontario, and land was available at Guelph, a place said to be noted for "the strong moral and religious tendencies of its people."

But long before the Western provinces had established schools of agriculture the work of William Saunders, first Director of the Dominion Experimental Farms, was bringing science into the service of the farmer. Plant breeding was his chief interest, and recognizing the crying need for an earlier wheat, Saunders carried a search for appropriate varieties to many parts of the world. Each kind he tested at Ottawa. Some were too late; some were not good for milling; some were poor yielders. One after another was discarded; it looked as though Canadians must create a new variety to fit their own needs.

A crossing program was started in 1888 and much of the technical work was done by Saunders himself and his two sons, Charles E. and A.P. Saunders. For parent strains, Ladoga, a bearded wheat from Russia, Hard Red Calcutta from India, and Red Fife, were used extensively. The elder Saunders made the crosses from which Preston and Stanley varieties came and A.P. Saunders brought together the parents of Huron and Percy. Of these, Preston and Huron were introduced to the West in the nineties but they were deficient in milling qualities and did not last. The new wheat which the West needed and wanted was still undiscovered.

Charles E. Saunders became Dominion Cerealist in 1903. With a Vandyke beard, a pair of spectacles, and an endless fund of patience, this scientist began immediately to revive the search for better wheats. His first step was a re-examination of the crossbred lines, including some lost strains which he literally discovered on a dust-covered shelf in an Ottawa storage space.

Among single-headed selections made in that year of 1903 was one which came from a Red Fife father and a Hard Red Calcutta mother, mated at Agassiz eleven years before by A.P. Saunders and Thomas Sharpe. Charles Saunders was impressed. The seed from that head was marked for special attention. When the next crop was harvested, Saunders applied his "chewing test" for gluten strength and milling and baking qualities. Elasticity in the wheat gum indicated ability to make a big loaf and colour of gum was a clue to colour of flour. By every test, the new strain was good.

But it had to prove its worth under the trying field conditions of Western Canada. After the harvest of 1906, seed totalled forty pounds and twenty-three of those pounds were sent to the Indian Head Experimental Farm where Angus MacKay was superintendent. Said the Dominion Cerealist, "That canny Presbyterian MacKay is hard to convince. I want him to be the referee."

Two or three days after the seed arrived at Indian Head, near tragedy occurred. Somebody stole the bag containing those twenty-three precious pounds of wheat. Everything seemed to indicate that it was somebody who recognized the possible value of this prize, probably somebody working on the farm. But the superintendent didn't "blow up" and he didn't call the police. He did call his men together and issued a reasoned appeal. Here was seed which might bring relief to the struggling settlers right across this country and to the hungry people beyond Canadian shores. Said MacKay, "The storage granary will be unguarded and the door unlocked tonight." The appeal proved MacKay's wisdom because the next morning the bag of seed, all twenty-three pounds, was back in its place.

In 1907 and 1908, this wheat grown under MacKay's supervision gave a good account of itself. It outyielded Red Fife and was six days earlier. In one of those trial years, only the early maturing wheat escaped a late August frost and the merits of Marquis were increasingly plain. MacKay was not one to jump to conclusions but in 1909 he gave approval and distribution of Marquis was commenced.

The superior qualities of Marquis were recognized quickly. It was the favourite topic of conversation as farmers met in the livery stable or around the big-bellied stove in the general store. As fast as seed could be supplied, it swept over the prairies, east into Manitoba, west to the Foothills, south to cross the International Boundary, and north to force back the limits of wheat production, just as earlier varieties of corn had extended the bounds of the corn belt in the United States. Everywhere it replaced its parent Red Fife and won a dominant position in the continent's spring wheat belt.

The idea of exhibiting Marquis wheat in World's Fair competitions probably never entered the mind of its creator. Dr. Charles Saunders was a plant breeder, not an exhibitor. But exhibited by a skilful grower like Seager Wheeler, the new variety won its first world championship soon after being released and drew international attention to the Canadian Prairies. The biggest surprises were displayed right near home where men were asking: "Who is this Seager Wheeler?" and "Is this Marquis wheat all that good?"

In making Seager Wheeler a world champion, fate was dealing mysteriously. If he had been one inch taller he would have been accepted by the British Navy and given no chance to grow wheat on the Canadian Prairies. Bitter at rejection by naval authority, he resolved to leave the Isle of Wight where he had grown up with people who drew their livelihood from the sea and had more interest in the Blackgang Pirates, with headquarters nearby, than with planting and harvesting of crops.

While still smarting from the disappointment of being rejected by the "blooming nyvey," he received a letter from an uncle, homesteading near Clark's Crossing, north of Saskatoon. It brought an idea: he would join the uncle in that far part. It was springtime, 1885, when the seventeen-year-old lad reached his uncle's place, 180 miles by trail from a railway.

His decision was to remain in the country and get a homestead for himself. He worked on railroad construction out of Moose Jaw for awhile. Then, he saved some money, bought a wagon and team of oxen, and started north to his land.[1] His mother joined him to keep house in a lowly shelter made by placing poles in an upright position around a dugout on the riverbank.

Wheeler's first revenue came from gathering and selling buffalo bones—eight dollars per ton delivered. Bones paid for the groceries for most of the first two years. At the end of that time, the homesteader had some wheatland in production, but being less than satisfied with his homestead quarter, he made a change and bought a better place from the CPR near Rosthern, Saskatchewan. On it the little man made a home, planted trees, and struggled to have his Red Fife wheat mature before the fall frosts came. For one whose life and interests had been with ships and sailors, homesteading should have been completely foreign, but astonishingly enough he discovered an unsuspected fascination in the selection of crop plants and vegetables and flowers. The light from his kerosene lamp burned late at night as he hand-selected seeds. Neighbours, seeing him combing wheat fields for heads with special merit, said he was "odd." At one point he nearly lost his farm to a mortgage company; frozen wheat selling at twenty-three cents per bushel did extremely little to improve his security.

Conscious of the need for something earlier than Red Fife, Wheeler obtained Preston from Dr. William Saunders and saw it yield as high as sixty bushels per acre. But it was not the answer and Seager Wheeler admitted it.

At about this time, L.H. Newman, secretary of the Canadian Seed Growers' Association, visited Rosthern and spent some time with Wheeler. Together, they went into the fields, and Newman took time to explain experimental techniques, filling his pupil with resolve to become an expert in crop improvement.

During field exploration in 1910 Wheeler came upon a single head, obviously superior to plants around it. This head, with early maturity in its favour, was threshed separately and multiplied to give Wheeler the variety known as Red Bobs. From another selection he obtained the variety Kitchener which won some high honours, including the sweepstakes at the International Exposition at El Paso, Texas, in 1916.

It was the championship of 1911 that brought the clearest sounds of praise for Marquis wheat and the expanding Canadian wheat industry. Somebody who knew Seager Wheeler's skill with plants sent him a small sample of the new Marquis almost as soon as it was approved for distribution. It fulfilled expectations, and Seager Wheeler had enough seed for most of his planting in the spring of 1911. With almost parental devotion he watched tender shoots break through the soil, then stool, head, and ripen. Growth was about as high as Wheeler's head, and the little man knew what it was to become lost in wheat as he walked to remove weeds; it was like being lost in the woods. At threshing time he had the satisfaction of seeing golden grain pouring from the threshing machine spout, plump, clean, heavy, red, and hard. It was the best wheat he had ever seen and neighbours examining it in double handfuls said it should be sent to the Provincial Seed Fair at Regina. Cleaning a bushel or two to make it look its best was a labour of love, but he remained reluctant about entering a competition. Neighbourly coaxing triumphed, however, and Wheeler's entry went forward to Regina, there to win the provincial championship. After that, Wheeler did not have to be coaxed. Later in the year a sample of his Marquis wheat was on its way to the New York Land Show. It seemed like a bold adventure, but it was in line with the conviction of people like Sir Thomas Shaughnessy of the CPR who believed a Canadian entry had a chance of winning.

James J. Hill of Great Northern Railway offered a gold cup valued at one thousand dollars for the best exhibit of wheat grown in the

United States. Sir Thomas chided his railway counterpart, hoping the competition would be open to Canadian exhibitors as well as to those in the United States. Hill, adamant, repeated sternly: "Grown in the United States."

"All right," Sir Thomas replied, "if you won't do it, my company will give one thousand dollars in gold to the exhibitor of the best hard spring wheat grown anywhere in the world. We'll see what happens."

Shaughnessy's hunch was sound, and days later the news was flashed across the country: "Man From Rosthern, Saskatchewan, Wins World Wheat Championship For Canada." People in the homestead country were exuberant in their joy while those in more distant parts took out maps to determine the location of that place called Rosthern.

A short time after the New York Show, Calgary was the scene of a banquet at which a railway executive presented Seager Wheeler with one thousand dollars in gold coins. With twinkles in his eyes, the man from Rosthern then passed the money back to the railway official, saying: "Thank you for the thousand dollars. Now, you take it as the final payment on my farm which I bought from the CPR."

Adapted from *Between the Red and the Rockies* (1952)
and *Harvest of Bread* (1969)

Harrison's Dream Horse

Delia D entered Stanley Harrison's life with the dramatic suddenness of a high-diver's leap into a pool. Once enthroned in Harrison's heart, she was there to stay. Fifty years later, with the memory of her still clear and untarnished, the Captain proclaimed her "the most beautiful creature the Lord of Life ever fashioned." And as a foundation mare, her breeding record was something to match her beauty.

It was a summer morning in 1911, and Harrison, waiting to take the train from Regina to Qu'Appelle, lounged in one of the big leather-covered chairs in the lobby of the King's Hotel. Having been there before, he knew this chair as the one commanding the best view of horse-and-buggy traffic on the Regina street. Next to him sat an older man smoking a pipe. Without waiting for an introduction, Stanley proposed swapping a pipeful of his Old Chum tobacco for some of the Field and Stream from his neighbour's pouch. The stranger—a Scotsman, by his speech—agreed, and conversation turned slowly from tobacco to weather and then to horses.

"This is my favourite place to sit when I have some spare time in Regina," the twenty-six-year-old Harrison said. "I can watch the horses being driven back and forth, and I try to identify the breeds. You see all the kinds and combinations here, the big ones with Percheron and Belgian colours pulling drays, the Clydesdales with stylish white markings hauling farm wagons; then you'll notice a few Hackneys hitched to carriages and Thoroughbred crossbreds doing general purpose work and those half-civilized broncos popping up everywhere."

"Aye, I see ye have a serious interest in horses," the older man said with obvious satisfaction. "O' course, all you western people are horsemen;

ye have to be. Without horses, ye'd no be able tae grow wheat, an' ye'd still be messin' about with the fur trade. Ye wouldna settle for oxen an' ye couldna depend on the big steam tractors. Weel, I'll tell ye: I'm in the horse game tae. My name's Murdoch, an' I'm here wi' a carload of bonnie Clydesdale stallions I hope tae sell."

For the younger man, this was an agreeable surprise. Taking the pipe from his mouth, he introduced himself. "I'm Stanley Harrison. I'm helping to run some big farms for D.H. McDonald, and I've just bought a small farm for myself about forty miles northeast of here. I raise a few horses, partly because I need them in my work and partly because I love them. Often I think that good horses were Nature's finest creations. They make me want to paint pictures of them and write verses. Do you feel that way about them, Mr. Murdoch?"

"I like horses," the other man replied, "but I canna say I love them. They are my business an' the best thing about them is the shillings I make frae them. But tell me, laddie, what's your favourite breed?"

"Well," the young man replied, "I'm hoping to breed Clydesdales, Thoroughbreds, and Hackneys, but a good horse of any breed can cast a spell over me. I can like them all but to be honest, Mr. Murdoch, the old English Thoroughbred, the greatest improver of them all, just may be closest to my heart. I suspect that when I find my Pegasus or dream horse, it will be a Thorough—"

Harrison did not finish the word because his attention was arrested by what he saw passing on the street. Almost gasping, he said, "Did you see that?"

"I saw a team of horses hitched to a buggy," the Scot replied. "Why, what did you see?"

"That mare," Harrison answered. "The one on this off side.* She's Thoroughbred. I have to see. I have to overtake her and see if she's for sale. I might see you later, Mr. Murdoch." Absentmindedly leaving his

---

* A horseman's term for the right side of a horse or team.

pipe and cap on the arm of the big chair, the eager fellow dashed from the hotel to follow the horse. As he told it later, "I followed that buggy like a schoolboy after a circus. The mare's driver pulled up at the post office. He was, as I recall, a tall man and I had a long way to look up as I met his whimsical smile."

"Like her?" the owner, R.B. Heron, asked laconically as he prepared to get out of the vehicle.

"Lord, yes!" replied Harrison.

"She's quite a mare," the owner said. "I got her from Raymond Dale who picked her up at one of the Kentucky sales. She's in foal to his horse, Kelston."

"I see she's in foal," Harrison was saying as he recovered his breath. "A pity to drive her. But will you sell her?" What he was saying under his breath was *Mister, you are about to sell your mare because nothing will stop me from getting her, even if her purchase leaves me penniless.*

Waiting for the mare's owner to reply seemed to take ages, as Harrison stood partly hypnotized by what he saw, surely his dream horse, a rich chestnut, sixteen hands at the withers, with refined head and neck, a barrel-like spring of ribs, and grand muscling. The flat and flinty shank bones bespoke the mare's quality.

Finally, the owner named a price, $175, which was less than Harrison expected. As it happened, the man needed the money—something not uncommon among horsemen—and Harrison, with heart beating rapidly, took a hurried inventory of the contents of his wallet. What he found was a rail ticket to Qu'Appelle and five dollars. Impulsively, he passed the latter to the other horseman and promised he would be prepared to pay the balance before the end of the day. How he would get the $170 before sundown he did not know, but he was determined. By midafternoon he had made the payment, taken possession, and prepared to ride his prize to Fort Qu'Appelle.

For Harrison, it had been love at first sight. The more he studied her, the more he admired her. "Her luminous eyes were large and deeply blue, tipped with coral pink where most horses' eyes are white," he observed.

"There was no mistaking that look of conscious greatness. I knew that she was kind as well as brave. I thrilled to know that my first impression was confirmed. Not a point that failed to harmonize with her peerless head. She was truly magnificent. Here was a fragment of that eternal beauty for which the human heart has ever thirsted."

It wasn't until Harrison had the mare at her new home that he learned she was thirteen years old, having been foaled in Kentucky in 1898. But in Harrison's words, "the years were nothing to her. She was of the gods and perennial youth. At twenty she was a champion in one of the biggest show rings, and when barren one year, I showed her under saddle and carried off the highest award."

The new mare, to be sure, received the best care the home farm could offer. She was her owner's pride and joy. She drew him in his buggy and carried him in his saddle. She went to the local fairs, won laurels in Thoroughbred classes, and was her proud owner's entry in some of the first horse races in which he participated. He was so inspired by her quality and character that he sketched her picture and wrote verses about her.

Of course, he hoped she would give him foals of her magnificence. At fourteen, she might have been regarded as an aged mare, but she performed like a mare in her prime and produced the stallion foal that carried the name Merry Marquis. In 1916, she presented her stable with the filly Lady Rosalind. At that time, Stanley Harrison was on the front lines and Delia D in the care of Stanley's brother. A year or more later, while Stanley was still away, the mare, once again in foal, strayed from the Stockwell farm and became lost. When a search for her failed, it was presumed that the great Delia D had died in some obscure part of the Valley or been the victim of horse thieves. The fact was that she had disappeared. There was nothing to be gained by worrying further about her.

Toward the close of the war, Captain Harrison was sent home to recuperate from wounds and, understandably, one of his first questions was about Delia D. He was shaken by the report that she had disappeared and was presumed to be dead. Oh, the bitter grief of "The Empty Stall."

Twilight descended o'er the drowsy fields;
From willowed sloughs and killdeer's plaintive cry
Came fitfully across the homeland wealds
Softly aglow beneath a saffron sky.
The teams from work, the mares and foals from play
Snorted content and munched their evening hay.

Each night the farmer from the bedding-shed
Came whistling in with great arms-full of straw
And made each horse a deep and shiny bed,
And when some eager colt would neigh and paw
His kindly voice would scold and bid it cease;
But no such protest came tonight for peace.

The shining light of just one thing we love
Can ease and brighten all we have to do;
No matter what it is we place above
All other things its gleam will aid us through.
As dreamers stand who see their idols fall,
He stood in grief beside an empty stall.

But there lingered the possibility that the great mare wasn't dead. With more hope than confidence, Stanley Harrison would conduct his own search. Questions brought a rumour of a stray mare of Delia D's colour and description having been seen at a straw pile about twenty miles from Stockwell. But the rest of the tale was most distressing. The stray mare had wintered in the open fields and then foaled beside the straw pile where she remained until she died, leaving behind a two-month-old orphan.

Harrison hastened to find the spot. Sure enough, there were a horse's bones, recently picked by coyotes, and a half-starved filly foal. He talked again with neighbours and became convinced beyond all doubt that the mare had been his fine Delia D and the emaciated foal was Delia's baby and his property. Neighbours agreed that the foal had done unbelievably well to survive. They told of it being suddenly deprived of its mother's milk and being obliged to shift for itself or starve. They had watched the dejected little creature wander up to a mile from the straw pile each day to forage for tender morsels, then return to spend the night beside the bones of its mother. What Harrison was told about the tragedy made him weep but filled him with determination to save this foal, though it seemed to be almost dead on its feet. Neighbours counselled that the little thing was not worth trying to save and apologized for their failure to destroy it when they saw the hopelessness of its position.

Such talk only annoyed Harrison. How awful to suggest killing Delia D's foal! He made it clear that the walking skeleton belonged to him, and he knew exactly what he would do about it. He would save the foal, even if it took all the resources he possessed; he could not do less for Delia's baby, and he wanted to hear no more about destroying it. Within two days, he had fashioned a horse-drawn stoneboat and hauled the pitiful creature to the stables at Stockwell. There it was allotted the best box stall, well bedded, and the choicest feed the farm could furnish.

The Captain's faith was justified, and the foal gained strength and muscle and life. The transformation seemed miraculous. The foal would never be a big and handsome Thoroughbred like her mother, but she might inherit her courage and character and pass them on to future generations. Harrison was happy, accepted her small size—and loved her. He called her Redwing and gave her the freedom of the barnyard and farm. She ran at times with her older half-brother, Merry Marquis, and they became staunch friends—perhaps too staunch because she had her first foal too early for an undersized and underdeveloped filly. But there was nothing wrong with Redwing's filly foal; the Captain called her Dusky at first and later renamed her Merry Minx.

What a mare was this one, Merry Minx! Stanley Harrison, sensing her speed and personality and quality, felt more than ever rewarded for his efforts in recovering the Delia D family line. Out at two years of age, Merry Minx won futurity races at Calgary and Edmonton and went on to gain more racing fame. Her fibre and stamina became ever more apparent. She seemed indestructible. Later, when Harrison's horses were racing in Cuba and were struck by a virulent infection, Merry Minx was one of the few survivors. Later still, when the Harrison racing string was in a train wreck and all the horses were reported dead, Merry Minx again survived. She was buried and bloodied but she was alive, a worthy daughter of Redwing, a worthy granddaughter of Delia D. And at Winnipeg, just a few days after the wreck, Merry Minx was one of the racing contestants and one of the winners.

Nor did the influence of the Captain's dream horse end there. It continued on through other great racing and breeding Thoroughbreds like Bend Oria, Merry Melody, Scarlet Runner, Chiron, Druma Doon, Mystic King, Merry Centaur, Sans Regret, and Safanard. They were like majestic branches springing from the parent trunk, bringing both joy and inspiration to Stanley Harrison. If fondness for horses was the principal force in setting his artistic flame aglow, his first loves—Delia D and members of her family—must have been the prime factors behind his output of poetry, prose, and pictures.

From *The Rhyming Horseman of the Qu'Appelle* (1978)

Historic Harvest Scenes at the Cameron, 1920

Farm tempo quickened at the harvest season when crop recovery across the West appeared to resemble a mad rush against time and changing weather. It was ever thus. Daylight hours were becoming shorter, and working hours were longer for men, women, and horses. Breakfast was earlier; supper was later; and bedtime for workers with tired muscles was sweeter in those rushed but unforgettable days that began annually with cutting and stooking and ended when the big steam-driven threshing machines gobbled up the last of the sheaves and members of the well-organized threshing crews were paid off.

Never were those harvest scenes more dramatic than on the Noble land in that autumn of 1920 when the operations engaged the chief and as many as 160 hired helpers and three hundred horses and mules. Never before was one Canadian farming enterprise conducting harvest on as much land, and never had there been an indication of as much threshed grain. And in the light of extensive farm expansion and near crop failure in the previous year, it may be that no debt-ridden farmer had ever experienced greater need for a good crop return.

A reporter visiting the Foundation farms in August thought he saw a "million dollar crop on the Noble fields."[1] He might have been right if it had not been for falling prices. When the short-lived Canadian Wheat Board terminated its dealings and trade was resumed by the Winnipeg Grain Exchange on 15 August 1920, wheat prices strengthened slightly to $2.85 a bushel at Fort William and then began their long and disastrous decline. The country was entering a postwar slump, and before threshing was completed, wheat and other grains were on the skids.

But threshing came before marketing and Charlie the chief was noticeably more intense. His stride was longer and bolder, and people around him wondered if he was getting any sleep and when he was taking his meals. Only a few understood the burden he was carrying or realized that the task of directing the work force required to harvest a good crop on twenty thousand acres of prairie land would probably match that of a field marshal commanding a battlefield campaign.

The year's harvest began with the cutting of roughly six sections of winter rye, that cereal for which Noble was finding greater use and greater respect on account of its soil-saving value. The thick stand and heavy heads reinforced his belief that winter rye was not only a relatively reliable crop but also one of the most useful in furnishing cover and protection for the soil in the spring season when wind erosion was a major threat.

The field of rye that made the chief chuckle was not his best producer but rather one which he did not expect to give him anything. It was a six-hundred acre area seeded on new breaking two years earlier. In the dry and disappointing year of 1919, it yielded only seven or eight bushels per acre, and it was Noble's intention to plough the stubble and summerfallow the ground in 1920. But to his surprise, the spring brought a fine stand of volunteer rye and ploughing was delayed so the area could be used as an early season horse pasture. Then, when the volunteer crop continued to show vigour, Noble decided to give it a chance to mature. The final result was a volunteer crop giving twenty bushels of excellent rye per acre.[2]

Again Mr. Noble invited members of the Lethbridge Board of Trade to visit the farms on a day in August when harvesting was in progress. This time, the Calgary Board of Trade membership received the same invitation, and about 250 visitors from the two cities drove to the Cameron Ranch farm on 18 August and saw harvest operations such as they had never witnessed before and would never see again. Those who completed the farm tour could have seen sixty binders, hauled by 240 horses and mules, cutting into the nineteen thousand acres of crop and might have made their own wild and inconsequential guesses about probable returns in terms of bushels or dollars. Whatever the exact dollar return, it would be the biggest and most valuable crop to come from one farm anywhere in the British Empire in that year or any previous year.

Overawed visitors learned that the Noble Foundation farm land at that moment totalled 33,090 acres, of which 28,689 acres were under cultivation and the rest was in use for grazing. They might have surmised that since the formation of the Noble and Harris Land Company—a Noble Foundation subsidiary with Charles Noble as president, J. Harris as managing director, and E.C. Cranstoun as secretary—intended to handle purchases and sales, total acreages could fluctuate from day to day like the weather.

There were some unprecedented speeches within the sound of grain binders. The visitors heard Mr. Noble explain his farming ideals and the methods by which he hoped to conserve his soil and bring a complete halt to drifting. He believed that farmers should be keeping more closely in touch with experimental and scientific developments and made a significant plea for what he called "agricultural advisers." These informed individuals would be trained public servants, constantly available to farming people to advise about crop varieties, seeding methods, cultivation, soil management, livestock production, and so on.[3]

His plea was significant because he was again ahead of his time in making a public request for the kind of advisers who were provided ultimately in the agricultural representative services of the provincial departments of agriculture in the West.

The guests were impressed, also, by the remarks made on the same occasion by G.R. Marnoch, president of the Lethbridge Board of Trade, when he pronounced Mr. Noble as one of the best neighbours any rural–urban community could have. His mind is always open to discovery, the president said, and when he has tested something new and found it good, he is anxious to share it with others who can benefit. "A community that has one man of the calibre and experience of W.H. Fairfield, superintendent of the experimental farm here, and another farming on such an extensive and highly efficient scale as C.S. Noble, is very fortunate."[4]

The host of the day was sorry and the visitors were sorry that they were a few days too early to see five steam threshing outfits—two on the Nobleford places and three on the Cameron—starting to work. They were also some days too early to see the recent Noble invention, the cable car, designed to move grain across the Old Man River as a means of shortening the delivery distance to a railroad shipping point. But about the latter they would hear much.

As soon as the winter rye was dry enough and hard enough for threshing, just two days after the sixty binders completed cutting the wheat, the Reeves steamers and the Red River separators moved into threshing positions, and binder operators hitched to bundle wagons and stookers became field pitchers and spike pitchers.

Robert Gratz, who hired with Noble in 1920 and became a farm foreman, spent most of that harvest season working in the elevator at Chin, which the chief was leasing from the Bawlf Grain Company. In that position, Gratz was taking delivery of four to five thousand bushels of Foundation grain every working day and keeping closely in touch with all the threshing operations on the Cameron. As he explained, each threshing outfit was supported by twenty-seven workmen and fifty-four horses.[5] Thus, the five threshing crews employed 135 men. Teamsters were paid $8.00 a day and spike pitchers $9.60, making a total payroll of at least $1,500 per day. Horses and mules in harness for the threshing numbered about four hundred.

It was a harvest exercise such as the Canadian countryside had not seen before.

Noble was fair to his men, as most of them were quick to declare, and thoughtful for his horses and mules, but he demanded efficiency and organized to insure it. Each threshing outfit had one engineer, one separator man, one fireman, two tankmen who drove four-horse teams in hauling water for the engine, one "flunky" who used part of his time hauling straw for fuel to the engine, four spike pitchers at the feeder, two men handling the Stewart sheaf loaders, three men with 125-bushel grain tanks and four-horse teams hauling grain from the separator, one or two cooks, and, according to Robert Gratz, up to twelve teamsters with bundle racks hauling from the sheaf loaders to the separator. When the sheaf loaders were abandoned late in that season, they were replaced by eight field pitchers.

An inventive feature of Noble's threshing methods of that time was the unloading arrangement at the feeder of each separator. Each machine was provided with a big wooden platform at the feeder end on which the bundle racks unloaded automatically with a feeder extension that brought the feeder within a couple of feet of the ground, making it easier for spike pitchers to work from the platform.

To facilitate this feeder-end arrangement, each bundle rack was provided with a loose or movable gate which rested against the front of the rack until the teamster drove onto the platform, at which time he completed a connection between the gate and a cable anchored to the steam engine. Having fastened the gate or end gate to the engine, he drove away and saw the load of sheaves being dragged off his wagon and deposited on the platform from where the sheaves would be fed into the elongated feeder by the spike pitchers.

Generally, two threshing outfits operated close to each other on the Cameron Ranch farm, enabling the crews of both to share the same movable camp for sleeping and dining. Distances on the Cameron were great, and it would not do for men and horses to be spending a big part of their time moving back and forth on the trails. To remove such an extravagance, movable threshing camps were set up close to the machines. These caboose and tent camps were moved every time the threshing outfits moved, and workmen and horses remained in the fields, close to their work, day and night.

But it was the overhead tramway to carry grain across the river that captured public interest more than any of the other harvest innovations. The long haul from the Cameron place to an elevator that would receive grain—either at Taber or Retlaw—was one of the objections to the property, perhaps one reason why the property had not been developed sooner. When the small amount of grain grown there in the previous year was hauled to an elevator, it had to go twenty-five miles—fifty miles round trip for the teams and teamsters. Again and again Mr. Noble and his men said: "Oh, for a bridge across the Oldman River that would allow us to take our grain to Chin on a trail of less than ten miles."

Chin was straight south of the mouth of the Little Bow River, but to reach it from the north side of the Oldman River by way of existing bridges or ferries would entail more trail miles than going to Taber. A shorter haul would be easier on horses, necessitate less granary space on the farm, and make more efficient use of labour. Something had to be done. Mr. Noble vowed that something would be done.

It was the kind of challenge he seemed to enjoy, the way a mountaineer enjoys a climb to the top. He considered building a bridge but cost would make it impractical. He thought of installing his own ferry, but it would not be reliable under the circumstances of changing weather. He eventually hit upon the idea of storage bins on both sides of the river with cable cars to convey the grain from one side to the other.

As recorded by Mrs. Lillian Noble, his daughter-in-law, "Consulting engineers were brought in from Vancouver to advise as to the feasibility of a cable car to carry grain across the river. They advised that it could not be done. Dad said it must be done and so work was started."[6]

First, it was necessary to find a river location with a high and steep bank on the north or farm side and a broad valley with adequate access for wagons on the south or Chin side. Having fixed upon a site, a fifty-thousand-bushel storage bin was built on the steep side and a five thousand-bushel elevated storage bin was built on the south side, about eight miles north of Chin. A cable and cable car or bucket with sixty-bushel capacity was then installed to convey the grain from north side to south side, whence the horse-hauled wagons could be loaded by gravity for the relatively short haul to Chin.

But it was more complex than that. A load of grain from the threshing machines dropped on the north side would fall into the long fifty-thousand-bushel bin constructed on an angle of about thirty-five degrees so grain would slide to the lower end where a mechanical device would release sixty bushels or fifty-five bushels as required into the car or bucket. The loaded carrier would then be propelled across the river on the cable with power from a donkey engine and dumped automatically into the elevated storage on the south side.

It was an eighteen thousand dollar installation and was ready to use on 15 September 1920. Those who were present to judge its initial performance said it worked perfectly, and every bushel of grain taken across the river was benefiting by a reduction in delivery distance of about fifteen miles.

Noble had an excellent grasp of practical construction principles and chose to supervise the work going into the erection of his own buildings. When the cable car bins were under construction, he personally supervised the making of the long structure resembling a grain elevator lying at a precarious slant on its side, but he could not be on both sides of the river at the same time and left the supervision of the south side building to a foreman.

Whatever the reason—inadequate reinforcing, faulty materials, or excessive wind pressure—trouble overtook the structure on the south side, and at a moment when it was full of grain, its sides collapsed. Nobody was injured, but five thousand bushels of grain had to be shovelled from the ground into wagons and there was a delay of two or three days while the bin was being repaired and retrussed. But the invention then returned to giving unfailing service, and people drove for miles to see it.

The first grain moved across the river on the cable was a quantity of rye. Robert Gratz said that about eighty carloads of rye were shipped that year, most of it from the Cameron land and most of it through the elevator at Chin where he was working at the time. This grain was brought to Chin by twelve eight-horse teams—each team pulling two grain tanks—and four four-horse teams hauling single grain tanks. Altogether, according to Gratz, they were delivering about six thousand bushels per day. The teams made two round trips one day and one trip the next to avoid overworking the horses. An auxiliary team or "snatch team" of four horses was kept at the south side bin at all times to provide assistance needed to take the loaded wagons up the hill and out of the river valley.

While the twelve teamsters and over a hundred horses were hauling rye from the river to Chin and getting most of the public attention, there were the members of the other crew hauling from the threshing machines and field bins to the river. Observers like Robert Gratz marvelled at the coordination reflecting Noble's skill. And the famous overhead conveyance constructed at a remote and lonely point on the western countryside to take a ton and a half of grain across the river every three minutes was working well. Apart from the brief delay when the south side bin suffered a break, there were no problems, and Mr. Noble believed that the installation saved so many miles of heavy hauling, it more than paid for itself in a single season.

Members of the board of trade travelling in a party were too early to see the rye and other grains taking the aerial route across the river, but they read in their newspaper on 16 September that the eighteen thousand dollar apparatus of Charles Noble's creation was in service: "The first trial of the carrier was made yesterday and it worked splendidly."[7] The news brought hundreds of visitors from as far as Medicine Hat, Camrose, and even Great Falls in Montana. And sixty years later when nothing remained except the carefully chosen site with a high and almost forbidding bank on the river's left side, some concrete footings, and a few rusted cast iron gears, visitors were still travelling far out of their way to see where Charlie Noble installed his famous aerial tram to be a link in the transportation of nearly half a million bushels of grain in one year. Although it probably did not even enter his thoughts, he had also built a monument to human resourcefulness.

From *Charles Noble: Guardian of the Soil* (1983)

Stampeding on the Streets

Calgarians watched with partial disbelief as the giant Jack Morton and his cowboys from beyond Hussar stormed the city streets and avenues during stampede week, 1923, acting as though they were at home on the range. What could not be recognized at the time was that the friendly invaders were helping to establish a pattern for city conduct in succeeding stampede seasons. An annual one-week "reign of terror" was being inaugurated which, according to a reporter, "was just what the thousands of people who thronged the thoroughfare wanted."[1]

Morton set up a rope corral on Ninth Avenue in which to temporarily confine his chuckwagon horses, and carelessly scattered hay from there eastward to the Palliser Hotel. He spread his blankets on the sidewalk beside the corral, as he might have done in a quiet coulee far back in the Wintering Hills, and invited anybody needing accommodation to bed down beside him. When reprimanded for burning the cx brand on a telephone pole in front of the Yale Hotel, he replied, "We do it at Gleichen and Hussar. Does Calgary want to be backward?"

The news reporter witnessing Morton's takeover of the city's business section wrote, "Just how many of the city's bylaws and statutes were broken by the howling, whooping, rip-snorting bunch of cowboys that he brought with him will never be known, and it is not likely that anybody will ever enquire."[2]

The downtown capers began early in the week when Calgary, according to press headlines, was "Captured by Indians; Mayor a Prisoner; City Hall in Hands of Redskin Warriors."[3] Escorted by a posse of mounted cowboys and cowgirls, Indians from the Sarcee, Blackfoot, and Stoney tribes converged upon city hall and seized the offices of

Mayor George H. Webster, the city commissioners, and City Solicitor L.W. Brockington. The mayor was removed from his official chair which, to symbolize seizure, was then occupied momentarily by Chief Weasel Calf of the Blackfoot. The mayor was escorted to the street where he was placed on a horse and roped to the saddle, to be paraded like a convicted rustler on his way to a wild west execution. When the game had been carried far enough, the bewildered mayor was released to return to his civic rank and dignity, and spectators were left to ponder the new frivolity that had overtaken the city.

The next day brought street theatricals with a somewhat different tone, in which Morton was the leading actor. His role was that of the rancher dispensing rural hospitality, doing it at the heart of a city, and in his own distinctive way. If there remains any doubt about who started the tradition of the complimentary chuckwagon breakfast on downtown streets during stampede week, the *Calgary Herald's* report written at the time and given front-page treatment should settle the question:

> When Jack Morton, the man who wears the brightest orange shirt yet exposed to view, galloped the cx chuckwagon down Eighth Avenue on Friday morning, he started the final performance of the "morning stampede" in a way that Calgary will never forget. . . . Four plunging horses dragging behind them a complaining chuckwagon, flanked by howling cow punchers who rode across the tracks as if such modern improvements did not exist, made the turn around Traffic Officer Dan Finlayson and pulled up with a jerk on the south side of the avenue, between Centre Street and First Street West. Out came the old cookstove and soon the pungent odour of wood smoke filled the air, to be followed shortly by the inviting aroma of sizzling hot cakes. "Who wants 'em—Who's hungry?" queried the cook. They wanted them and were hungry. Spectators fought to get to the front in order to bite into the luscious flapjacks that

were being turned out by the outfit's cook. The boys supplied their eager guests with butter and maple syrup, introduced them to their two tame badgers and told any kind of stories [the guests] wanted to hear.

It is fine to sit up in the grandstand watching these cowboys perform at a distance but it is a grand and glorious feeling to get right down with them. Calgary crowds demonstrated that they wanted to meet the cowboys, talk to them, risk being kicked by their horses. They warmed to the personal touch.[4]

Other chuckwagon race participants caught the idea of taking the spirit of the Old West to the streets and followed Morton's example. And so was born a Calgary Stampede tradition.

The "trial marriage" of exhibition and stampede at Calgary in 1923 was judged a success. Directors, confirming faith in the union, hoped that the unpaid people who carried the reckless and hospitable spirit of frontier range years to the streets would come back.

Would Jack Morton, who led that friendly invasion of the downtown parts in the initial year, return to give Eighth and Ninth Avenues the odour of frying pancakes, sizzling coffee, and sweating horses? Before the exhibition and stampede week of 1924 was many hours old, the business section of the city had the answer. The big rancher wearing the yellow shirt with a cx brand emblazoned on it was again the most conspicuous figure on the main thoroughfare. Again, his booming laugh could be heard above the clang of streetcars. His wild horses, hating every second of their servitude on city streets, were as restless as ever. The unpolished wood-burning stove with two lengths of battered stovepipe was there again to prove that tasty hot cakes can be made on shabby equipment, just as good tunes can be made on old fiddles. And there, too, were the two tame badgers that were not really tame at all.

The stage properties were the same, and nobody had reason to expect that Jack's performance would be unchanged. The curious and hungry pressed closely around the cx wagon on the first morning of the new stampede week. They saw the rancher and his helpers, slightly spattered with batter from buckwheat flour and buttermilk, presiding over the two big coffee urns on the hot stove. Most of those crowding in upon the wagon reached eagerly for the breakfast rations and pronounced them "excellent." One guest to whom a helping of hot cakes was passed shook his head disdainfully and soon discovered that it was the wrong thing to do. Noting that the man had not even said "no thank you," Jack Morton was annoyed. To the amusement of the more appreciative guests, he seized the ungallant fellow and shoved a whole pancake into his mouth, very much as he might have forced a bit into the mouth of a green bronco.

Most guests asked for second helpings, at least until they witnessed another Mortonism such as Jack's friends had grown to expect from time to time. At a moment when one of the big coffee containers became empty, and the eager eyes of a hundred coffee-drinking spectators were fixed upon the second pot, Jack removed the lid from the latter, reached in, and pulled out a dripping dead cat, holding it aloft by the tail. Women shrieked and men turned away, some of them vowing they would never drink coffee again.

It explained the search for a cat, but for those guests with strong stomachs, Jack had a third coffee pot in temporary hiding, from which he was able to pour a hot, clean, and appetizing beverage, the only kind he had ever actually served.

"You'll find no cat hairs in my coffee," he assured both those who remained to laugh and those who returned after being convinced that the coffee Jack was serving was as clean as the best dispensed at the hotel.

Anticipating a busy week on the avenues, Jack was wishing he had a better stove for making coffee and frying hotcakes. The heavy one with stovepipes leaning like the Tower of Pisa was inconvenient. A compact, kerosene-burning stove would be handy, but Jack did not have time to go shopping for one. Next morning, however, when driving his wagon and team from Victoria Park to the Eighth Avenue location at which he would serve his breakfast wares, he recognized a nicely polished kerosene stove in a collection of sale articles being displayed on the sidewalk in front of an Eighth Avenue second hand store. His immediate thought was to stop and buy it, but having nobody with him capable of holding the fractious horses while he visited the store, he knew he must dismiss the hope of getting the stove, or find another way of acquiring it.

He realized that if he failed to get the stove at once, some other person would likely buy it. He was convinced that he needed that stove more than any other prospective purchaser, and also more than the dealer needed to make a sale. At the next intersection, instead of continuing westward, he turned to the right and jogged around the city block to pass the second hand store again. This time he drew the team close to the sidewalk and reached out to measure the distance between the stove and his place on the wagon, confirming his hunch that the stove was beyond his reach while the wagon was in motion. As Robin Hood might have reasoned, Jack thought of the hundreds of people he hoped to cheer with hotcakes, butter, syrup, and coffee that day and convinced himself that he had to have the stove.

Again he encircled the city block. When about to pass the store for the third time, he collected the driving reins in his left hand and, with his right, he swung his lariat and dropped the loop over the stove, making a perfect catch. Without slackening their pace, the horses jogged on, and Jack drew the stove closer to the wagon, the way an angler would draw in a fish, until he could seize it and lift it into the wagon.

The stove was bruised but not damaged, and for the remainder of the week the kerosene burner served Jack Morton and the people on the avenue very well.

Was it a case of theft? Well, not really, because at the end of the week Jack drove past the second hand dealer's premises and, using almost the same technique, unloaded the stove at exactly the same spot on the sidewalk where he had first seen it, and drove on. As far as is known, the dealer never learned where his stove had spent the week, but he probably found a pound of Morton's surplus coffee dropped where the stove was deposited, a sort of rental payment.

All the while, Jack's badgers were winning as much attention as the grand champion Hereford bull at the exhibition. He brought two of them when he came to the stampede in the previous year and now, whether he had the same ones or a different pair, his badgers were making more trouble than ever.

Wherever Jack Morton went during the week, the badgers accompanied him, sometimes in their cages, sometimes on leashes, sometimes without restraint. In the Palliser Hotel, they scampered across the lobby and dived for shelter beneath leather-covered chesterfields and under the flowing skirts of terrified ladies. This would not do, and when the angry manager invited Morton to gather up his wild pets and leave the hotel, Jack feigned surprise and asked, "Why? None of us has dirtied your floor." But he obeyed, and with a badger under each arm went across the avenue to make his first stop at the restaurant where he took most of his meals. There he hoped to find understanding.

Patrons gazed with glee at the entry of the big man who had suddenly become about as well known as Guy Weadick and exhibition manager, E.L. Richardson. Reacting to the public interest and approving smiles of restaurant patrons, Jack released the two frightened badgers on the long counter; it was almost as long as the bar of record length in the old Alberta Hotel on Eighth Avenue. What the badgers did was exactly what any wild animal will do with freedom; they ran, using the counter as their runway.

But badgers are not the most graceful animals in their movements, and the polished counter top did not offer very good footing. The result was disaster. As the badgers dashed toward the far end of the counter, hoping, no doubt, to find cover, dishes were dislodged and dashed to the floor. Guests leaning on their elbows to study the native animals withdrew in sudden fear. Teapots and coffee cups were scattered in all directions. Customers splashed with cream, gravy, and hot soup shrieked and swore at Morton and ran for the exit like people in panic at the warning of fire.

Jack, wearing an expression of surprise and guilt, strode to the end of the counter to retrieve his pets, and was at once confronted by the excited and irate manager, waving his arms and making threats of violence.

"I could kill you, Morton. You break my dishes. You spill my sugar. You drive away my business. I would like to kill you. I will sue you. Take your animals and don't you ever come here again."

Jack, still grinning sheepishly, said he was sorry. "But don't burst a blood vessel. Just gather up the broken dishes and tell me what it will cost to replace them. I'll pay you for them. It's not that serious, you know. Nobody got hurt. Can't we have some fun in your dull city?"

As good as his word, Jack did pay for the broken dishes. The bill was a big one. But Jack and the badgers continued to take in the stampede together, posing for pictures and trying to keep trouble to a minimum.

Guy Weadick and the exhibition officials thought so much of the downtown entertainment as a useful adjunct to the main show that they began to offer prizes for performances in certain categories. If there had been a prize for the most disruptive individual on the streets for the week, the judges would have been hard pressed to decide between the rancher from Hussar and the colourful reporter and man-about-town, Buffalo Child Long Lance. It was he who led the local Indians on the "scalping raid" against city hall. City Solicitor Leonard Brockington was the first "victim" and was left with a yellow wig to compensate for the loss of hair he may have suffered.

If there had been an award for the person who had successfully dropped his lariat over the largest number of Calgary city police officers—including the chief of police—without being arrested for irreverence, the most eligible candidate would have been Jack Morton.

As it was, members of the Morton family collected a big share of the honours, especially in the downtown category. Charlotte Morton, the second of the Morton daughters, won first prize for the best-dressed cowgirl under sixteen years, just as her older sister Lucy had won a similar award at the Gleichen Stampede in 1915.

Jack Morton was not a winner in the chuckwagon races of that year but he won some other wagon awards that pleased him just as much. He placed first for driving skills as demonstrated in the races, and first prize and a Stetson silver trophy for the best ranch outfit as judged on the streets. Still another Morton, Darcy, Jack's nephew and unfailing outrider in the races, was the winner in the contest for the best-dressed cowboy in the street performances.

It was a good year for the Morton contenders, and there were to be more good years because the rancher loved rodeo and enjoyed crowds of people. "Jack Morton," said a reporter in 1926, "could no more stay away from the Stampede than he could stop taking his meals."[5]

So it was until 1938, which was Jack's last year to be actively involved in the chuckwagon events at Calgary. The last race of that year ended with an accident involving Jack's outfit. Some observers could not help seeing something appropriate about such a concluding race in a career that had been marked by so many bumps.

The Calgary press did not overlook Morton's long and unbroken record. It was not a record of race victories—quite the opposite, but it was scarcely less significant.

"Big Jack Morton of Hussar," a reporter noted, "one of few cowboys to have driven in all the chuckwagon races since the race was inaugurated in 1923, is in Holy Cross Hospital suffering from three broken ribs as a result of a spectacular pile-up in the second heat of the rangeland derby at the Stampede last night."[6]

It was Jack's last race, spectacular and rough for a 240-pound man in his sixtieth year. But he refused to concede that it was his last. He insisted he would race again and if he had had his way, he would have been back. Nobody knew better than he that wagon racing was a dangerous pastime, but it was still his favourite sport. Age did not change his determination that he could never be satisfied to play games which were totally without risk and danger. He talked like a man who would rather die with his horses and chuckwagons than live without them.

From *Wildhorse Jack: The Legend of Jack Morton* (1983)

Horse Race Down the Mountainside

Williams Lake, 325 miles or 540 kilometres northeast of Vancouver, claimed the first rodeo in British Columbia and some of the richest rodeo traditions in Canada. Local enthusiasts told visitors very seriously that the last rodeo—whenever it will be held—will likewise be at Williams Lake.

The first rodeo was in 1920 and, two or three years later, the wild mountainside race was added as an annual feature. It was, without a doubt, the most spectacular and most nearly "vertical" horse race the world has known.

An Eastern visitor, seeing it for the first time, asked: "Why don't they use parachutes?" The reply explained that the riders didn't want parachutes because they were more concerned about making speed than making a safe landing.

Horse lovers couldn't be expected to like it, but for sheer outdoor roughhouse competition there was nothing like the Williams Lake mountain race, which started a quarter of a mile high and ended on the flat ground reserved for the fair and rodeo.

Ken Liddell, a well-known writer with the *Calgary Herald* for many years, wrote in October 1957: "It is a good thing the Highway and a housing development that now parallels the Williams Lake rodeo grounds put an end to the wild west attraction before the Calgary Stampede chuckwagon races, by comparison, got the reputation of being a kids' soap box derby with horses."[1]

Liddell went on to say that: "Considering the vertical track, it is not surprising that cow ponies have streaked the mile in one minute and twenty-nine seconds, a time that would throw rocks aplenty in the face of Citation which did the mile in 1:33 3/5 seconds. A flat mile, that is."

Contestants in the Williams Lake classic took their time getting their saddle horses to the top and were rewarded for their efforts with a perfect "bird's eye view" of town, fairground and endless rugged scenery, unlikely to be equalled except from a plane or balloon.

The race began with a shot from the starter's pistol and at once all was dust, noise and commotion. For the short duration of the race, nobody caught more than fleeting glimpses of the horses and riders as they came into view amid the big trees and disappeared just as suddenly in the mountain forest. But whether seen or unseen, nearly everybody could hear and interpret the sounds of falling rocks, cracking deadfall wood, shrieks from boisterous riders and hoofbeats from galloping, stumbling and leaping horses as they plunged toward the level ground and the finish line within the bounds of the exhibition ground.

Two minutes after the starting gun barked the beginning, the race was over and officials were listing the winners and finishers. Surprising as it seemed, very few horses and riders were ever seriously hurt. It spoke well for the sure-footed and tough cow ponies and equally well for the hardy cowboys and cowgirls.

The winner was an instant hero. Some of the contestants, like Joe Fleigier, became repeat winners and perennial heroes. Nor was it exclusively a man's race. At least one woman, Mrs. Olive Matheson, was among the contestants and finishers in each of three years. An older woman, who remains unnamed, is remembered for having lost her stirrups and her reins but still riding to the finish with hands high as if reaching for clouds and shrieking triumph in tones that drowned out most others.

For a few years after the mountain race was forced to discontinue because of highway and urban development priorities, many visitors to the town asked to be escorted to the spot at which the race contestants emerged from the rock and tree-covered slopes to dash to the finish. Their intention was to climb to the top on the course over which the horsemen and horsewomen had ridden down, just to test the difficulties.

Most of them climbed far enough to satisfy themselves that it would be easier and safer to learn the facts of the mountainside from residents of the Capital of the Cariboo than attempt the course, either up or down.

Local people said it convincingly that their contest was the fastest horse race in the world, explained satisfactorily by the old law of gravity.

From *Coyote Music and Other Humorous*
Tales of the Canadian West (1993)

The Pulling Contests

Horse pulling competitions were no respecters of breeds. Breed colours, conformation, or pedigree mattered not at all. Nothing counted except a contesting team's strength and will to move the near-impossible loads.

Horses would have had the best of reasons for hating the gruelling tests of strength and sometimes there was injury. But organized pulling became popular public entertainment. As a local pastime it wasn't new. Unscheduled barnyard pulling matches were probably as ancient as cockfights.

Hauling rocks from farm fields with stoneboats and teams offered useful training for competition. The work of picking and hauling stones was tedious, tiring, and uninspiring and needed something like an occasional on-the-spot test of horse strength with a bit of betting money to enliven it.

Every farmer had a stoneboat and most had field rocks, but if stones were not available, it was never difficult to resort to bags of gravel or cement blocks. Still, the lack of a scale to measure pulling force was a handicap, making it practically impossible to obtain a mathematical assessment of a performance to permit comparison with pulls in the next municipality or the next province. Supervisors, by requiring the use of the same stoneboats an as nearly as possible the same loads of stones, did well to minimize inequities. Without complete uniformity of pulling conditions, competitions could create as many disputes as they settled.

It could have been argued that horse breeds and breeding were not factors in determining a contest's outcome, but it was clear that the desire on the part of breeders to see representatives of their favourite breeds being called to the winner's circle at the pulling competition was fully as intense as at the conventional showring.

There were some exciting and spectacular private pulls before 1924 but it was not until that time that the awkward looking four-wheel vehicle—suggesting a hybrid offspring from a farm truck as one parent and an army tank as another—appeared to change the whole character of the contests. It was the heavy dynamometer of a kind first constructed at Iowa State College and then remade under the direction of Prof. A.E. Hardy of the University of Saskatchewan.

Horse pulling entered suddenly upon a new era of excitement, and for the next few years it would have been difficult to imagine either a horse race or a horse show holding more rural appeal than the western pulling events. One of the astonishing yet significant Saskatchewan headlines of 1925 announced: "Heavyweight Championship Of The World Goes To Lumsden." Nobody in the rural West at that time would confuse the editor's message with a prize fight.

All the big western exhibitions scheduled pulling competitions in 1924. It was a matter of yielding to public demand, although the fever of excitement didn't reach a climax until August of the next year when the two giant breeds and two proud prairie cities were locked in battle.

Saskatchewan could boast a million farm horses and every farmer had a breed preference. Brandon was still the horse capital of Canada—if not of the world—and might be expected to parade up to two hundred draft stallions from the city's sales stables to mark the official opening of a winter fair. Heavy horses still ruled in Canadian farm fields and still ruled most human hearts and lives.

With the adoption of the dynamometer, competitions in pulling could be conducted with the same rules as those in use in the United States. Comparative pulling results astonished everybody. An American team had pulled 2,500 pounds on the dynamometer for the full regulation distance of twenty-seven and a half feet to make what was considered a record. But at the Calgary Exhibition that summer, close to the beginning of the show season, a team of southern Alberta Clydesdales won with a registered pull of 2,615 pounds, accepted as a world record.

Edmonton was next on the exhibition circuit and there a Percheron team pulled 2,600 pounds. Then, in the next week it was Saskatoon's turn and previous pulling records tumbled when R.B. McLeod's big Percheron geldings, Dan and Tag, settled professionally into their twenty-eight-inch collars and brought shouts of glee when the dynamometer dial recorded a pull of 2,900 pounds, a new championship with pounds to spare.

This was but the beginning of the excitement. When the special midway train departed for Regina on Saturday night, the dynamometer was taken along to that community in which horsemen believed they had horses capable of outdoing the best pulling performances between Calgary and Saskatoon. Among the local horsemen who had been doing well in the stoneboat leagues were Gibbs Brothers of Lumsden whose massive Belgian geldings, Jumbo and Barney, had shown a team weight of 3,790 pounds. The Regina people became so inspired that they were almost ready to expropriate the Belgians and annex the town of Lumsden.

As that last of the scheduled pulling contests of the 1924 season turned out, the Gibbs team was a decisive winner, having pulled 3,100 pounds for the full distance. It was another world record, the third to have been made by Canadian horses in four weeks. Saskatoon horsemen were loath to surrender their supremacy of only a few days and to yield to a Regina contestant would be humiliating. They wished the two great city teams could be brought together for a showdown match.

There was still one day left in the Regina Exhibition program and Manager Dan Elderkin, never one to miss an opportunity to fill his grandstand, had an idea. He placed a telephone call to his poker-playing friend, Sid Johns, manager of the Saskatoon Exhibition, urging him to act at once to have Bob McLeod load his pair of Percheron geldings on the midnight express bound for Regina, to participate in a pulling battle of champions in front of the grandstand next day.

No doubt Sid Johns gasped and remarked that it would be costly to ship two tons of Percherons to Regina at the express rate. But Dan replied that the investment would be returned with dividends and, besides, his board of directors would assume the full cost. Johns agreed and, acting on behalf of his friend McLeod, he issued a challenge for the Lumsden horsemen to present their Belgian team and pull against the Saskatoon Percherons for the thousand dollar prize the Regina Exhibition was prepared to provide.

McLeod accepted the challenge and undertook to have his team ready for the overnight journey. The Saskatoon Percherons were in Regina early the next morning and by noon everybody in the south seemed to know about the unlisted heavyweight championship and everybody wanted to see it. The afternoon grandstand show was revised to accommodate the heavy horses and by 1:30, the Regina turnstiles were clicking to make Elderkin smile.

Determined by the toss of a coin, the Belgian team would pull first. The Belgians had the advantage of weight and home town support. On their first pull, they registered at exactly 3,000 pounds for the full twenty-seven and a half feet, not quite as good as they had done the previous day, but the partisan crowd roared approvingly. It was then for the Saskatoon Percherons to show what they could do and they made precisely the same score as the Belgians. The judging committee called for the second pull and both teams started the dynamometer at 3,100 pounds, but neither succeeded in sustaining the forward thrust for the distance. Inasmuch as the McLeod Percherons had moved the 3,100 pound load for the greater distance, namely eighteen and a half feet, they were declared the winners and the cheque for one thousand dollars was presented on the spot. The Regina fans became silent while the visitors from Saskatoon acted as if they had just won the Grey Cup.

There was still something unsatisfactory about the outcome; although the Saskatoon horses won fairly on the day's performance, the Belgians had made the best pull of the week and were still the world champions. It may have suited Dan Elderkin better than he was admitting and he had something more to say; "There'll be another year," he shouted, "and there'll be another prize of a thousand dollars for the best pull from the Saskatoon and Regina champions. Don't you people forget to come back. It'll be the biggest show you ever saw!"

The two big teams were taken to their respective homes to be conditioned for the test of 1925. No horses or athletes in the country were assured of better feed and care, with just enough pulling to keep them fit. Dan Elderkin made sure that everybody across the West knew the dates for the "Battle of the Heavyweights." Weight was important and both teams were heavier in 1925. The Gibbs Belgians weighed in at two tons even, two hundred pounds more than the Percherons.

The Saskatoon team pulled first and made 3,200 pounds over the required distance, thereby establishing a new world record for Canadian horses. Sid Johns waved another ten dollar bill inviting an additional bet and waited only a few seconds to see it covered. Then the Gibbs team pulled 3,300 pounds—a fresh and most convincing world record.

That was it: the Lumsden Belgians were the 1925 champions and their owners collected the thousand dollar prize. The Gibbs horses pulled again to see if they could better their own record—and sure enough, they did, pulling 3,350 pounds to make a third world record in one day.

Canadian horsemen representing all breeds were pleased with the demonstration that led to an article in the Breeder's Gazette, published in Chicago. The title question was: "Does Canada Have Better Draft Horses Than The United States?" The author offered the opinion that on the strength of the pulling records, Canada did have better horses.

The popularity of the pulling contests rose and fell. When it was presumed that the big and cumbersome dynamometer would not be needed further, it was considerately retired to the Western Development Museum in Saskatoon. But pulling had not lost its appeal. It was still easy to generate enthusiasm, but Canadians had to admit the surpassing records made by American horses in recent times. The report of the National Horse Pulling Contests held at Hillsdale, Michigan, on 11 and 12 October 1949, proved two points: first, a lasting interest on the part of horsemen and, second, the apparent ease with which biological records can be raised and broken. Entries from eleven states and Canada totalled 112 teams battling for five thousand dollars in prizes. Of these, sixty-eight were in the lightweight category, in which a pair of Belgians from Ohio weighing 2,995 pounds won on a pull of 3,400 pounds for twenty-three feet, eight inches.

In the heavyweight class, forty-four teams from nine states and Canada were in the field. The seven heaviest of them had team weights ranging from 3,960 to 4,950 pounds. Two of the teams—one weighing 4,475 and the other 4,950—pulled the equivalent of the world's record of 4,250 pounds. To break the match tie, the required load was set at 4,275 pounds and both teams moved the load but neither took it the required twenty-seven and a half feet. Although both teams had equalled the world record, the match decision was made in favour of the team of sorrel Belgians weighing 4,475. They pulled the load for a distance of twenty feet, eleven inches, while the heavier team, also matched sorrel Belgians, pulled the same load nineteen feet, two inches.[1]

Canadian horsemen shook their heads and muttered, "Incredible!"

From *Heavy Horses: Highlights of their History* (1986)

The Herders and Their Dogs

There appears to be a subtle difference between a sheep herder and a shepherd, even though both terms refer to those individuals who are entrusted with the care of sheep. The word shepherd commands the greater esteem, especially in church and academic circles. Church ministers aspire to be "the shepherds of their congregational flocks," never the "congregational herders." But out in the sheep country, those practical fellows who are normally known as herders and are entrusted with the responsibility for the safety and welfare of a thousand sheep on a remote range for seven days a week, rain or shine, will probably win more friends than the ones who conform to the flute-playing shepherds of song and tradition.

Be that as it may, every sheep owner knows that the herder with good judgment and good conscience in carrying out his duties is likely to deliver heavier and better lambs at weaning time and is the best single key to flock success. The herder, with skill and honesty in his favor, should be granted readily, the right to be eccentric to the point of liking his sheep and loving his dogs more than the humans he sees only occasionally. If he finds preference for the quiet life in which his voice and judgment are the only signs of human intrusion upon silent nature, he should not be discouraged.

As a rangeland herder, he can expect to see his employer for a few minutes or an hour about once a week when the regular delivery of food and supplies is made: traditionally bread and butter, oatmeal, sugar, jam, eggs, bacon, cheese, condensed milk or skim milk powder, prunes, salt for both the herder and the sheep, drinking water and personal mail, if any. Depending upon the herder's interests, the weekly delivery would include a recent copy of a newspaper. Some of the herders liked to read, some did not.

Altogether, it was a simple list of food and other needs and from it the herder would feed his two or three dogs as well as himself. The dogs, by nature, were carnivorous, but most Border Collies, after years of necessity, had adjusted to the same basic foods as consumed by the herders, largely oatmeal porridge with some milk, buttermilk, or powdered skim milk mixed with it. In the light of their working association with sheep and lambs, the taste for blood and flesh was not to be encouraged.

At best it was humble fare served in the no-less humble home on wheels. Stein Gleddie, who ran a sizable flock near Tilley for many years, had constant need for a minimum of three herders, one for each of three bands of a thousand or twelve hundred ewes, and generously shared his recollections of herding and herders. The Gleddie herders were given two weeks of holidays each year and thereby the herder's home for 351 days per year was the caboose or sheep camp wagon on wheels. It was eight feet wide and fourteen feet long and was, along with the big night corral, the point from which the day's operations began at sunrise and the point at which they ended at sundown. For many herders it was the only "Home Sweet Home" to which they laid claim.

The moment after the sheep were corralled for the night, herder and dogs had time for their supper. There being no time-consuming household duties, man and dogs could then go promptly to bed, and generally did. In demonstrating the degree to which household labour saving could be carried, that camp wagon was a model in its own peculiar way. The narrow bed was built against the wall and the tabletop, when not in use at mealtime, was under the bed. There were storage shelves and cupboards on the other wall and the resident could make his bed, set his table for breakfast, find his hat and jacket for the day and fix bread and cheese sandwiches for a noon snack, and do it all without taking a full step in any direction. The little "house" was heated in winter with the help of a coal or wood stove, and bathroom facilities were "over the hill." But herders insisted upon being different and at least one of Gleddie's men was "very neat" in his care of the camp wagon and his bedsheets and pillowcases were said to be "snowy white." That particular herder did not allow his dogs to share his bed.

Herders, wrote Mr. Gleddie, always had a calendar, on which they would carefully mark off each day, because otherwise, if they missed a few days, the error could be perpetuated for the rest of the year. Visitors, as practical jokers were known to "mark off" some additional days, causing a herder to celebrate Christmas up to a week too early. In later years, radio became a great boon to the herders. But some herders grew to like isolation so much that they didn't want to see anybody except the person who delivered the supplies.

It became general opinion that herders used their holiday time for drinking sprees. That was only partially correct, of course. Some of the holidayers celebrated in a boisterous manner but there were just as many who found the holiday period too long and asked to be allowed to return to herding duties as quickly as possible. Now and then the spree was so uproarious that the herder was obliged to answer to the magistrate. There is an undocumented account of a Saskatchewan herder who celebrated handsomely and after being apprehended by the law, became properly repentant. His good fortune was in facing a sympathetic magistrate who might have been a sheep herder at some time. After listening to the story of the herder who had gone berserk on the city street, the understanding official asked, "Have you had enough of city life?" To which the herder replied, "Your Honour, I just want to go back to my sheep and dogs as fast as I can and if they'll forgive me, I promise them I'll never leave them again until three days before my funeral."

One of Mr. Gleddie's men who was employed as a summer herder only, contrived through one misdemeanor or another to be sent to jail each year for the cold months and was satisfied with the arrangement. "The jail," he said seriously, "is warm and has a good library."

The average herder's housekeeping and way of living would never win public applause and that amazing person didn't care. He was satisfied with his lot and would have been ready to fight to protect his lifestyle and safeguard his bosses property against storms, fire and predator dangers. Many stories of herder heroism were told and some deaths recorded. One account of a near tragedy that occurred in a severe snowstorm near Maple Creek in 1899 was rather typical. The sheep drifted with the blast and the falling snow destroyed all visibility. It became impossible to hold the flock and almost impossible to see it. The herder, Blair by name, was ill prepared with clothes but managed to follow and exercise some influence in keeping the sheep together. The storm lasted for three days and three nights and Blair and his dogs persevered, hoping to overtake a deep ravine or other shelter. No shelter was found but as the storm abated, search parties went out to find Blair, his dogs and sheep. They did find them and thanks to what seemed like a miracle, man and dogs were alive and not one sheep was missing.[1]

Nothing in the story of herding can surpass in sentiment the loyalty between the herders and their dogs, generally the little black and white Border Collies. The men proved to be excellent trainers and the dogs became unbelievably proficient and ready to work their hearts out to please their masters and qualify for two bowls of porridge and skim milk powder per day.

"One of our herders," Mr. Gleddie wrote, "always referred to his dogs as 'my boys.' Once when I came out to the camp, on an extremely cold and windy day, neither the herder nor dogs were in sight. But when I got closer, the herder stood up and the dogs came out from under his coat. . . . That herder became especially attached to one of his dogs, Scottie, and was planning to retire and live comfortably with him elsewhere. But one day when I came out to tend camp, the herder was silent and weeping. I guessed right away that something had happened to Scottie. He had been struck by a truck and died. The herder never really got over this blow. He retired earlier than planned and he followed Scottie to the grave soon after."

Most sheep dogs might have preferred to spend their sleeping hours outside, except in extremely cold weather, but many herders wanted to have one or two inside to share his bed.

In recognizing the wonder of good sheep dogs, Stein Gleddie told of one of his ranch neighbors whose herder died unexpectedly and it was several days before the death was discovered. When the truth was known, the owner felt added concern for the welfare and safety of his big flock left for days without the benefit of the herder. He hastened to investigate the state of his flock and found to his surprise that the sheep hadn't scattered and hadn't suffered in any perceivable way. The fact was that the dogs had remained diligently on duty and "looked after the flock." The flock had been brought to the corral at night and back to grazing in the morning. The only unanswered question was: "Who opened and closed the corral gates?" It was finally concluded the the big frame gates were not needed because the dogs had positioned themselves at the corral entrance and acted as a gate.[2]

The herder with whom this writer had the longest association was John Eastman, the shepherd and herder, from 1938 to 1950, at the University of Saskatchewan farm on the outskirts of Saskatoon. The flock with which he worked through all seasons consisted of five to seven hundred head of breeding ewes, predominantly Rambouillet. The flock wintered at the University farm and as soon as lambing and shearing were completed in the spring, it was trailed south to summer range in the sand hills south of Beaver Creek and west of Dundurn.

The ever-faithful John, like many of the best sheepmen of his generation, gained his early experience in the Scottish Highlands. He was no longer a young man. His exact age had never become public information but it didn't matter. The essential point was that he liked his work and would ask for nothing better than being left alone on the range. He loved his dogs, loved the sheep under his care and his "castle on wheels," which, he declared, was the ideal size and shape for a man and two dogs. He wished he could live there all winter and escape the necessity of wintering so close to city people, "that they could hear him talking to himself and saying his prayers."

When a Saskatoon salesman called, hoping to sell an annuity, he began, "Mr. Eastman, do you never think of retiring and living in the city?" The old man answered sharply, "Not on your life. My dogs and I get along better with our Cheviots than we would do with the 'sheep' on your street."

"Well," said the visitor, "I don't know how you can survive the way you live."

"Survive?" said John. "I'm not thinking of dying. The way I have it figured, the good Lord doesn't want me yet and the Devil is so over-crowded with salesmen that he hasn't room for me."

There were hundreds of other good and loyal herders whose names have vanished from the public records. Not all were born to be heroes but they proved that they could be uniformly useful without being homogenous. Some were companionable, some were not. Some chose to be tolerably good housekeepers and about the same number seemed to follow the rule of washing towels every first of July and sweeping camp wagon floors every time there was a change of government in Ottawa. But the silken threads that remained in herder performance were, devotion to a shepherd's duty, a true fondness for the simple way of life and an unselfish feeling for sheep, dogs and all of God's living creatures.

From *Highlights of Sheep History in the Canadian West* (1991)

A Cowboy's Horse

The cutting horse is a highly trained specialist—like a piano tuner or goalkeeper in human society—and often a high-priced one. A Texas horse seen in Western Canadian cutting competitions in 1961 was said to have been bought as a four-year-old for fifty thousand dollars.

Most showyard contestants have been Quarter Horses, simply because animals of that breed seem to possess a special aptitude for western saddles and stock work, like Border Collies for sheep herding, and Cocker Spaniels for flushing game birds. The fact is that cutting horses can be of any breed or any colour. Morgans, Arabians, Thoroughbreds, Palominos, Appaloosas and horses of unknown ancestry have appeared as professionals in the cow country art of cutting. The cutting horse, it should be noted, is an individual more than a breed. In this instance, it is performance and that alone which counts.

Somebody said cutting horses are "born rather than made." The statement is only partly correct. No doubt the intelligence and disposition necessary for top performance are present as inherited characteristics; likewise, heredity will have something to do in determining the desired muscling, nimble feet and that all-important quality known as "cow sense."

But regardless of aptitude, no horse gains distinction without long and intensive training. Teaching begins lightly at about two years of age, calling for a patient rider and repetitious practise in running, stopping, turning quickly and pivoting.

The colt must be taught to neck-rein at a light touch, slide hind feet into position to stop suddenly and change leads appropriately at the gallop. In running, a horse leads naturally with the foreleg on the inside of the circle and any animal failing to change leads with change of direction is in danger of being caught off balance with all the dire consequences. Correct lead is important in all saddle horses but especially so in cutting horses where footwork counts for much.

The horse in training must learn to interpret the feelings of pressure from the rider's legs. In competitions, horses work without any perceptible guidance from riders—sometimes even without bridles or hackamores. At best, a horse doesn't reach a state of "finish" for two or more years. And the animal is not "finished" until able to work amid the glare and noise of a strange arena as well as in the quietness of home surroundings. The fact is that most horses selected for training never reach competition calibre, while those which do succeed become highly valuable.

The competitive test consists of taking one protesting steer or heifer at a time from the herd in the arena and effectively blocking its eager attempts to return. Horse and rider enter the herd quietly and, having selected the animal to be cut out, the horse is turned to move it away from the other cattle. Then, when the segregated critter finds itself isolated from herd-mates and makes a frantic attempt to return, the good cutting horse, with eyes fixed firmly upon the cattle victim, unwinds like lightning to frustrate every bovine plunge to achieve its purpose. It can be beautiful to watch as cutting horse displays the foot action of a tap-dancer, turning, twisting, leaning, blocking and ever in balance. The spectator will find it easy to agree that here is the finest of all examples of teamwork between a horse and its rider. And, if one may judge, the trained horses seem to enjoy the sport, enjoy outguessing the cattle against which they find themselves pitted.

Cutting horse competitions became popular in the 1940s and 1950s. In 1954 the Canadian Cutting Horse Association was formed and the increasing number of shows and entries after that date gave evidence of the rising interest. In 1961 there were fifty-five Canadian contests with sixteen thousand dollars offered in prizes. Western Canada, by that latter year, was said to have more top cutting horses than anywhere outside of the Western States.

But it would be wrong to convey any idea of all cutting horses being frequenters of the showring. Horses of the kind were working expertly on cattle ranches long before competitive cutting was introduced. Like industrious back-country cowboys who never indulged in yodelling or glamorously coloured shirts. they were indispensible at roundup time or whenever cattle were to be worked. Most of them lived and died on the job without ever seeing the inside of an arena or exhibition enclosure. But, worth their weight in mink coats to a rancher, those great horses of the range deserved the highest praise.

Indeed, thousands of those "skilled workers" served faithfully without ever becoming known beyond the home range. The first Canadian horse to be brought into the national or international limelight was a gelding called Keeno and he was nineteen years old—well beyond a normal span of life—before he left range routine on the Streeter Ranch at Stavely, Alberta, to indulge in the more frivolous activities of a public contest. The old horse was, in some ways, like a rancher who, after reaching retiring age, decided to travel and take part in the youthful pastimes he had missed in earlier and busier years. It appeared as a reckless adventure but the old horse brought one surprise after another and was finally hailed as the greatest cutting performer discovered in the Canadian Cattle Kingdom.

How was Keeno bred? The sire of the talented gelding, now a memory, was a Thoroughbred standing at Henry Sharples' ranch west of Claresholm. On the maternal side was Blackfoot Indian horse stock, mostly Mustang. It made for a fascinating pedigree: on one side an old English breed with speed and quality, and on the other, a long-time North American strain demonstrating the law of "Survival of the Fittest."

Keeno was foaled in 1927 and didn't attract any particular attention. Along with other Streeter Ranch horses of his generation, he was broken to saddle at three years of age although he received no special training. And until Keeno was in his twentieth year, nobody except the two Streeter brothers had ever thrown a leg over his well-muscled back.

From the time of breaking, however, Allie Streeter suspected he had a "one-in-a-million" horse; but he was more concerned about day-to-day work on the foothills cattle ranch than in seeking showring glories.

There was nothing phenomenal about Keeno's speed, nor about his beauty. But his sagacity and determination in working cattle set him apart. Always he did a big share in the thinking when cattle were being handled. Allie Streeter said, and his technique was nigh faultless. "He was too smart for critters thinking they could cut back on him."

And at the age of nineteen, instead of being retired, Keeno went to the shows. The Nanton Horse Show of 1946 was the farthest the old fellow had ever been from the home ranch. Understandably, a horse of nineteen years would be "set in his ways," and he didn't like the fair. But even while registering his dislike for the strange surroundings, he won both stock horse class and cutting contest against the best in the foothills.

Streeter's friends were impressed and one said: "That horse is good enough for Denver. Why not take him there for the big show?"

But Allie Streeter wasn't convinced that a rising twenty-year-old should be taken anywhere except back to the ranch. The idea of hauling the ancient horse to far-away Colorado was quickly dispelled. Along in December, however, Streeter met up with W.A. Crawford-Frost of Hereford fame and was persuaded to make the bold adventure, take Keeno to what was admittedly one of the strongest competitions in the world. The formal entry was transmitted to Denver by telegram and on the day after New Year's, 1947. Allie Streeter and Hal Sears loaded the horse in a trailer behind the former's car and headed southward.

Keeno was on wheels for the first time in his long life and didn't like it, didn't like leaving the grassy hills he knew so well and heading into the unknown at forty miles an hour. He was nervous, worried and annoyed. But after days of travel, men and horse arrived at Denver, forty-eight hours before the contests were scheduled to start on 9 January.

First there was the elimination contest, with twenty-seven contestants—twenty-seven of the best stock horses on the continent and most of them experienced under the distracting lights of a showring. Eliminations reduced the field to eighteen and Streeter and Keeno were "still in." So much, so good. For that two-minute period during which the Alberta horse was officially under the observation of judges. Keeno managed to hide his uneasiness about the strange and gaudy surroundings and worked well—extremely well for a newcomer to the big city. The old horse had probably worked more cattle than any two other horses at the show but never was he exposed to so many hand-clapping spectators and every time the crowd cheered, Keeno naturally wondered what it was about and momentarily his mind was off his work.

In the next competitive round, contestants were reduced to twelve, then to eight. The Alberta horse and cowboy were still in the race and when the winners were finally determined, Keeno was in seventh place. Under the circumstances, it was seen as one of the most notable triumphs in the history of those sturdy little horses which carry stock saddles.

And when Keeno and Allie Streeter arrived back at Nanton, ranchers, farmers and town people united at a banquet to celebrate the success and do honour to a cowboy and his horse. A presentation was made and with the gift went an inscription: "To Allie Streeter of the Nanton–Stavely district for the excellent showing made by him and his horse, Keeno, In the stock cutting contest at Denver, Colorado, USA, 9 January 1947, against the best on the continent. Nanton Agricultural Society and Nanton and District Board of Trade."

Back home on the range, Keeno was ready to forget the bright lights and high living; there was work to do and he would settle down to it as though he had never been away. At the time of the horse's twentieth birthday, Allie Streeter could say: "He's as sound as a bullet and still likes to buck a little when you first get on him."

The adventure to Denver had added glamour to Keeno's life but he was first, last and always a cowboy's working horse, reliable, skilful and tireless—like thousands of those faithful and indispensible animals which assist in the cattle industry and rarely leave the home ranges.

From *Hoofprints and Hitchingposts* (1964), republished in 2002 as *Our Equine Friends: Stories of Horses in History*

Personal Glimpses

Water Pleasure: A Raft on the South Saskatchewan

Some time ago I had the opportunity to talk to a former homesteader who had filed on a plot of land in the grasslands of southwestern Saskatchewan. In this arid region legend had it that frogs died without ever having learned to swim. A man of cheerful disposition, the homesteader still held on to many happy memories of water recreation during the time he spent in the region. The foremost of these was that of his annual spring shower baths, which he said consisted of "one or two sprinkling cans of warm, soft water hung on a harness hook in the horse stable."

If he liked it that much, I asked, why didn't he repeat it more often? "Because," he explained, "there wasn't any more soft water to spare." He may have been exaggerating, but probably not, Like many of his generation, he learned to swim in a Canadian Pacific Railway ditch. Some learned very well, especially those who came under the coaching influence of instructors like Joe Griffiths, trainer extraordinaire and Prince of Gentlemen who was for many years the director of physical education at the University of Saskatchewan. "Making swimmers out of prairie kids," he said, "was my lifetime goal."

Young prairie people of the frontier years were, for one reason or another, likely to terminate plans for high school studies. The distances between farm houses and high school facilities were, of course, a principal reason. But this was a temporary situation and many of the drop-outs heard the call to return to schools after they began offering gymnasiums, playing fields and even access to indoor swimming facilities. As the years advanced, new schools were built with their own pools. But if Joe

Griffiths had been a spectator of this change, he probably would have repeated his conviction: some of the best swimmers Canada had ever sent to international competitions were kids who had learned to dog-paddle in a railroad ditch in the Palliser Triangle.

Even in the 1930s, when drought and economic depression were tightening their cruel grip on much of the world, when the prairies became a dust bowl and wheat prices collapsed, when university employees who usually took summer holidays gave them up, water recreation was still available for little or no cost. One late August evening in 1931, Alister Ewen, my new colleague at the University of Saskatchewan, and I had an idea for an inexpensive holiday. It occurred to us as we were walking to our living quarters across the broad South Saskatchewan River. Why not take a rafting trip down the South Saskatchewan River just like in the days of the fur trade? Henry David Thoreau, who said "the man is the richest whose pleasures are the cheapest," would have nodded his approval of the plan. Al Ewen quickly warmed to the idea even though he didn't know exactly what to expect from the proposed log raft expedition. A graduate of the University of Edinburgh, he was a versatile athlete, a strong swimmer and a former heavyweight boxing champion of the Scottish universities. He knew nothing about the Saskatchewan River but would be an excellent partner on the journey.

Plans were completed in the half hour it took to walk home that summer evening, and everything fell into place like a well-oiled army manoeuvre. I happened to know somebody in the service of the Saskatchewan Telephone Company and was sure I could buy three or four discarded telephone poles at a bargain price and have them delivered early on the same day. After these sixty-centimetre-thick poles were delivered to a Saskatoon river bank and cut in half, the budding raft mariners had eight raft poles three-and-a-half metres in length. Our material investment had been nominal: a dollar each for the four ageing poles with an additional dollar spent on rope for lashing them together. The assembled raft weighed close to three-quarters of a ton.

Thankfully, the raft, cumbersome on shore, became agreeably submissive once it was eased into the water. We would later come to understand how we had overestimated the stability of our raft and underestimated the power of the river.

Mounted with a packing-box shelter, the raft was pushed into midstream at 3:30 PM on launching day, leaving behind on the shore some twenty envious kids and one snarky fellow who wanted to know how the merry adventurers were going to find their way back to the city.

The first full night on the river had an almost divine peacefulness about it. The only person in sight when the travellers awakened was a farmer who had driven his horses to the river to drink. Eager to know how far the raft had travelled during the night, Al asked him how far it was to Saskatoon. "Heck man, you've passed Saskatoon," the farmer replied. "You'll never get there now."

The second night on the water was more alarming. First there came a storm that seemed to be trying to blow the travellers back to Saskatoon. Following a lull, another storm hit, this time accompanied by lightning. The drenched travellers found some solace in the knowledge that the safest place to be in a lightning storm might well be on a raft in the middle of a river.

For the intrepid rafters of August 1931, there were new experiences and water adventures at every bend in the river. A heavy raft riding peacefully on quiet water is not likely to make trouble. On the other hand, the same raft with a great weight of angry water behind it can easily perform an aerial flip. Disaster struck near Fenton Ferry just minutes after we had bought our mid-journey groceries. The crowning glory was a four-pound can of peach jam that was supposed to furnish a special meal-time treat for the next few days. The treacherous water ahead seemed innocuous enough to two mariners who now thought themselves thoroughly seasoned. After all, the loaded raft represented almost a full ton of weight and promised stability. MacEwan, with his seven-foot staff, was at the front and would be the first to sense danger and change navigational orders accordingly if necessary. It was the job of the man at the front to decide which side of an exposed rock appeared to be the safest for the raft.

A threatening rock was indeed sighted, but merely sighting it was to no avail. As the roar of water about the rock grew more deafening, it became obvious that it would be impossible for us to change course. All self-assurance about the stability of the heavy raft evaporated like a spray of hot water in the desert.

It isn't difficult to explain what happened. Locked in the rush of the current, the front of the raft struck the protruding rock like a battering ram, slid up one side of it and tilted, sending everything aboard cascading into the turbulent waters; blankets, clothing and the four-pound can of peach jam hit the water along with the hapless adventurers. Luckily, when we resurfaced we caught the two lower corners of the upended raft. We clung to it dangerously until we could find a way of shifting the raft slightly, creating a new imbalance sufficient to cause it to right itself and fall flat again. Through sheer determination, we succeeded in doing so and then retrieved as much of the inadvertent jetsam as possible. Sadly, the four-pound can of jam had sunk like a stone to become a treasure lodged forever beneath the current. To this day, this author can remember exactly where the accident took place and confidently predicts that, given favourable circumstances, he could still retrieve the jam and enjoy the meal he never had on that fateful day in 1931.

Over the course of six days we had drifted 160 kilometres down the broad river. The entry in this author's diary following the grand adventure read: "It was a great holiday, simple, thrilling and cheap. The entire outing, including the cost of the raft and equipment, food, return train fare, and a few incidentals, cost the travellers just twelve dollars each."

As for the historic South Saskatchewan, it remains as beautiful and capricious as ever. Al Ewen and I intended, at one time, to return to study the history of the forks area of the North and South Saskatchewan Rivers in greater detail. Sadly, fate and circumstance intervened and a second trip was never undertaken. Nevertheless, we were able to declare publicly that, in spite of a few errors and hazards, the 1931 log raft expedition on the South Saskatchewan River was the most memorable water holiday of our lives. If Henry David Thoreau had been present, he probably would have said with a smile, "What did I tell you?"

From *Watershed: Reflections on Water* (2000)

Interview with J. W. Grant MacEwan
8 August 1983
MAX FORAN

You know that my background was markedly orthodox. My parents, and particularly my mother, were Scottish Presbyterians, which meant that you really kept the Sabbath; everything that had to be done ceased on Saturday night. If you were going to whistle on Sunday, you whistled a sacred tune. If shoes happened to be dirty, they could wait 'til Monday. We milked the cows and fed the horses, but we didn't do anything that we could escape from doing on that day. My mother would take the kids to church. My father didn't necessarily accompany us very often. He was somewhat more of a free thinker. He was a man of action. He saw more to criticize in the modern church than mother or any of us did. I think he was ahead in that respect. Yet he had his philosophy and I inherited more of it than for a long time in my life, I realized.

One of Dad's purposes in life was to leave his farm better than he found it. That meant that the fences had to be kept up, and the soil kept free from weeds and that the fertility be maintained. I think that is not very different from the purpose of the young Grecians coming up to citizenship more than two thousand years ago. They committed themselves to a program of work and athletics, and they took an oath to leave Athens better than they found it. It was for them to figure out how that was to be done. I think today, that most of our people—I don't say this unkindly—feel that the greatest achievement in life is to take as much as possible out of the land and convert it into money. If the resources are poorer and their bank account is richer , then they are satisfied. But that is not leaving Athens or Canada or Alberta better than we found it. I think my father left his farm better than he found for the next people who came along.

If you want my philosophy in a word, and I guess I can assess it myself, I'm a conservationist. The concept of conservation that I have and which has come to mean a great deal to me, took the place in my thinking of the conventional church-going philosophy of my youth. It was commonplace thinking in those years that if you believed in the Lord Jesus Christ, nothing else mattered. You could exploit the soil; you could overwork your horses. You might get away with it. I tended to accept this philosophy. I was a good church man for a time and as long as my mother was alive, I think she was very happy to think that I took up the collection in Knox Church, did some ushering and was a member of the board. It took up considerable time as I obediently followed the teachings of my mother's family. I had one of the greatest mothers in the world, and today I wouldn't change anything. But it wasn't for me to remain in that line of thinking.

It was when I left Saskatoon that a major change occurred. I had been anticipating it, but I was so involved with the conventional church that it wasn't easy just to walk away. But when I left Saskatoon, I decided that, for a period of time anyway, I was not going to be a regular church attendant. I was going to think this thing over. I did not return to the church, but I needed to find something else to take its place. It was after 1946 that I developed a new concept of purpose.

I always felt that everyone should have a purpose—whether it was to make a million dollars or to be the best farmer in the community or to have the best horses on the road—everybody should have a purpose, and in some way most people do. It can be selfish or it can be noble. It can be something with a good moral foundation. At that time I was looking for a more satisfying link with my Maker. It didn't happen overnight, but took shape gradually. I came to the conclusion that I could not serve my God better in anything than in conservation; taking care of His garden, His household, His world of nature, His resources, His soil, His trees, His water, His air, His iron ore and so on. Of course this new line of thinking played a degree of havoc with the conventional concept of prayer and the like. My mother was a praying person and raised me to be the same. There was never a break in that and there won't be. But, instead of saying that there is a God of love who demands certain things from His children, I began to determine how I could serve Him in a sensible way.

What has He got to tell me that He would not tell any other person, whether they were raised in the church or not? I was raised in the church, but I guess that a majority of the world's people, at that time, were not raised in the church. I couldn't conceive of a great overriding power that would give me an advantage. The Almighty didn't make any attempt to create all people Presbyterians. He didn't create them with denominational views. There are a thousand denominations with strong convictions. Why should I have an advantage in working out a moral concept or purpose just because I was born within a denominational group?

Basic to all living things is instinct. My instinct and I think, human instinct, points to a higher power—call Him a Great Spirit if you're an Indian, or call Him God if you belong to some other group. I think there is something in humans, if they allow it expression, which is akin to your foal born in the snow three years ago and which was the most helpless thing that ever tried to stand up. But it did, and furthermore, something told that helpless creature where to find some milk. I think there are pointers in my life. Instinct would be one of my working materials— my working resources. Second would be conscience. I think I was born with a conscience. I think everybody is, but that is not to say that it is always given an opportunity to express itself. I think it's there and I think it should be cultivated. Third, there is reason. It may not always seem like very good reason, but it's mine and I inherited it. And with instinct, conscience and a sense of reasoning, I can establish a contact with something bigger than myself.

If I had never heard of doctrines, I think I could have satisfied myself that I was serving a spiritual purpose by looking after the soil, by looking after trees and birds and animals and fellow humans, and my own body, of course. This is part of the God-given resource. So, over the years this concept took form, and it did more for me by far than anything that happened to me when I was going to church. I went to church in a perfunctory sort of way and just like the people around me, we stood at the right moment, we sang hymns with gusto and we put twenty-five or ten cents on the plate when it came around and then went home and forgot about the purpose of it all. People must have purpose. I have a completely different purpose to my mother, for example. But it satisfies me and I think it has given me a better spiritual base. I *think* I am ready to be a good steward in His household.

From *Grant MacEwan's Journals* (1986)

Endnotes

Introduction

[1] Most of the biographical information contained in this Introduction draws on the two biographies of MacEwan published to date and biographical material contained in *Grant MacEwan's Journals*, all listed in the bibliography (p 238). Other materials are footnoted if the source is not obvious. A somewhat different version of this article, fully footnoted, appeared in *Grant MacEwan: A Tribute*, the special edition of *Alberta History*, 49.4 (Autumn 2001).

[2] D.W. "Tracing the Course of Western Agriculture," *Saskatoon Star-Phoenix*, 22 November 1952.

[3] See for instance the reviews in the *Toronto Star*, 11 October 1952; *Montreal Star*, 13 December 1952; *Calgary Herald*, 3 January 1953; *Winnipeg Free Press*, 19 September 1953. The review in the *Toronto Globe and Mail*, 20 December 1952, is less enthusiastic. Copies of the reviews can be found in the Grant MacEwan fonds, University of Calgary, Special Collections/ Archives, Acc. No. 392/86.14, 2.54.

[4] Hilda Neatby, "Review of *Between the Red and the Rockies*" by Grant MacEwan," *American Historical Review*, 58.3 (April 1953).

[5] Grant MacEwan to B.F. Neary, President, Thomas Nelson and Sons, Toronto, dated 605 Maclean Building, Calgary, 22 January 1957; Grant sent a previous letter to Mr. Neary on 22 December 1956. Grant MacEwan fonds, University of Calgary Library, Special Collections/Archives, Acc. No. 444/89.06, 1.23. References to the rejections by the Toronto publishers also appear in this file.

[6] "Alberta: The Bad Old Days," *Time*, 23 December 1957.

[7] C.W.M., "Life of Bob Edwards Scholarly, Exhaustive," *Albertan*, 7 December 1957.

[8] "Calgary Rich in History," *Calgary Herald*, 25 May 1957.

[9] Grant MacEwan quoted in Bob Harvey, "Lieutenant-governor is hooked on writing—he just can't stop," *Edmonton Journal*, 28 March 1969.

[10] "MacEwan to teach history at U of C," *Calgary Herald*, 25 July 1974.

[11] The research files for one of Grant's books, *Frederick Haultain* (1985), three thick files, are held in the Grant MacEwan fonds, University of Calgary Special Collections/Archives, Acc. No. 420/88.01, 3.62, 3.63, 3.64.

[12] Interesting academic reviews of Grant's later books include the two cited here:

> Gary Pennanen, "Review of *Sitting Bull: The Years in Canada* by Grant MacEwan," *Canadian Historical Review*, 56 (1975); and

> John Herd Thompson, "Review of *Charles Noble: Guardian of the Soil* by Grant MacEwan," *Canadian Historical Review*, 65 (1984).

Other valuable commentaries include:

> R. Douglas Francis, "Review of *The Best of Grant MacEwan*, edited by R.H. Macdonald," *Prairie Forum*, 8 (1983).

> David C. Jones, "Review of *Charles Noble* by Grant MacEwan," *Prairie Forum*, 10 (1985).

> David Hall, "Review of *Frederick Haultain: Frontier Statesman of the Canadian Northwest* by Grant MacEwan," *Canadian Historical Review*, 67 (1987).

> R. Bruce Sheppard, "Review of *Heavy Horses: Highlights of Their History* by Grant MacEwan," *Prairie Forum*, 12 (1987).

[13] Quoted in Bradley Bird, "Grant MacEwan takes run at fictionalized history," *Winnipeg Free Press*, 6 October 1984.

[14] David Kilgour tells this story in, "Chapter Ten: Grant MacEwan, Ongoing Legend," in *Uneasy Patriots. Western Canadians in Confederation* (Edmonton: Lone Pine, 1988).

[15] John W. Berger, "What it's like to be Mayor of Calgary," *Senior's World*, January, 1995.

[16] Quoted in the press release of the Writers Guild of Alberta, issued after the Alberta Book Awards Gala in Calgary, 6 May 2000.

Anthony Henday

[1] Arthur S. Morton, *A History of the Canadian West to 1870–71* (Toronto: University of Toronto Press, 1973).

[2] Ibid.

Laidlaw's Pigs

[1] William Laidlaw, letter to Lord Selkirk, 22 July 1818. Selkirk Papers, National Archives of Canada.

Maski-pitoon

[1] *Regina Leader*, 10 December 1885.

Storms without Shelter

[1] James Walker, "The Coming of the NWMP, 1874," speech to the Alberta Military Institute, 14 March 1924, 971-23005ALB, Calgary Public Library, Main Branch.

[2] Fred Bagley, "Diary of North West Mounted Police Trumpeter, 1874–84," M44A.BI46A, Glenbow Archives, Calgary.

[3] James Walker, no title, *Scarlet and Gold,* (Vancouver: RNWMP Veterans' Association), December 1919.

[4] Ibid.

[5] E.H. Maunsell, "The Great Trek of '74," *Scarlet and Gold,* Diamond Jubilee Edition (no date).

[6] George French, *Commissioner's Report for 1874* (Department of Justice, January, 1875).

[7] James Walker, "The Coming of the NWMP."

[8] Ibid.

[9] George French, *Commissioner's Report for 1874.*

The Inglorious Return

[1] *Saskatchewan Herald*, 24 March 1879.

[2] Zachary MacCaulay Hamilton and Marie Albina Hamilton, *These are the Prairies*, Regina: School Aids and Textbook Pub. Co., 1948.

[3] Adrien Chabot, *History of Willow-Bunch, 1920–1970*, Winnipeg: Canadian Publishers, 1970.

[4] John Peter Turner, *The North-West Mounted Police 1873–1893*, Ottawa: King's Printer, 1950, vol. 1.

[5] *Fort Benton (Montana) Weekly Record*, 11 August 1881.

[6] *Benton River Press*, 24 August 1881.

The Great Clarence

[1] Clay, John, *My Recollections of Ontario*, Private printing, Chicago, 1918.

[2] *Farmer's Advocate*, London, 1 February 1883.

[3] Clay, John, *Recollections.*

[4] *Canadian Live Stock Journal*, Hamilton, January, 1885.

Trader Burns

[1] Abstract of Titles, Land Titles Office, Neepawa, 3 August 1977.

[2] Pax Crawley, whose father had farmed two miles north of the Burns farm, corroborated this account in a personal letter, 10 November 1957.

[3] *Minnedosa Tribune*, 25 September 1885.

[4] Ibid., 11 September 1885.

[5] Ibid., 12 March 1886.

[6] Ibid., 6 August 1885.

Meet Sir Frederick

[1] Sir James Barrie, "Courage," from the Rectorial Address at St. Andrews University, 13 May 1922 (London: Hodder and Stoughton, 1922). Quoted by Sir Frederick at the University of Saskatchewan Convocation, 12 May 1934.

[2] James Clinkskill, manuscript presented to the author.

Bedson's Buffalo

[1] *Manitoba Daily Free Press*, 19 April 1889.

[2] Ibid, 18 December 1888.

[3] *Grand Forks Plaindealer*, as copied by the *Manitoba Daily Free Press*, 18 December 1888.

[4] *Manitoba Daily Free Press*, 12 September 1890.

The Alberta Hotel

[1] *Calgary Eye Opener*, 12 May 1919

[2] *Calgary Herald*, 10 February 1905

Ernest Cashel

[1] *Calgary Herald*, 24 December 1889.

[2] Ibid., 27 October 1903.

[3] Superintendent G.E. Sanders, *Report of the North West Mounted Police, 1904* (Ottawa: King's Printer, 1904).

[4] Ibid.

[5] *Calgary Herald*, 2 February 1904.

[6] *Calgary Eye Opener*, 8 March 1913.

"To Hell With Ottawa"

[1] House of Commons Debates, 15 April 1910.

[2] *Edmonton Bulletin*, 6 July 1910.

[3] *Grain Growers' Guide*, 8 November 1911.

[4] Ibid, 11 January 1911.

[5] Ibid, 18 January 1911.

[6] Ibid, 25 January 1911.

Education, Experiment and an Unlikely Champion

[1] Seager Wheeler's homestead beside the South Saskatchewan River was eighteen miles notheast of Saskatoon. After proving up that homestead, he bought the Rosthern farm from the CPR for three dollars an acre.

Historic Harvest Scenes at the Cameron, 1920

[1] *Lethbridge Herald*, 19 August 1920.

[2] Ibid., 2 August 1920.

[3] *Calgary Herald*, 19 August 1920.

[4] Ibid.

[5] Robert Gratz, interview conducted by O.S. Longman, 30 July 1957, Charles Noble Files, Glenbow-Alberta Archives.

[6] Lillian Noble, "The Noble Story," Nobleford and Monarch History Book Club, *Sons of Wind and Soil* (Calgary: D.W. Friesen and Son, Ltd., 1976).

[7] *Lethbridge Herald*, 16 September 1920.

Stampeding on the Streets

[1] Editorial, *Calgary Herald*, 13 July 1923.

[2] Ibid.

[3] Ibid, 12 July 1923.

[4] Ibid, 13 July 1923.

[5] Ibid, 5 July 1926.

[6] Ibid, 13 July 1938.

Horse Race Down the Mountainside

[1] *Calgary Herald*, 18 October 1957.

The Pulling Contests

[1] H.F. Moxley, "Report of the National Horse Pulling Contest," *Percheron News*, January 1950.

The Herders and Their Dogs

[1] *Nor'-West Farmer*, Winnipeg, 5 June 1899.

[2] Gleddie, Stein, *When Grass Was Free*, privately printed and circulated manuscript, September, 1988.

Bibliography

Books by Grant MacEwan

1) *The Science and Practice of Canadian Animal Husbandry* (with A.H. Ewen). Toronto: Thomas Nelson & Sons, 1936. Revised 1945, 1952.

2) *General Agriculture* (with A.H. Ewen). Toronto: Thomas Nelson & Sons, 1939.

3) *Breeds of Farm Live-Stock in Canada.* Toronto: Thomas Nelson & Sons, 1941.

4) *Feeding Farm Animals.* Toronto: Thomas Nelson & Sons, 1945.

5) *The Sodbusters.* Toronto: Thomas Nelson & Sons, 1948, Second edition, Calgary: Fifth House, 2000.

6) *Agriculture on Parade: The Story of the Fairs and Exhibitions of Western Canada.* Toronto: Thomas Nelson & Sons, 1950.

7) *Between the Red and the Rockies.* Toronto: University of Toronto Press, 1952.

8) *Eye Opener Bob: The Story of Bob Edwards.* Edmonton: Institute of Applied Art, 1957. Second edition, Saskatoon: Western Producer Prairie Books, 1974.

9) *Fifty Mighty Men.* Saskatoon: Western Producer Prairie Books, 1958. Second edition, 1985. Third edition, Vancouver: Greystone Books, 1995.

10) *Calgary Cavalcade: From Fort to Fortune.* Edmonton: Institute of Applied Art, 1958. Revised edition, Saskatoon: Western Producer Prairie Books, 1975.

11) *John Ware's Cow Country.* Edmonton: Institute of Applied Art, 1960. Second edition, Saskatoon: Western Producer Prairie Books, 1973. Third edition, Vancouver: Greystone Books, 1995.

12) *Blazing the Old Cattle Trail.* Saskatoon: Western Producer Prairie Books, 1962. Second edition, Calgary: Fifth House, 2000.

13) *Hoofprints and Hitchingposts.* Saskatoon: Western Producer Prairie Books, 1964. Second edition, as *Our Equine Friends: Stories of Horses in History,* Calgary, Fifth House, 2002.

14) *Poking into Politics.* Edmonton: Institute of Applied Art, 1966.

15) *Entrusted to My Care.* Saskatoon: Western Producer Prairie Books, 1966. Revised edition, 1986.

16) *West to the Sea* (with Max Foran). Toronto: McGraw-Hill Ryerson, 1968.

(Simultaneously released in paperback as *A Short History of Western Canada*)

17) *Tatanga Mani: Walking Buffalo of the Stonies*. Edmonton: Hurtig, 1969.

18) *Harvest of Bread*. Saskatoon: Western Producer Prairie Books, 1969.

19) *Power for Prairie Plows*. Saskatoon: Western Producer Prairie Books, 1971.

20) *Portraits from the Plains*. Toronto: McGraw-Hill Ryerson, 1971.

21) *Sitting Bull: The Years in Canada*. Edmonton: Hurtig, 1972.

22) *This is Calgary* (photographs by Toby Rankin). Calgary: Calgary Real Estate Board Co-operative, 1973.

23) *The Battle for the Bay: The Story of the Hudson Bay Railroad*. Saskatoon: Western Producer Prairie Books, 1975.

24) *And Mighty Women Too: Stories of Notable Western Canadian Women*. Saskatoon: Western Producer Prairie Books, 1975. Second edition, as *Mighty Women*, Vancouver: Greystone Books, 1995.

25) *Memory Meadows: Horse Stories from Canada's Past*. Saskatoon: Western Producer Prairie Books, 1977. Revised edition, 1985. Third edition, Vancouver: Greystone Books, 1997.

26) *Cornerstone Colony: Selkirk's Contribution to the Canadian West*. Saskatoon: Western Producer Prairie Books, 1977.

27) *The Rhyming Horseman of the Qu'Appelle: Captain Stanley Harrison*. Saskatoon: Western Producer Prairie Books, 1978.

28) *Pat Burns: Cattle King*. Saskatoon: Western Producer Prairie Books, 1979.

29) *Grant MacEwan's Illustrated History of Western Canadian Agriculture*. Saskatoon: Western Producer Prairie Books, 1980.

30) *Métis Makers of History*. Saskatoon: Western Producer Prairie Books, 1981.

31) *Alberta Landscapes* (photographs by Rusty Macdonald). Saskatoon: Western Producer Prairie Books, 1982.

32) *The Best of Grant MacEwan* (ed. by Rusty Macdonald). Saskatoon: Western Producer Prairie Books, 1982.

33) *Highlights of Shorthorn History*. Calgary: Alberta Shorthorn Association, 1982.

34) *Charles Noble: Guardian of the Soil*. Saskatoon: Western Producer Prairie Books, 1983.

35) *Wildhorse Jack: The Legend of Jack Morton*. Saskatoon: Western Producer Prairie Books, 1983.

36) *Marie Anne: The Frontier Adventures of Marie Anne Lagimodière*. Saskatoon: Western Producer Prairie Books, 1984.

37) *100 Years of Smoke, Sweat & Tears*. Calgary: Calgary Firefighters Association, 1984.

38) *French in the West/Les Franco-Canadiens dans l'Ouest*. Saint-Boniface: Éditions des Plaines, 1984.

39) *Frederick Haultain: Frontier Statesman of the Canadian West*. Saskatoon:
Western Producer Prairie Books, 1985.

40) *Grant MacEwan's Journals* (ed. by Max Foran). Edmonton: Lone Pine, 1986.

41) *Heavy Horses: Highlights of their History*. Saskatoon: Western Producer
Prairie Books, 1986. Second edition, Whitewater, WI: Heart Prairie
Press, 1991. Third edition, as *Heavy Horses: An Illustrated History of the
Draft Horse*, Calgary: Fifth House, 2001.

42) *He Left Them Laughing When He Said Good-bye: The Life and Times of
Frontier Lawyer Paddy Nolan*. Saskatoon: Western Producer Prairie
Books, 1987.

43) *Colonel James Walker: Man of the Western Frontier*. Saskatoon: Western
Producer Prairie Books, 1989.

44) *Grant MacEwan's West: Sketches From the Past*. Saskatoon: Western Producer
Prairie Books, 1990.

45) *Highlights of Sheep History in the Canadian West*. Calgary: Alberta Sheep and
Wool Commission, 1991.

46) *Coyote Music and Other Humorous Tales of the Early West*. Calgary: Rocky
Mountain Books, 1993.

47) *Buffalo: Sacred and Sacrificed*. Edmonton: Alberta Sport, Recreation, Parks
and Wildlife Foundation, 1995.

48) *Watershed: Reflections on Water*. Edmonton: NeWest, 2000.

49) *A Century of Grant MacEwan: Selected Writings*. Calgary: Brindle & Glass,
2002.

Biographies of Grant MacEwan

Grant MacEwan: No Ordinary Man, by Rusty MacDonald. Saskatoon: Western
Producer Prairie Books, 1978.

Everyone's Grandfather: The Life and Times of Grant MacEwan, by Donna Von
Hauff. Edmonton: Grant MacEwan College/Quon Editions, 1994.

Blazing the Old Cattle Trail

Western Canada has a long history of cattle drives. In *Blazing the Old Cattle Trail*, historian Grant MacEwan has brought together an entertaining collection of history and tales from these trips. Originally published in 1962, this classic book recounts many stories starting with the first cow and steer to arrive in Manitoba to later, more challenging trips through the Rocky Mountains into British Columbia.

Filled with details about the cowboys, thieves, cattle, and even the odd sheep who braved Canada's western trails, *Blazing the Old Cattle Trail* preserves the spirit of the Old West for contemporary readers.

Fifth House Publishers
ISBN 1-894004-63-9 • $14.95 PB
http://www.fitzhenry.ca/fifthhouse.htm

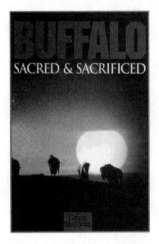

Buffalo: Sacred and Sacrificed

Buffalo: Sacred and Sacrificed is the remarkable account of where the buffalo once roamed—and its comeback from the brink of extinction. It's a story too good to miss.

Federation of Alberta Naturalists
11759 Groat Road
Edmonton, Alberta   T5M 3K6
Phone: 780-427-8124
E-mail: info@fanweb.ca

The book is also available from Red Deer Press and many book stores in Western Canada.

Alberta Sport, Recreation, Parks and Wildlife Foundation
ISBN 0-9699355-0-1 • $24.95 HC
www.fanweb.ca

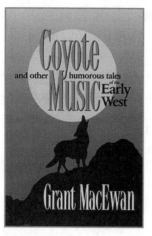

Coyote Music and Other Humorous Tales of the Early West

In this lighthearted and charming collection of stories, popular historian Grant MacEwan captures the homespun humour, the outrageous antics, and the colourful characters that brought laughter and joy into the often difficult lives of the early pioneers.

Among these pages you will meet the likes of: Pegleg Paul, king of woodenleg mirth and permanent fixture at the Fleet Livery's Hot Stove Liars' League; and Tom Sukanen, inventor and mechanical genius, obsessed with the singlehanded construction of a 43-foot, 15-ton seaworthy ship on the banks of the South Saskatchewan River.

Rocky Mountain Books
ISBN: 0921102-26-7 • $17.95 PB
www.rmbooks.com

Our Equine Friends: Stories of Horses in History

In this collection historian Grant MacEwan looks back over the history of the horse, tracing its beginnings and telling stories that illustrate the many different ways horses have affected our lives. From the famous examples of Napoleon's white Arabian Marengo, and Alexander the Great's Bucephalus, to stories of rural horses who have kept their young riders safe during blizzards, MacEwan celebrates the special friendship that has kept the paths of horses and people so closely intertwined through the years.

Our Equine Friends was originally published in 1964 under the title *Hoofprints and Hitchingposts*.

Fifth House Publishers
ISBN: 1-894856-01-5 • $19.95 PB
http://www.fitzhenry.ca/fifthhouse.htm

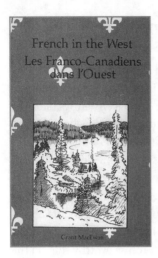

French in the West/Les Franco-Canadiens dans l'Ouest

In this bilingual (facing-page translation) book, Grant MacEwan brings to life the role the Canadiens played in the colonization of the West. From the hundred years' struggle for the control of Hudson Bay, through Louis Riel and the mixed blessing of Confederation, to the fight for the survival of a culture, *French in the West* is the fascinating and oft-forgotten story of one of the West's founding peoples.

Éditions des Plaines
0-920944-45-0 • $12.95 PB
www.plaines.mb.ca

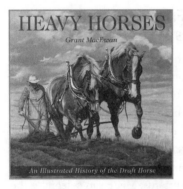

Heavy Horses

MacEwan pays tribute to the strength, beauty, and endurance of the draft horse in this fascinating collection of history, breeding information, stories, and photographs. He celebrates Clydesdales, Percherons, Belgians, Shires, Suffolks, and Canadien horses, as well as the dedicated breeders, keepers, and enthusiasts who nutured them and made them famous.

Heavy Horses is filled with information about the introduction of draft horses to North America, their European origins, and their changing roles on the farm and in the show ring over the decades. Originally published in 1986, this award-winning book has been completely redesigned and includes a new Foreword by Bruce Roy, editor of *Feather and Fetlock*.

Fifth House Publishers
ISBN: 1-894004-74-4 • $21.95 PB
http://www.fitzhenry.ca/fifthhouse.htm

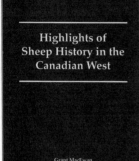

Highlights of Sheep History in the Canadian West

Many books have been written about the romance of the Western cattle industry, yet this was the first book to describe the history and contributions of the Western shepherd. If you are a sheep producer or a history buff this book is well worth a look.

Alberta Sheep and Wool Commission
Agriculture Centre
Bag Service #1,
Airdrie, Alberta T4B 2C1
Tel: 403 948 8533 / Fax: 403 912 1455
E-mail: aswc@therockies.com

Alberta Sheep and Wool Commission
$30.00 HC
$15.00 PB

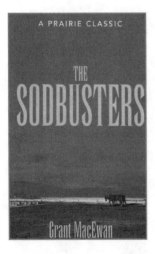

The Sodbusters

Originally published in 1948, *The Sodbusters* is Grant MacEwan's tribute to the men who transformed the prairies from rough, unbroken land into a breadbasket for the world. This entertaining collection of stories captures the strength, determination, and adaptability of the first people to explore, settle, farm, and ranch the Canadian prairies.

For MacEwan, the mark of a "sodbuster" lay in his relationship with the land. While some, including the Barr Colonists and John Sanderson, were farmers, just as many were ranchers, pioneers, and visionaries. From Captain John Palliser to Pat Burns and William R. Motherwell, the people in this book earned the title of "sodbuster" through their hard work and dedication to developing the western frontier.

Fifth House Publishers
ISBN: 1-894004-62-0 • $14.95 PB
http://www.fitzhenry.ca/fifthhouse.htm

Watershed: Reflections on Water

"We begin as almost pure water."

—Grant MacEwan

"Few of us even think about the water we drink, unless we're a curious child with a dry throat on a summer day, or a fine, old man with a thirst for change." —*Edmonton Journal*

In his last book, Alberta icon Grant MacEwan draws from his broad knowledge as an agriculturalist and his vast life experience to tell us "what every Canadian should know about water." Intended to encourage Canadians to value a natural resource taken for granted, *Watershed* highlights the importance of water in our daily lives and questions the stability of the earth's water supply—a pressing issue in the world today. This timely commentary on water is a book every "water-rich" Canadian should read.

NeWest Press
ISBN: 1-896300-35-9 • $19.95 PB
www.newestpress.com

JOHN WALTER GRANT MACEWAN was born in 1902 near Brandon, Manitoba, grew up near Melfort, Saskatchewan, and was educated in Guelph, Ontario and Ames, Iowa. He served on the faculties of the Universities of Saskatchewan and Manitoba, as mayor of Calgary, and as lieutenant-governor of Alberta. Renowned across Canada as a livestock judge and lecturer on agricultural topics, he became a tireless advocate of conservation and regional historical awareness, themes which drove his astonishing output of writing. The man described as "the Western Canadian of the Twentieth Century" died on 15 June 2000.

≈